Exploring Creation

with Chemistry and Physics

by Jeannie K. Fulbright

Technical Editorial Contributions:
Jonathan D. Sarfati, B.Sc. (Hons.), Ph.D., F.M.
Kristy L. Plourde, M.S.

Exploring Creation with Chemistry and Physics

Published by Apologia Educational Ministries, Inc.
1106 Meridian Street, Suite 340
Anderson, IN 46016
apologia.com

© 2013 by Jeannie K. Fulbright

Scientific content reviewed and edited by Dr. Jonathan Sarfati, Ph.D., F.M.,
of Creation Ministries International USA, www.creation.com.

Printed in the United States of America
by LSC Communications
Fifth Printing: April 2018

Cataloging-in-Publication data

ISBN: 978-1-935495-98-7

Apologia's Young Explorer Series
INSTRUCTIONAL SUPPORT

Apologia's elementary science materials launch young minds on an educational journey to explore God's signature in all of creation. Our award-winning curriculum cultivates a love of learning, nurtures a spirit of exploration, and turns textbook lessons into real-life adventures.

TEXTBOOK
Apologia Textbooks are written directly to the student in a highly readable conversational tone. Periodically asking students to stop and retell what they have just heard or read, our elementary science courses engage students as active learners while growing their ability to communicate clearly and effectively. With plenty of hands-on activities, the Young Explorer Series allows young scientists to actively participate in the scientific method.

NOTEBOOKING JOURNAL
Spiral-bound **Apologia Notebooking Journals** contain lesson plans, review questions, full-color mini-books, puzzles, and much more to keep students actively engaged in learning while keeping them organized.

JUNIOR NOTEBOOKING JOURNAL
Designed for younger students and those who struggle with writing, **Apologia Junior Notebooking Journals** cover everything in the regular notebooking journals, but at a more basic level and with primary writing lines. With simpler vocabulary pages, and additional coloring pages, junior notebooking journals make science enjoyable for even your youngest student.

AUDIO BOOKS
Some students learn best when they can see and hear what they are studying. Having the full audio text of your course is great for listening while reading along in the book or riding in the car! **Apologia Audio Books** contain the complete text of the book read aloud to your student.

FIELD TRIP JOURNAL
Apologia's Field Trip Journal is a fun and exciting way to record those moments when textbook lessons turn into real-life adventures. You and your students can successfully prepare for field trips, map the places you visit, and document entire field trips from planning stage to treasured memory.

At Apologia, we believe in homeschooling. We are here to support your endeavors and to help you and your student thrive! Find out more at apologia.com.

Scientific Speculation Sheet

Name _____

Date _____

Experiment Title _____

Materials Used:

Procedure: (What you will do or what you did)

Hypothesis: (What you think will happen and why)

Results: (What actually happened)

Conclusion: (What you learned)

Contents

INTRODUCTION

Welcome to *Exploring Creation with Chemistry and Physics*. This unique course explores the world God made using engaging text, many hands-on demonstrations, projects and experiments, and exciting activities, as well as proven methods to help your students remember what they've learned. The text is written directly to the students, making it very appealing to kids from six to thirteen. The material is presented in a conversational style that will make science enchanting and memorable for your students and create an environment in which learning is a joy.

Lesson Increments

This text includes fourteen lessons. Each lesson should be broken up into manageable time slots depending on your schedule and the ages and attention spans of your students. The *Chemistry and Physics Notebooking Journal,* designed to accompany this text, includes a suggested schedule that spreads each lesson over two weeks.

Narration

Narration is an ancient and effective educational method in which students are asked to retell what they have just heard or read. This focuses their attention, engages them with the material as active learners, helps them retain more of what they learn, and enhances their ability to communicate clearly and effectively. Throughout each lesson, students are asked to tell or narrate what they have just learned. The "What Do You Remember?" questions near the end of each lesson can be used for oral narration.

Notebooking Activities

Notebooking facilitates retention and provides documentation of your students' education. It is superior to fill-in-the-blank worksheets and tests because the unique personal written and artistic expressions incorporate both sides of the brain. Notebooking is flexible and allows for multilevel learning: A twelve-year-old student may write an essay and make an elaborate illustration, while a six-year-old may write one sentence with a stick-figure drawing. Notebooking assignments at the end of each lesson include activities such as recording fascinating facts, illustrating concepts, creating comics, and writing stories.

Projects and Experiments

"Try This!" activities throughout the text help students understand the concept learned with a hands-on demonstration. In addition, every lesson ends with a project or experiment. Though many experiments use items you may already have on hand, such as paper clips and string, some require special science supplies. You may wish to purchase a science kit, available through many suppliers. A supply list is provided on pages 255-260. Be sure to gather all necessary supplies ahead of time and designate a box or shelf where you can store them. You may wish to obtain nonperishable supplies for the whole year, one semester, or a few lessons at a time.

Be sure to provide adult supervision for all "Try This!" activities, projects, and experiments.

Caution: Set aside equipment to be used *only* in experiments, not for cooking. Never experiment and cook/eat with the same items! Thrift stores are a good source of inexpensive equipment.

Notebooking Journal

The *Chemistry and Physics Notebooking Journal* provides a place for students to complete assignments and creates a lasting record of their work. It includes templates for the "What Do You Remember?" questions that can be used for written narration or testing, notebooking assignments, and reports on experiments; Scripture copywork; book lists; and fun activities such as minibooks, additional experiments, and vocabulary crossword puzzles. A junior version for younger students also includes age-appropriate features such as coloring pages, cut-and-paste vocabulary exercises, and primary writing lines. Students may create their own notebooks, but the notebooking journal simplifies the process and enhances learning with additional activities.

Course Website

Take your learning to the next level by visiting websites that bring the concepts to life. The course website allows your students to dig even deeper into chemistry and physics. It includes resources mentioned in the text as well as additional links for other resources.

www.apologia.com/bookextras

You will see a box on the page. Type the following password into the box:

Godmadeitall

Make sure you capitalize the first letter, and make sure there are no spaces in the password.

How To Use This Book
A Step-By-Step Guide

1. Purchase a supply kit or scan the supply list on pages 255-260 to see what you need for the lesson you are going to do. Always check the supply list for each lesson in advance so you'll have everything you need.

2. Begin by reading the lesson to your students. (Older students may read the lesson themselves.) Narration prompts throughout the lesson ask students to tell or narrate what they have learned up to that point. These are not written narrations; they are impromptu oral presentations.

3. Each lesson includes "Try This!" activities to give students a hands-on model to demonstrate a point made in that section of the book. Ideally, the project should be done right then. However, don't be discouraged if you do not have the materials. You can always go back and do the project later. The *Chemistry and Physics Notebooking Journal* includes pages students can use to record experiments and projects. This helps prepare them for high school lab reports. They can include a picture or an illustration if they wish.

4. Unless you are following the schedule in the notebooking journal, continue reading until you feel a natural break is at hand. Each family will differ in the amount of reading done in each session. Some families become extremely engrossed and want to read an entire lesson. Most families read a quarter to half the lesson at one time; there are many natural stopping points within each lesson. This flexible schedule allows you to complete the book in a year in the way that works best for your family.

5. When you end for the day, ask your students to orally tell you what they learned. If you wish them to do so, they may spend a few minutes recording their learning in their notebook.

6. At the end of each lesson, the "What Do You Remember?" section provides specific questions to ask your students to prompt their memories about the lesson. Don't expect young children to be able to answer most of these, and don't expect older children to answer all of them. However, this is a great time to discuss what they learned and remind them of what they may have forgotten. These are also oral, not written.

7. If students have not yet written down the fascinating facts they learned throughout the lesson, they should do so at the end of the lesson. The "Fascinating Facts" pages of the notebooking journal provide a place for students to write down what they enjoyed or want to remember from the book. There are no right answers. Don't require students to record every detail of the lesson or write down what you want them to remember. Let them decide what they thought was interesting and important and express their own learning as they see fit. This gives them autonomy and keeps science fun. For nonwriters or slow writers, you can type or write what they tell you.

    Don't pressure your students or feel discouraged if they can't remember anything. If they struggle to recount their learning, you can encourage them with questions. Eventually, through patience and encouragement, they will be able to remember what they learned and accurately recount it in writing.

8. Have students do the notebooking assignment.

9. The last thing students should do is the project or experiment for the lesson.

10. The notebooking journal includes other activities your student might also enjoy, such as additional experiments, vocabulary work in the form of crossword puzzles, copywork, additional book and DVD suggestions, and full-color lapbook-style minibooks they can put together.

Chemistry and Physics Matter

You are embarking on an adventure—an adventure filled with fascinating facts, exciting experiments, dynamic demonstrations, and power-packed projects. On this journey you'll learn about two of the most interesting fields of science: physics and chemistry. They're the sciences God created to make everything around you operate as it does. You're about to learn how God made the world work. Are you excited? Well, you might be wondering, "What on earth is physics?" and "What exactly is chemistry?" Those are great questions—important questions. In fact, even if you haven't asked these questions, I'm going to answer them for you!

Chemistry and **physics** are the studies of matter and energy. But what *are* these things called matter and energy? Simply put, matter is anything that takes up space. Regardless of how small that space is, if it takes up *any* amount of space, it's matter. Is a dust particle flying through your house matter? Yes, it is! Is a microscopic germ on the back of a flea matter? Indeed, it is! *Anything* that takes up space is matter. In this book, we'll study matter and all the things God used to make everything you see around you.

Energy is what makes everything in the world work, move, and do things. When your oven heats your food, it's using energy. When the sun warms the earth, that's energy. When you sing, the air passing by your vocal cords vibrates. That's energy too. When the earth spins on its axis or revolves around the sun, it's energy that keeps it moving. How about the ocean waves and the wind in the trees? All these things are moved by energy. You'll learn all about it in this book.

In the grand scheme of things, physics and chemistry are really the studies of how God put the world together and made it work.

In the Beginning

Do you remember what the Bible says after "In the beginning"? Let's say it together: "In the beginning, God created the heavens and the earth" (Genesis 1:1, ESV). Think about it! That means God created *matter* in the very beginning. The Bible tells us God created everything in six days and then rested. He started by creating light. Then He separated the sea from the sky. After that, God made the land appear and plants grow on it. He then made all the animals. Finally, God made human beings in His image. All that matter uses energy in some way, so matter and energy were created in the beginning. Now you know why chemistry and physics are important sciences to study. Every other science depends on them!

Let's read an important passage in the Bible that you should probably memorize. It speaks about our Lord Jesus. It's one of my favorites because it shows us who our Creator really is. "He is the image of the invisible God, the firstborn of all creation. For by him all things were created, in heaven and on earth, visible and invisible, whether thrones or dominions or rulers or authorities—all things were created through him and for him. And he is before all things, and in him all things hold together" (Colossians 1:15–17, ESV).

How many things were created by Jesus? Look at the second sentence. It says *all* things. Look at the last

Although scientists aren't exactly sure what energy is, they know that energy is what makes these flowers and these girls grow.

sentence again. Who holds it all together? The Lord Jesus does! And guess what? He used energy to create it, and we'll soon discover in this book that He uses energy to hold it all together.

We'll be studying a whole lot about energy in this book. As you learn, I want you to remember this one thing: Scientists don't know exactly what energy is or where it comes from; they only know how it works. When you study energy, remember that God created it. The Bible tells us God holds all things together. Scientists have learned that energy holds all things together. Since God created everything, including energy, we know that He's the author of chemistry and physics! Chemistry and physics all boil down to one single thing—God!

Take time right now to read Genesis 1:1–2:4. After you're done, continue reading this lesson.

Forming the World

Fill in this sentence: In the beginning, the earth was _____. Some Bible versions say "formless." Some say "without form." Both mean the same thing. What things can you think of that have no special form or shape? There are some things in the world of chemistry that have no special form. One of those things is liquid. A liquid takes on the form of the container it's in. When you pour a glass of milk, the milk takes on the form of the glass. When you spill milk, it forms itself to the table or floor. It really has no form of its own. Gas also has no form. So in the beginning, the earth was probably one of these two things. Which do you think it was? The next verse tells us: "The Spirit of God moved upon the face of the waters." Aha! In the first chapter of Genesis, we're introduced to a special and important liquid called water. Remember that I said chemistry and physics are the study of matter and energy. Water is matter.

Before God created the dry ground and all you see around you, the earth was without form and empty.

It's a particular kind of matter formed when two different substances bond together. Those two substances are hydrogen and oxygen. Have you ever heard water called H_2O? H is for hydrogen, and O is for oxygen. The 2 after the H just means there are two hydrogen atoms. H_2O is called a molecule, which is a collection of bonded atoms. We're going to learn all about atoms and molecules in the next few lessons, but first let's take some time to learn all about matter.

Everything Matters

Have you ever played the game 20 Questions? While I was growing up, my family spent hours playing this game. One person would think of an object—any object in the world. Then the rest of us would ask yes-or-no questions to discover what that object was. The first thing we'd ask was, "Is it an animal, vegetable, or mineral?" "Vegetable" refers to anything that grows from plants. "Animal" refers to any living, moving creature. "Mineral" refers to something that has never been living. Then we'd ask, "Is it bigger than a bread box?" A bread box holds a loaf of bread. We could ask only 20 questions to discover all the properties and uses of the object. So we really had to think of specific questions that gave us a great deal of information. This is what scientists do all the time. They're full of questions about everything they see around them, and they figure out ways to find the answers. They're always interested in the different **properties**—those special features, traits, or attributes of materials found in the universe. Knowing the properties of something helps scientists identify what it is.

How would you describe each item in this picture? How are the items similar? How are they different? What properties does each have? Scientist are always seeking to describe matter according to its properties.

Being able to describe the properties of matter is an important skill. What are the properties of a tree? What are the properties of a cat? Can you describe the properties of a street sign? What about lake water? Is ocean water different from lake water? Everything has different properties. Some things have similar properties. Knowing how to find the properties that separate one thing from another is important.

Try This!

Find a companion and try playing another version of the 20 Questions game called "I Spy." Look around and choose an object in the room. Then say, "I spy with my little eye something that is _____." (Name the color of the object or another property.) Your companion will ask you yes-or-no questions about the object. Remember, only 20 questions are allowed. With each question and answer, you'll be describing the properties of the object. Take turns doing this with one another and have fun spying!

As you can see, the properties of matter are important. Scientists always look for certain properties when they explore matter. Let's study these special properties of matter.

Matter Matters

I told you earlier that matter is anything that takes up space. Scientists say that **matter** is anything that has volume and mass. Do you know what volume and mass are? You're about to find out. But before we talk about volume, mass, and their cousin, density, I want to tell you a little bit about atoms. Do you know what an atom is? Atoms are the particles that make up everything around you. In the next lesson, we're going to get to know atoms quite well. But for now, you just need to know they exist and that everything you see around you is made up of them. Everything—whether it's hard, soft, wet, sticky, or microscopic—is made up of tiny particles called atoms.

Although atoms are too small to see, artists draw them to look something like the image here. (Drawing not to scale)

Did I mention that they're teeny tiny? Take a look at the dot below:

That little dot is made up of atoms. How many atoms do you think could fit into that dot? Believe it or not, it would take 7.5 trillion atoms to fill up the dot, so you can imagine how small they are. They'll be mentioned a lot throughout this book. For now, just remember these little particles called atoms make up every single thing in the world.

Let's explore properties now!

Turn Up the Volume

When I bake bread, sometimes the bread rises beautifully. It's big, light, and fluffy. It fills my bread box to the top. It has a lot of volume. But sometimes the bread doesn't rise at all. It's thick and compressed. It has the same amount of bread in it because I used the same recipe, but it doesn't have much volume. It doesn't take up as much space in my bread box.

The amount of space something takes up is called its **volume**. Anything that's matter takes up space, so all matter has volume. That's really important to remember. A fly takes up space, so a fly has volume. Even a germ takes up space, so it has volume. A fly has a much greater volume than a germ. People have a much greater volume than a fly. Do you take up much space? Some people have a lot of volume. Some have only a little bit of volume. Who has the greatest volume in your family?

The larger fly has more volume than the smaller fly.

When this family gets out of the hot tub, the water level will go down.

In our backyard we have a hot tub. It's filled with water almost to the top. I can tell who has the most volume in our family by how much the water level rises when people get into the hot tub. When I get in, the water is displaced, rising a little. Then, when all four of my children pile in, the water level rises a lot more. Together, they take up a bunch of space. They're displacing the water even more. You can probably guess what **displace** means. It means to replace matter with another kind of matter—or to move matter. When things are moved by something, they're being displaced. In this case, a liquid (water) is being displaced by solid objects (my children). Eventually, Daddy sees the fun and decides to join us. Guess what happens next? He gets in, and the water flows out of the hot tub onto the deck. He has a huge amount of volume, taking up even more space. So he displaces the water right out of the hot tub!

We can sometimes measure how much volume something has by using water. An ancient Greek mathematician named Archimedes discovered this. The story goes like this: Archimedes' king gave a pure gold to a crown maker. He asked him to make him a crown using all that pure gold. When the king received his crown, he didn't believe that *all* the gold was used to make the crown. He wondered if perhaps the crown maker had taken some of the gold and replaced it with an equal weight of silver. How could he tell

that the gold in his crown was the same amount of pure gold that was given to the goldsmith? To find out, he sent for Archimedes, the greatest scientific thinker in his country. Archimedes arrived but was unsure how to find the truth. He couldn't eat or sleep or even bathe for days as he pondered the problem at hand. He was getting really smelly. Finally, he gave in to the pressure of those around him and took a bath. When he got into the bathtub, he was astonished to see the water rise. He realized the amount of water that was displaced was a way to measure volume and calculate density, which we'll talk about shortly. It was said that Archimedes jumped out of his tub and ran immediately to the king without getting dressed. He cried, "*Eureka!*" which means "I have found it!" Archimedes was then able to answer the king's question. Sadly for the crown maker, the story does not have a happy ending.

Let's try a similar experiment with water so you can see what I mean about volume.

Try This!

You will need: An adult's supervision, a graduated cylinder, water, and a small, solid object that doesn't absorb water (such as a rock).

To begin, fill the cylinder about halfway with water and take note of where the water level is. Now drop your object into the cylinder. Observe where the water level is now on the cylinder and take note of its measurement. Subtract the first volume measurement from the second volume measurement to find the volume of the object. You now know the exact measurement of how much space that object takes up.

Note: The volume of a liquid is measured in a unit called a liter, while solids are measured using cubic centimeters. You'll convert liters to cubic centimeters to get the correct unit for solids. $1 \text{ mL} = 1 \text{cm}^3$ (1 cc).

Look at the images above. For each pair, identify which has more volume.

I want you to remember two important things about volume before we study mass: Matter has volume, and volume is how much space something takes up.

Now that you know what volume is, let's study mass!

Mass Matters

Have you ever held a baseball and tennis ball at the same time? They're about the same size, aren't they? The balls have about the same volume. They take up about the same amount of space. However, one ball is heavier. What about a golf ball and a ping-pong ball? They have about the same volume, but again, one is heavier. Why do you think it's heavier? The baseball and golf ball are heavier because they both have more matter packed inside. A tennis ball and a ping-pong ball are empty on the inside. If something has more matter inside it, we say it has more mass. **Mass** is a very important property of matter that tells us how much matter is inside something.

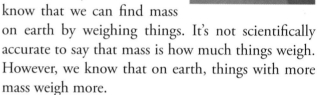

Since I mentioned weight with the baseball and golf ball, you may be tempted to think of mass in terms of how much things weigh. That's true here on earth. But imagine if you were traveling around in outer space and decided to get out of your spaceship to play some tennis. You get out, taking your tennis ball with you. Your fellow astronaut brings his baseball because he doesn't want to play tennis. There they are—the two balls—in space. Do they weigh anything? No. They weigh nothing in space. However, the baseball still has more mass. Mass doesn't change, but weight does.

Now you know what mass is, but you should also know that we can find mass on earth by weighing things. It's not scientifically accurate to say that mass is how much things weigh. However, we know that on earth, things with more mass weigh more.

Here's the important thing to remember: Matter has mass and volume. That's the actual scientific definition for matter. Anything with mass and volume is matter. Volume refers to the space it takes up, and mass refers to how much stuff is inside it.

Wow! You've learned a lot and are well on your way to becoming a physicist! Before we move on to density, let's review what we've learned.

Tell someone in your own words what matter, volume, and mass are.

The gold bars have more mass than the soap bars.

Density Matters

Density is another important property of matter. In order to understand density, let's try an experiment.

 **You will need:** An adult's supervision, safety goggles, 2 glasses, 2 eggs, ½ cup of salt, and hot water.

First, run the sink water until it becomes hot. Next, fill both glasses about halfway. Add ½ cup of salt to one of the glasses and stir it well. Now, make a hypothesis (a guess) about what will happen if you drop the eggs in the glasses. What will the eggs do? Go ahead and drop an egg in each glass to see what actually happens.

Were you surprised by the results of the experiment? What happened? Really and truly, density happened! Density is related to mass and volume. In fact, **density** is how much mass is in a certain volume of matter. Does that make sense? I'll try to explain so that you understand.

Let's go back to my bread. The mass of my bread was the same whether it had a lot of volume or not. I used the same amounts of flour, water, and everything else to make both loaves. But one loaf rose and produced fluffy bread with a lot of volume. The other loaf fell and did not have as much volume. But they had the same amount of mass.

Now let's add density to this equation. Which bread was denser? Which bread had more mass per volume? Well, the bread that fell had the same mass packed inside that smaller volume. It was dense. The fluffy bread had more volume, but the mass was spread out more, so it was not as dense.

Here's how it works: If something is really dense, there are a lot of particles inside the particular volume of that object. For example, in my bread, the particles are tightly packed together. In the experiment you just did, there was a lot of matter—a lot of extra particles inside the glass with salt in it. There were not as many particles inside the glass with only water.

Think of when you pack a lunch for yourself. If you put a couple of things in your lunch box (like a sandwich and a juice box) and close it, you'll have a lot of space between the items in your lunch box. Not a very dense lunch, if you ask me. There's a lot of room in that lunch box. It's a light lunch box. Now if you

The same amounts of flour and other ingredients were added to both of these loaves of bread. However, the one on the left has more volume than the one on the right. That's because it rose during baking, while the other did not.

decide you'd rather have a dense lunch box (and who wouldn't?), you could add a banana, a box of raisins, yogurt, a spoon, a cheese stick, some crackers, an extra bottle of water in case you get thirsty after you finish your juice box, and, of course, a package of cookies. Make that *two* packages of cookies. Now that's a lunch with density! When you close your lunch box, you'll find that all the things inside are closely packed together. Since it's denser, it's also heavier.

Let's get back to the eggs. Eggs have more particles packed inside them than water. The egg was denser than plain water, so it sank. But after adding salt to the water, the egg floated.

Which lunch box is denser—the one on the left or the one on the right?

The salt made the egg less dense than the water.

When you get into water, you're usually more dense than the water—so you sink. That's why you had to learn to swim. One time, my family and I went to a part of the ocean that was extremely salty. It was dense water. When we swam out into the ocean from the beach, we just floated in the water without swimming!

Let's try a few more experiments to find out more about density.

Ice is less dense than water. That's why icebergs float in the water. However, 90% of the iceberg is found below the surface of the water.

This man is able to float in the Dead Sea because he's less dense than the very salty water.

Try This!

You will need: An adult's supervision, safety goggles, a clear plastic straw, very warm water, food coloring (red, blue, green, and yellow), 4 plastic cups, measuring spoons, and 10 tablespoons of salt.

Begin by filling all the cups ¾ full of very warm water. Make sure the water level is equal in all the cups. Now place several drops of a different color of food coloring in each cup. Next, add 1 tablespoon of salt to the blue water and stir it until the salt has dissolved. Put 2 tablespoons of salt into the red water and stir. Next, add 3 tablespoons of salt to the green water and stir. Finally, put 4 tablespoons of salt into the yellow water and stir.

Place one end of the straw about 1 inch into the blue water, and place your index finger over the other end of the straw. Pull the straw out of the water, keeping your finger at the top so the water stays in the straw. Without releasing your finger, lower the straw into the red cup about an inch lower than the blue cup (about 2 inches). Now carefully release your finger from the top of the straw. The red liquid will push the blue layer up to the level of the water in the cup. Press your finger firmly on top of the straw and remove the straw. Next place the straw 3 inches into the green cup and carefully release the straw so that it fills with green liquid just a bit. Put your finger back over the top and remove the straw. Next, do the same with the yellow liquid. Put it inside the cup an inch lower than all the others, and allow some liquid in. You now have four layers of colored water in your straw!

Try This!

You will need: An adult's supervision; safety goggles; a tall, thin glass or vase, honey, corn syrup, 100% pure maple syrup; whole milk; dish soap; water; vegetable oil; rubbing alcohol; 8 plastic cups; a turkey baster; food coloring; a popcorn kernel; a die from a game; a cherry tomato; bead; a piece of a plastic straw; and a ping-pong ball or marshmallow.

Pour 8 ounces of each liquid listed above into a separate cup. Place a drop of a different color of food coloring into each cup except the cups with the oil and honey. Write down the color for each liquid. (Example: maple syrup: red, water: green, etc.) Next, pour the following cups of liquid very, very *slowly and carefully* into the center of the glass container one at a time in the following order (*make sure the liquids do not touch the sides of the container while you are pouring*): honey, corn syrup, and maple syrup. For the next two liquids, use the turkey baster to *slowly and carefully* drip the liquids into the middle of the glass container: milk and dish soap. For the rest of the liquids, use the turkey baster to *slowly and carefully* pour the liquids down the side of the container: water, vegetable oil, and rubbing alcohol. Now make a hypothesis (an educated guess) about which items (popcorn kernel, die, cherry tomato, etc.) will land in which layer of liquid based on density. Write down your hypothesis. Finally, drop the items one by one into the glass container and watch which layers they rest in.

How did the colors separate in the first experiment? It was density! You added more and more salt to the water, making it more and more dense. The solution with the highest density (yellow) stayed at the bottom of the straw while the solution with the least amount of salt (and the lowest density) remained at the top. Because you increased the amount of salt in each cup (and kept the volume of water in each cup the same), each liquid had a different density. Therefore, the liquids separated into different layers.

Were you surprised by what you saw in the second experiment? Each object sank until it found a level that had more density than it did. Obviously, the die was the densest object and sank to the bottom.

Spend some time telling someone all you've learned about mass, volume, and density.

Try This!

You will need: An adult's supervision; a bowl of water; and several items from around the house, like a piece of wood, a cork, a piece of ice, some coins, and a few different plastic toys.

Predict whether or not each item you collected will sink or float. Now place the items one by one in the bowl of water. What happens? Are you surprised by the results?

Buoyancy Basics

When something floats in water, we say it's buoyant. **Buoyancy** is the ability of something to float. It's buoyant because of the upward push of the water. If you put a raft in a pool, the upward push of the water on the raft is strong enough to keep the raft afloat. But if you drop a nail in the pool, the upward push of the water is not strong enough to keep the nail floating. This goes back to density. If the density of an object is less than the density of the liquid, it floats in the liquid! Some objects may seem like they would be denser than water—metal, for example. But their shape changes their density. Boats are an example of this. They're shaped in a way that increases their volume, which decreases their density, allowing more air to fill them.

Shipbuilders design and build ships in a way that increases the surface area. The ship's metal is flat and spread out, with high sides. This enables the ship to go down into the water with a lot of air in the submerged part of the ship.

Try This!

You will need: An adult's supervision, safety goggles, a large pan of warm water, a few drops of blue food coloring, pennies, ¼ cup of salt, and aluminum foil.

Imagine that a pirate  ship was captured and you've been asked to bring all the treasures from the ship back to shore. You need to design a boat out of foil that can hold all that treasure. Your pennies will be the treasure! First, fill a large pan with warm water. Add the salt and food coloring. Next, design and construct a boat out of the aluminum foil. How many pennies do you think your boat can hold? Make a guess. Now float the boat in the water. Then place as many pennies in the boat as it will hold before it sinks. If you're doing this with others, have a contest to see whose boat can hold the most pirate treasure!

Spend some time explaining to someone what you've learned so far.
If you're finished reading for the day, write down in your notebooking journal
a few of the things you've learned. Be sure to include illustrations!

More on Matter

Now you know that matter has mass, volume, density, and buoyancy. But that's not all you need to know to identify matter around you. Consider the pillow on your couch or bed. How would you describe it? Consider the knife in your kitchen. What about the vinegar in your pantry? Each of these items has other properties that are unique. Some of the other important properties we should consider include color, shape, hardness, odor, and taste (although you shouldn't taste things that are not food because they might be poisonous). These features can help determine what it is we see around us.

Let's take a quick look at these other properties of matter before we close this lesson. Then we'll do a fun project.

The Golden Rule

Years ago, when gold was discovered in California, thousands of people poured into the hills and panned for gold in the rivers and streams. Sometimes they would see shiny gold in their pans and believe they had hit the jackpot. Hooray! They would never have to work again! They were rich! But many times what they thought was gold was really a gold copycat called iron pyrite—later known as fool's gold. Iron pyrite looks like gold, but it's not. How could you discover whether you had real gold or iron pyrite? Well, you would need to explore the physical properties of the golden material you found. We'll be looking at luster, color, shape, hardness, and odor to discover the properties of gold versus iron pyrite.

Prospectors poured into California to pan the rivers for gold. Many times they would find substances that only looked like gold.

Many times gold miners would mistake iron pyrite (left) for genuine gold (right). They had to know the special properties of each not to be fooled.

Luster Matters

Have you ever noticed that some things shine while other things don't? Look around the room you're in. What would you say is the shiniest thing in the room? Do you have a brass lamp or light hanging from the ceiling? Is someone wearing a shiny ring? The amount of shine something has is called **luster**. It's really hard to tell fool's gold from real gold based on luster. That's because fool's gold is really shiny—maybe even shinier than real gold.

Most metals are quite lustrous. Both gold and fool's gold—as well as silver, aluminum, copper, brass, and other metals—are shiny or lustrous. So although luster is an important property of matter, it's not going to tell you whether your piece of golden matter is valuable or not. But you can look at the color and find some clues to identify the material.

Although these coins are made out of different metals, they're all quite lustrous.

Color May Matter

All matter has its own special color. Pure gold has one color, and pure silver has another. Aluminum is similar to silver in color, but not exactly the same. Look at the images of silver and aluminum on this page. Their colors closely match, but they're not identical.

Silver   Aluminum

However, some materials are exactly the same color. Therefore, you'll have to look at other properties besides color to determine which material is which. Suppose you have a piece of silver and a piece of aluminum and aren't sure which is which. How do you tell? Well, the best way to tell the difference is to find the density of each and compare. Silver is almost four times denser than aluminum.

Gold   Iron pyrite

Gold and iron pyrite don't match as closely as silver and aluminum. Look at the pictures on this page of gold and iron pyrite. Do you notice that gold looks more yellow than iron pyrite? We might say iron pyrite has a silvery gold or brass tone. If you had a piece of real gold, you could compare the color. But what if you don't have a piece of real gold? Density is an excellent test here as well; gold is almost four times denser than iron pyrite. Iron pyrite might look like real gold if you don't have any gold with which to compare it. But there are other properties you can explore if you still aren't sure which material you have found.

Let's look now at the property of shape.

Try This!

If you have a rocky yard or know of a place where a lot of rocks can be found, go out there today and explore to see if you can find rocks with geometric shapes. Try to find as many different types of shapes as you can. Draw pictures of the rocks or take photos for your notebooking journal.

The Shape of Matter

Shape can be an important clue to discover what element you've found. Look at the shapes of the different pieces of gold on this page. Do you notice that iron pyrite is shaped more symmetrically than gold? It typically forms in a particular pattern or structure, with geometrically shaped pieces stuck together. We say it's crystallized or it forms crystals. We'll talk more about crystals later and even make some! But real gold is found in nuggets. They're often odd, uneven-shaped pieces. In fact, gold can be found in sheets, in flakes, or even in grains. If the golden material is oddly shaped, you may be in the money! If it looks geometric, it's probably fool's gold.

But maybe you still aren't sure. Well, there's another property of matter you can explore to get more information that will help you get to the bottom of the mystery. Let's look at how hard or soft the materials are.

Iron pyrite has a geometric shape.

Gold has an odd, uneven shape.

Hardness Matters

Every material in nature has a different hardness to it. A wood floor is pretty hard. But would you rather fall on a wood floor or a granite floor? Granite is a lot harder than wood. The Bible tells us that the streets in heaven are paved with gold. Pure gold is really soft. That means if we fall down on the streets in heaven, it'll probably make a dent in the street but won't hurt us.

Hardness is an important property to explore when determining whether or not you need to keep searching for your pot of gold. As I said, pure gold is soft and bendable. We call bendable materials **malleable** (**mal** ee uh buhl). We sometimes call this **plasticity** (pla **sti** si tee). This means a material can be changed into a different shape without breaking. Does the word plasticity remind you of anything? You probably thought of the word plastic. Well, plastic gets its name from this property. Plastic items can be molded into almost anything. We'll learn all about plastics in lesson 4. If you pound gold with a hammer, it will bend into different shapes. It can also be pounded into extremely thin leaves. This isn't true of iron pyrite. Therefore, iron pyrite is harder than gold. If you pound iron pyrite with a hammer, it'll smash into pieces because it's brittle.

Scientists also talk about **ductility**, which is whether or not the object can be made into a wire. Many metals—such as gold, silver, and copper—can be formed into a wire. We say they're very ductile. But you can't form iron pyrite into a wire. Actually, you can't form it into anything.

Although they're made of metal, these cans are able to be crushed rather easily. This tells us that the metal used is malleable.

A copper piggy bank would be difficult to break open.

Copper is very ductile because it's easily shaped into wires. Most wires are made of copper because copper has many properties needed for wires.

Rate the materials in the picture below in the order of how hard they are. Put the hardest material first and the softest material last.

Wood

Rock

Aluminum foil

Clay

You can definitely decide whether you have gold or fool's gold depending on what happens if you hit it with a hammer.

What if you don't have a hammer? Well, you could always smell the golden chunk! Yes, indeed, you could smell it!

Try This!

You probably have a lot of metal objects in your house such as coins, hardware, tools, and more. Gather some now so you can discover the different smells of metals. Which ones smell and which ones do not? You can find out by rubbing the metal objects with your fingers and sniffing to see if an odor lingers on your hands. Wash your hands and try with other metals. It may be helpful to have a damp paper towel handy to clean your hands between objects.

Smell Matters

Believe it or not, you can tell whether or not you have fool's gold or gold by the odor of the golden chunk in your possession. Gold actually has no smell at all. But if you rub iron pyrite on a hard, scratchy surface, it will give off a boiled-egg-like odor. This is because both eggs and pyrite contain sulfur atoms and produce the foul-smelling gas hydrogen sulfide.

So far, you've learned a lot about the differences between gold and iron pyrite. If you were panning for gold, you could find out pretty quickly whether or not that shiny matter in your pan was fooling you. There are also some other properties of matter you could use to discover the contents of your pan. Let's look at those before we close this lesson.

We often use the sense of smell to discover the identity of things. This girl is smelling basil leaves to determine what they are.

More Properties Matter

Not all objects stick to magnets. Objects that stick are made of iron.

There are two other ways to help decide what material you have: check the density and check the magnetism. Gold will sink in a swirling pan of water, while iron pyrite may be washed away. This is because gold is one of the densest substances on earth—19.3 times denser than water. When panning for gold, prospectors would add more water to the pan, swirling and swirling the pan. The heavier substances would then sink to the bottom. This is how they collected their gold nuggets, or more often gold flecks.

Another property of some iron pyrite is magnetism. Gold will not stick to magnets. If you had a strong magnet handy, you could tell whether you had gold or not.

We'll study magnetism in great detail in another lesson. But let's take a few minutes now to learn a little about it in this experiment. Are you ready to find out what items in your house are magnetic?

> # Try This!
> **You will need:** An adult's supervision; a strong magnet; and several items from your home, such as needles, tacks, tools, hair accessories, and more. First, take a guess which items are steel (made of iron) and which are not. Can you tell which of the items are magnetic? Test them out with a magnet to see if you're correct!

Some metals are not magnetic, as you were able to see. This tells us much about their properties.

If you still aren't sure whether or not you have gold, you could perform a chemistry experiment to see how your golden chunk reacts to certain chemicals. However, these types of experiments should not be done at home. For example, you might pour hydrochloric acid on your golden material. Iron pyrite will foam and dissolve when this extremely dangerous and caustic acid comes into contact with it. (The foaming gas is hydrogen sulfide, which is quite toxic in such amounts.) Gold won't change a bit.

There are other chemical tests people can perform to determine what substance they have in front of them. The chemicals used in these tests cause reactions that help scientists discover what the material is. For example, if I had two very light, silvery metals in front of me, how would I know whether I had potassium or aluminum?

You probably have aluminum foil in your house right now, but hopefully you don't have pure potassium. It looks similar to aluminum, but potassium is so soft you can easily cut it with a knife. An easy chemical test to do is to toss both substances in water. Potassium will react and could create a fire, but aluminum won't be affected. Now you know why I was hoping you didn't have potassium in your house! Some pans are made out of aluminum. Do you think they tried to make potassium pans first? No, I don't think so.

Final Matters

Isn't it wonderful how God created so many different things when He made the earth? You're going to be amazed as you continue your journey through chemistry and physics! God's world is filled with matter, and the more we learn about all that He made, the more we understand Him and how much He loves us.

See if you can remember some of the things you've learned by answering the questions below. After that, you'll do a fun notebooking activity followed by an entertaining project.

What Do You Remember?

Physics and chemistry are both the studies of _____ and _____. Matter is defined as anything that has _____ and _____. What is mass? Why is mass not always measured by weight? How can we measure volume? Which is denser—a cube of wood or the same size cube of gold? Why? Name as many properties of matter as you can recall.

Notebooking Activities

Your first notebooking assignment is to write down and illustrate some of the fascinating facts you want to remember about matter. If you have the *Chemistry and Physics Notebooking Journal*, a template is provided for you to use. After you've recorded your facts, do the following notebooking activity.

Have you ever been to a play? If not, have you seen a television show or watched a movie? All the actors perform the lines that were written by a playwright or screenwriter. A playwright writes plays, and a screenwriter writes scripts for movies and TV shows. A script tells each actor what to say and when to say it. Sometimes the script even includes stage directions, which tell actors things they should do or where they should move.

For your notebooking activity you will become a playwright. You are going to create a script about Archimedes and the golden crown. Your play will reenact the events that took place when the king needed a new crown and hired Archimedes to discover whether he had been cheated or not.

The *Chemistry and Physics Notebooking Journal* includes a template that you may use to create your play. The example below shows what a play script might look like.

King: Crown maker, I'm so glad you came! I need a new crown! Use all of this gold to create my new crown. (King hands gold to crown maker.)

Crown maker: Yes, your Majesty.

King: Be sure to use every bit of the gold.

Crown maker: Of course, your Majesty. I would never cheat you, your Majesty.

King: That would be most unwise. I expect it to be ready next week.

A week passes

Crown maker: Your Majesty, here is your beautiful new crown.

Project
Lava Lamps

Let's have some fun with density by making our own lava lamps!

You will need:

- 3 tall, thin plastic bottles with caps, like a soda or water bottle (Be sure to remove any labels so you can see the lava more clearly.)
- a lot of water (or vinegar for a stronger reaction)
- food coloring (3 colors of your choice)
- a large bottle of vegetable oil
- Alka-Seltzer tablets (Get a whole box!)

1. Fill each bottle halfway with oil.
2. Now fill the bottles up to the top with water. (For a bigger reaction use vinegar.)
3. Drop 3 drops of a different color food coloring into each bottle. Shake each bottle up a bit so the color can break down through the oil seal and color the water. Give the oil and water (or vinegar) a few minutes to settle back down into distinct layers before moving on to the next step.
4. Drop 1 Alka-Seltzer tablet into each bottle and place the caps on the bottles immediately to prevent the lava from overflowing.
5. Have fun watching the lava bubble up!

What happened in this project? Alka-Seltzer tablets don't react in vegetable oil. So the tablets you dropped in the bottles fell down through the vegetable oil and into the water or vinegar. When the tablets touched the water or vinegar, the chemicals inside the Alka-Seltzer reacted with the water or vinegar. This reaction caused gases to form. These gases were less dense than the oil, so they floated up into the oil, creating a bubbly effect.

Be sure to save your lava lamps as we will be using them in lesson 5.

Moving Matter

Now that you've learned a lot about volume, mass, density, and the other properties of matter, let's continue our study by exploring the most important properties of matter—the states of matter.

There are three main states of matter—solid, liquid, and gas. We usually use water as an example because everyone has seen water in all three states. You've probably never seen gold as a liquid or a gas. You've probably never seen oxygen as a liquid or a solid. But almost everything can be either a solid, liquid, or gas. Let's explore how this happens with water.

When you see water coming out of the faucet, what does it look like? When you think of water in your freezer, what do you imagine? If water is up in the clouds, how does it appear? The clouds are made of liquid droplets that condensed from gaseous water.

Everything God made can be a solid, liquid, or gas depending on one thing—heat energy. Heat energy has to do with how hot or cold something is.

The three states of matter are represented in this burning candle: solid (the candle), liquid (the melting wax), and gas (the aroma that you smell in the air).

Can you identify the different states of matter in this image?

Moving Atoms

Do you remember that everything is made up of atoms? It's these little atoms that determine whether the substance is a solid, liquid, or gas. It really depends on how active the atoms are. Solids are not very active. Liquids are a little active. Gases are very active. Let's explore this.

Solid Sleep

Think of it like this: When you're sleeping, you're not very active. Your body doesn't need a lot of room to move around. In fact, you only need your bed. You can stay right in that one spot all night long. Perhaps you'll move around a *little*, but you're content to be in that one place for hours. That's like the atoms in a solid. They stay pretty still.

Atoms in a solid don't move much, similar to this sleeping child.

Atoms in a liquid move more than in a solid but are not as active as in a gas, similar to this family reading together.

Liquid Motion

When you get up in the morning, you move around your house. Most likely you eat breakfast, read books, listen to music, play games with your family, and pretty much stay in your house for a while. You stick close to your family members during this time—but you're moving around. You have more energy than you did when you were in bed sleeping. You're like liquid atoms! Liquid atoms flow around with more energy than solid atoms, but they do stay close together.

Going Gas

Eventually, you're fully awake and full of energy. You start moving around more than before. Maybe you get a little loud and start bouncing off the walls! If you're a girl, you may feel like doing some cartwheels and dance moves. If you're a boy, you probably feel like karate chopping something or jumping off the couch. Your mom says it's time to go outside because you're just exploding with too much energy to be inside. Your energy requires a lot more room than your house has. You're here; you're there; you're bouncing around everywhere! So the door opens, and you bound outside with all your energy. You need space. You're just like gas atoms! They need a lot more room to move around because they're full of energy—moving here, there, and everywhere. In fact, gas atoms will pretty much fill up any space you put them in. If it's a big space, they'll fill it up. If it's a small space, they'll push against the walls of that space with all their energy, trying to get outside.

As you can see, the real difference between the states of matter comes down to how fast the atoms in that substance are moving. Slow-moving atoms are solids. Medium-moving atoms are liquids. Fast-moving atoms are gases. Let's study these three states of matter in a little more depth.

Atoms in a gas are extremely active and prefer to have a lot of room to move around, similar to this active boy playing outside.

Solid Matter

The atoms in these ice cubes have reached the solid state.

What exactly is a **solid**? Well, it's anything that has a specific shape and size. Unlike clouds and water, ice has a specific shape and size. The water molecules are not free to move about because they're frozen into a solid form.

The atoms in a solid aren't *perfectly* still because atoms always have *some* energy. Yet atoms in a solid are frozen in place. Because the atoms *stay* in place, the object is rigid and doesn't change shape. Have you ever frozen water? The atoms in water freeze into a solid when put in the freezer. Water needs to be 32°F (0°C) or below to be a solid. Jell-O needs to be about 50°F (10°C) to be a solid. Butter will stay a solid as long as it's below 90°F (32°C). Why do you think we use metal and glass to cook in our oven or on our stove top? Well, steel and many other metals—as well as glass—will remain solid even if the temperatures are above 1,000°F (537°C)!

The temperature that makes a liquid turn into a solid is called its **freezing point**. Butter is frozen at 90°F, even though it's not cold to our touch. Jell-O is frozen at 50°F. Water is frozen at 32°F. If it's above 32°F, water melts. It turns from ice into liquid water. That's the **melting point**. The freezing point of water and the melting point of water are the same temperature. If the temperature is a fraction above 32°F, water melts. If it's 32°F or below, water freezes into ice. As you can see, every substance on earth has its own specific freezing and melting point temperature.

Try This!

Let's do a simple experiment to discover which substance will freeze the fastest in your freezer.

You will need: An adult's supervision, 5 identical plastic cups, 1/4 cup of salt, Epsom salt, rubbing alcohol, Jell-O, water, a freezer, and a clock.

First, prepare the Jell-O according to the package directions, but do not put the Jell-O in the refrigerator. Next, fill three of the cups with ¼ cup of very warm water. Add ¼ cup of salt to one cup and stir. Add ¼ cup of Epsom salt to another cup and stir. Add nothing to the third cup. Pour ¼ cup of rubbing alcohol into the fourth cup. Pour ¼ cup of the Jell-O into the last cup. Now make a hypothesis (a guess) about which substance will freeze first, second, third, fourth, and fifth. Write this down in your notebooking journal.

Next, put all the cups in the freezer and write down the time. Check the cups every hour to see which items freeze first, second, third, fourth, and last. Write down the time that each freezes (if it does freeze).

As you noticed, salt and other substances lower the freezing point of water. This is why we put salt on the streets when the temperature outside drops to 32°F or below and it's snowing. It makes it safer to drive on the streets.

Can you explain to someone what you've learned so far?

Liquid Matter

As you know, when solids melt, they become liquids. Think about liquids for a moment. How would you describe a liquid? Scientists say that **liquids** are substances that are free to flow, with no particular shape. They do have a particular volume, but they take on the shape of whatever is holding them. Even though liquids always take on the shape of whatever is holding them, they don't change volume when they are poured from one container to another. They only change shape! You can prove this by pouring a cup of water from a large measuring cup into a small single-cup measuring cup.

Let's do an experiment with an interesting substance. You'll need to decide whether this substance is a liquid or a solid.

Try This!

You will need: An adult's supervision, cornstarch (16 ounces), a cake pan, water, and a measuring cup to pour the water.

First, pour the cornstarch into the cake pan. Next, slowly add water. Stir or mix the cornstarch with your hands. Continue adding water in small amounts until you get a mixture that has the consistency of honey. Once it's thoroughly mixed, hold your hand flat over the top of the pan and slap the mixture without splattering it. Next, stir the mixture slowly with your finger. How fast can you stir? Now sink your entire hand into the mixture and attempt to grab the fluid and pull it up. Grab some out and attempt to form a ball between your palms, as you would clay. Finally, flatten your hand out and allow the mixture to sit on your hand.

Do not dispose of the mixture in the sink; it will clog your pipes, or worse! Throw it in the trash when you're done.

Solid Liquids and Liquid Solids

What did you notice about this substance? Is it a flowing liquid or a solid? Read on to find out why this substance behaves as it does!

So what did you decide? Liquid or solid? Well, that's a bit tricky. This substance is called an **amorphous solid**—that's Greek for a solid without a shape (*a* = without; *morph* = shape). Sometimes it's called a **non-Newtonian liquid**. We'll talk about Newton in just a moment. A non-Newtonian liquid is a liquid that doesn't behave like other liquids. Instead of becoming a solid when it gets cooler, it becomes a solid when you put pressure on it. When you squeezed or smacked the substance, it froze into a solid. That's a pretty strange substance, isn't it? It's both a solid and a liquid. Most liquids don't have both characteristics. Let's look a little more closely at the active liquids before we move on to those wild and woolly gases!

Try This!

You will need: An adult's supervision, a piece of waxed paper or plastic, and water.

Drop a spot of water on the waxed paper or plastic. Now move the drop of water around with your finger. Try to separate the drop of water into two or more drops, then try to combine them again. Could you do it?

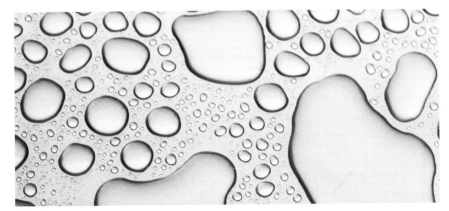

Did you notice that the atoms in the liquid prefer to stick together? It was harder to separate them than to put them back together again, wasn't it? That's because even though liquids are active atoms, they are "friendly" atoms that tend to stay close to each other.

Surface Tension

Water molecules have special bonds that hold them together. As the molecules on the surface of the water stick together, they form an invisible "skin" called **surface tension**.

This is why water striders and other insects can walk on water without sinking. The surface tension is strong enough to hold them. The insects' feet make small indentions in the surface of the water, but they don't break the invisible skin of surface tension.

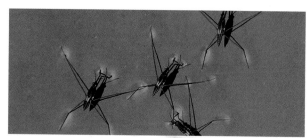
These water striders are insects that spend time resting on the surface of ponds, using surface tension to stay above the water.

Try This!

You will need: An adult's supervision, water, a bowl, a needle, and a single piece of toilet paper.

First, fill the bowl with water. When the water is still, place the needle on the tissue and carefully lay it in the water. Do not bump the bowl. Watch what happens. Did you see the surface tension in action? The needle is suspended above the water because of surface tension.

Viscosity Values

Remember when we explored the non-Newtonian liquid we made from cornstarch? That substance was named after Isaac Newton, a brilliant scientist who discovered the law of **viscosity** (vis **kos** i tee). What on earth is viscosity? It's the thickness or resistance to flow in a fluid. Have you ever tried to pour honey? It resists flowing from the jar or measuring cup; it has a high resistance to flow. Newton taught that we can change viscosity by changing the temperature. If you put honey in the microwave for a few seconds, you'll change its viscosity. That's because you're adding heat to the atoms in the honey, and they start moving more than before. As you saw earlier, a non-Newtonian fluid changes viscosity according to pressure. When you squeeze a handful of the cornstarch goop, its

viscosity increases—so it acts like a solid. When you release the pressure, the goop behaves just like a liquid. That's why you should not pour the mixture down the sink. The pipes will apply pressure, and the mixture will clog your drain!

Every fluid has a different viscosity. Some are more viscous than others. That means they resist flowing more. Honey is more viscous than water. Can you think of some other very viscous substances? Which do you think is more viscous (flows more slowly): honey, olive oil, ketchup, or salad dressing? You would have to experiment to find out. What would happen to each of these substances if you put them in the freezer for an hour? What if you heated them in the microwave? Why do you think that is? Read on to understand more about this.

Heating Up

Why do you think the atoms in a liquid are more energetic than they are in a solid? It's because they're warmer. How do we turn a solid into a liquid? Simple. We add heat. When it reaches its melting point, it'll turn from a solid into a liquid. When you take an ice cube out of the freezer, it won't be long before the heat from your house begins to melt the ice cube, turning it into a liquid. When heated, the atoms begin to move around more and more until they turn into a liquid. If you put the ice cube in the sun, this happens a lot faster. To turn water from a liquid to a solid, what

These icicles will begin to melt when the sun's heat causes the atoms to become more active.

Steel mills put steel in huge vats and raise the temperature above 3,000°F (1,645°C) to melt it. The steel is then poured into containers that will shape it into the kind of steel structure that's needed. There, it cools and hardens (or freezes) into that shape.

do we do? Can you remember what temperature water needs to be able to freeze? Yes! The freezing point of water is 32°F.

As you know, when some liquids become solids, they may not feel freezing to us. They may actually feel hot, yet they're still frozen. For example, iron melts and freezes at 2,795°F (1,535°C). If an iron bar is 2,000°F (1,093°C), it's frozen solid, but it's far too hot for us to touch! Can you think of any other substances that are frozen but don't feel cold to the touch? Look around you. Every solid you see is frozen. That reminds me of a childhood game I played called Freeze Tag. We would all run around trying to get away from the person who was "it." That's because **whoever** that person touched had to freeze in place. This game went on until everyone was frozen. We looked like statues in the yard!

Try This!

You're going to make a frozen dessert called sorbet!

You will need: An adult's supervision, 1 cup of fruit juice, 2 cups of ice, 1 cup of salt, 1 cup of water, a small zippered plastic bag, and a large zippered plastic bag.

First, pour the juice into the small bag. Now seal the bag. Next, add the ice, salt, and water to the large bag. Now place the bag of juice inside the large bag of ice and seal it up. Shake the bags for about 15 minutes until the sorbet is the consistency you want. (Make sure the ice is covering the juice during this time.) Remove the inner bag and rinse it off in the sink with cold water to get the salt water off. Pour the sorbet into a bowl and enjoy!

What happened? Well, salt lowers the freezing point of water, causing ice to melt. As I mentioned earlier, this is why salt is poured on icy roads and sidewalks. When salt is put with ice, the freezing point of the ice is lowered. The more salt you add, the lower the freezing point. For example, water usually freezes at 32°F. A 10% salt solution freezes at 20°F (-7°C), and a 20% salt solution freezes at 2°F (-17°C). By lowering the freezing point of the ice, you made the mixture much colder, which allowed the juice to get cold enough to freeze into sorbet!

Explain all that you've learned so far about freezing point, melting point, amorphous solids, surface tension, and viscosity.

The intense heat inside the earth melts the metals in the outer core and the rocks surrounding the core. This makes the outer core liquid metal. But in the inner core, the pressure is so great that it's solid.

Gas Matter

Before we talk about gas, let's do a simple experiment.

Try This!

You will need: An adult's supervision, a clear plastic cup, a small piece of paper, a piece of gum (or peanut butter), and a sink or large bowl full of water.

First, wad up the paper and put it in the cup. Now turn the cup over. The paper should not fall out. If it does, use gum or peanut butter to stick the wad of paper to the bottom of the cup. The paper should only cover ¼ of the cup; the rest should be air. Now, still holding the cup upside down, keep it straight while you submerge it into the water. After a few seconds, remove the cup from the water, making sure the cup remains upside down. Now check inside the cup.

In the Air

What happened? The paper should have stayed dry. Why is this? It's because the air around you is matter, called gas. Gas is a substance you can't see, but it's actually full of moving atoms—mostly oxygen and nitrogen. The matter in the air stayed in the cup, keeping the paper dry. The water could not get up into the cup because it was blocked by another material—air!

Gas is the state of matter we have a hard time seeing, but we can sometimes smell it! When your mother is cleaning the kitchen, you can often smell the cleaning products from another room. That's because the cleaning products produce gases that move around in the air. As you know, when a gas is in the air, it moves like crazy. It's just hoppin' and boppin' and dancing and prancing about—filling up the whole room with its acrobatics. It's like a child who needs a lot of room to play. The more room you give him, the more room he'll use.

Gases have faster moving atoms than liquids. When a liquid becomes a gas, it's because the atoms were infused with energy. How does a liquid become a gas? Well, if you've ever boiled water, you've watched gas in action. Becoming active is the atom's response to heat. As the stove slowly heats the water in the pan, the water molecules begin to move. Soon, the atoms begin to jump around. If you've ever looked in a pan of boiling water, you saw those water atoms going crazy with all kinds of energy. They were jumping around in the pan! We call this **boiling**. Eventually, when they got hot enough, those jumping atoms started jumping right out of the container and into the air, changing from a liquid to a gas. They became a vapor or **steam**. Those little atoms began moving, moving,

As this candle burns, it releases gas molecules into the air. Eventually, the entire candle will melt away, changing to gas molecules.

moving until they needed more room than that small pan provided.

We call the temperature that makes something change from a liquid to a gas the **boiling point**. Like the melting and freezing point, every material has a specific boiling point. As you've noticed, water becomes a gas fairly easily. The boiling point of regular water is usually 212°F (100°C). However, most of the elements God made have such a high boiling point they're almost never found as a gas. In fact, gold would have to reach over 5,000°F (2,760°C) before it would turn into a gas.

The boiling water in this kettle is changing from a liquid to a gas.

Atoms Together and Apart

Most solid atoms are lined up in an orderly way and are frozen in place very close together—usually in a very structured manner. Liquid atoms are not structured or as close together as solid atoms. Gas atoms are actually separated from one another. Look at the images below to see what the atoms might look like in each of these states.

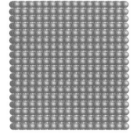

The particles in a solid are arranged in a way that gives solids a definite shape and volume.

The particles in a liquid are free to flow. They have a definite volume, but not a definite shape.

Gas particles do not have a definite shape or volume. They are spaced as far apart as they can get.

Now let's add another science concept. Do you remember that when something takes up more space, it has more volume? This is true of gas as well. Gas has more volume than liquids and solids. You see, the gas molecules are not attracted to one another. It's as if they don't like each other. So they fly around with a lot of energy trying to stay away from one another. If they're in a container and find one little opening, they fly out. You see, gas molecules always tend to escape the container that holds them. If the container is small, the gas volume will be small. If the container is large, the volume will be large. The gas's volume will equal the volume of the container.

Gas is defined as a state of matter with particles that don't have a specific volume or shape; the particles take on the volume and shape of the container.

Voluminous Expanding Gas

Have you ever noticed that when a woman sprays perfume on herself, it's not too long before you can smell that perfume from across the room? What happened? Well, the gas molecules carrying the fragrance of the perfume move with a tremendous amount of energy all the way across the room to your nose. They move through the room because gas can fill a space—even a large space—as the gas molecules fly about. Basically, the gas expands or grows in volume, filling up the entire room. Let's explore this concept a little more.

What does the word "expand" mean? It means to get larger. The individual gas molecules (the atoms that make up gas) don't actually get larger. However, as I've said, each atom or molecule takes up more space, filling that space up with all its active flying about. That is why we say gas expands. It gets larger. When a liquid becomes a gas, it needs more room to move. It won't stay put in the container anymore. The hotter the gas gets, the more room the molecules need—and the more the gas will expand.

Let's do an activity to watch this in action.

Try This!

You will need: An adult's supervision, a balloon, a small bottle of soda, and a packet of Pop Rocks candy.

First, pour your Pop Rocks into the balloon. Now carefully, without spilling the candy into the soda, fit the opening of the balloon over the opening of the bottle of soda. After the balloon is snug on the bottle, lift up the balloon and carefully shake the Pop Rocks into the soda. Watch to see what happens next!

What happened in this experiment? After coming in contact with the soda, the rough surfaces of the rock candies provided a place for the carbon dioxide bubbles to form easily—and they bubbled their way out of the solution and into the air. Some of the carbon dioxide from the soda escaped as well. These things together caused a lot of gas to move around above the liquid. Because the gas needed more space, it pushed against the balloon, causing the balloon to inflate with expanding gas. The balloon was hard and firm because the gas molecules were putting pressure against the sides of the balloon. They would have escaped if you'd given them the chance.

You've learned a lot about matter! Can you explain what you've learned to someone else?

Try This!

You will need: A piece of bubble gum.

Chew a piece of bubble gum until it's soft. Next, put the gum over your tongue, holding it with your teeth. Now blow a bubble. Once you've blown your bubble, explain what happened and why your bubble expanded. To learn how to blow a bubble, visit www.apologia.com/bookextras.

Bubble Power

When you blew a bubble with your gum, you filled the bubble gum with gas molecules—the very gas that was located in your lungs! Because gases are full of energy, they also have tremendous power—enough power to stretch out your gum and fill up your bubble!

Expanding and Escaping Air

You already know gas needs more room as it heats up. The hotter it gets, the less likely it is to stay in the container it's in. In fact, once I left a can of soda in my car. The temperature of the car reached above 140°F (60°C) because it was in direct sunlight on a very hot day. The can of soda was filled with a gas called carbon dioxide. This gas got so active that the can exploded in my car! That was because the gas needed to escape its container.

As fire heats the air inside the balloon, the air expands and much of it escapes, causing the balloon to be lighter than the air surrounding it.

This balloon is floating in the sky because it is less dense than the air outside it.

This is how hot air balloons get off the ground. You see, below the giant balloon is a heater that sends heat up into the balloon. This causes the air atoms inside the balloon to be filled with a lot of energy and to move about at a rapid pace. This means the gases in the air begin to take up more space. After all, they need more space to move, move, move when they get hot, hot, hot! Actually, a lot of this wildly busy, energy-filled air escapes out of the hole in the bottom of the balloon. Guess what happens when the air inside the balloon escapes? The remaining air inside the balloon becomes less dense than the air outside the balloon. With fewer molecules floating around, there's less matter inside the balloon than outside it. What happens when something is less dense? It floats! It's the same with air as it is with water. The heated air inside the balloon causes the balloon to suddenly become lighter than air. Then up, up, up the hot air balloon goes into the sky. Pretty cool, huh?

Let's look at what happens when we won't let gas escape.

Compressed Gas

What do you think would happen if you took all that gas energy that wants to take up a lot of volume and squeezed it into a tiny space? Well, you would end up with compressed gas. We use compressed gas all the time. You see, when we put a little nozzle on a can of compressed gas and open the can a bit, gases and sometimes liquids spray out. This is how hairspray works. Compressed gas mixed with sticky liquid is

put in the hairspray can. The gas helps the product spray out of the can and onto your hair. Compressed gas is also added to cans of whipped cream so that you can release it nicely.

How does compressed gas help create products that spray out? The actively moving molecules in the compressed gas rush out of any opening they can when the opportunity is presented to them. They don't like being confined in such a small space. They need space to move!

Gas to Liquid to Solid to Liquid to Gas

We have explored gases quite a bit. Remember that everything can change from a solid to a liquid and from a liquid to a gas. But that's not all! The whole process also goes in the other direction. Gases become liquids and liquids become solids. How does this happen? Removing heat can cause matter to change states. We know that water boils and becomes a gas at 212°F, but it changes from a gas to a liquid at the same point. If the temperature drops below 212°F, the gas will become a liquid again. But what do we call it when a gas becomes a liquid? It's called the **condensation point**.

When a gas becomes a liquid, we say it condenses. In fact, the gas clouds in the sky are filled with water vapor and liquid droplets. When it rains, those droplets get bigger. Scientists call rain condensation. There are a lot of processes involved with clouds becoming rain, but condensation typically happens like this: As gas atoms begin to cool off, they slow down. When they slow down, they begin to find each other and stick together again. As they do this, they eventually become a liquid.

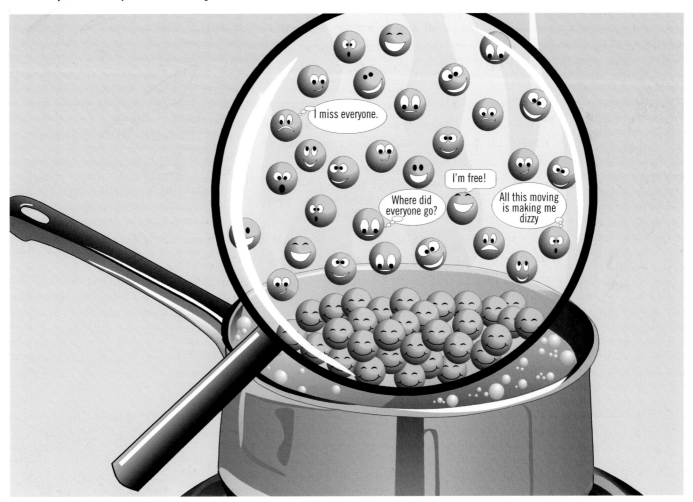

This image demonstrates molecules in a liquid heating up and moving apart as they form into gas in the air.

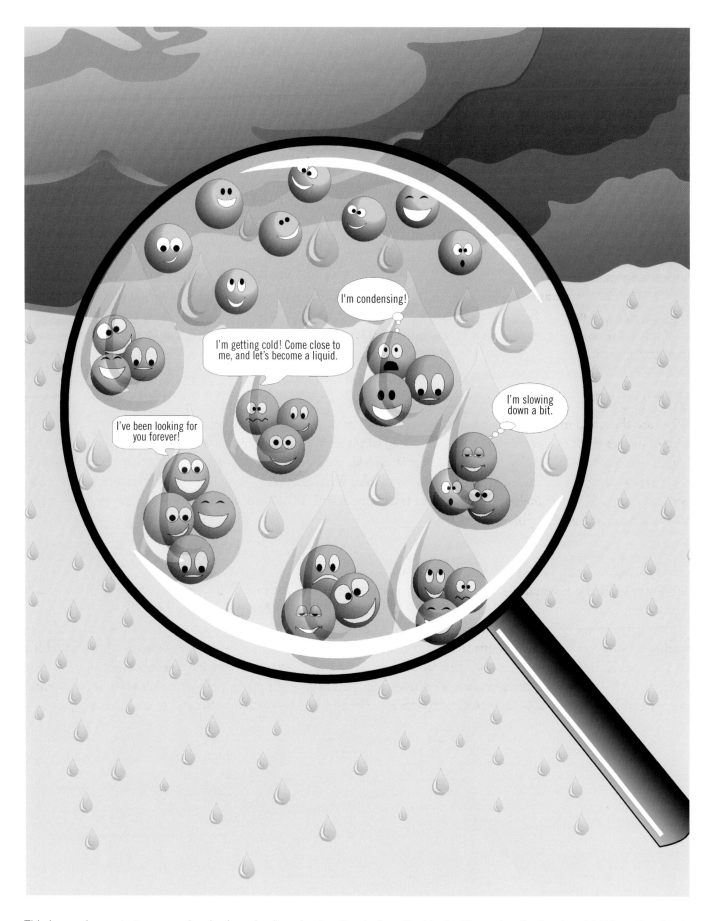

This image demonstrates gas molecules in a cloud coming together to form liquid rain. The molecules bond and fall from the cloud.

 Take a deep breath. Now get really close to a mirror or window. Open your mouth and exhale your hot breath onto the mirror or window. What do you think has happened? All that air has been in contact with the very moist surfaces of your lungs, windpipe, and mouth or nose. Some of the liquid water on those surfaces turned into gas. This became part of the air you breathed out. Then this gas hit the cold mirror and turned back into water. That's what's on your mirror or window! If you wipe it with your finger, you can see and feel that it's wet.

Final Matters

When God made the world, He created all three states of matter. I'm so glad He did, aren't you? Would you be surprised to learn there are more states of matter? In addition to solid, liquid, and gas, there are plasmas and Bose-Einstein states of matter. But you won't hear much about these until college.

Now it's time to review what you've learned in this lesson. After that, we'll do some notebooking activities and then an experiment.

What Do You Remember?

What are the three main states of matter? What causes one state of matter to change into another state? Which state of matter is composed of atoms that are frozen in place? Which state of matter is composed of atoms that are bound together but do not have a specific form? Which state of matter is composed of atoms that are freely moving about, expanding to take up as much space as is available? What is freezing point? What temperature is the freezing point of water? What is melting point? What is boiling point? What temperature is the boiling point of water? What is the condensation point?

Notebooking Activities

Write down all the fascinating facts you've learned in this lesson. Be sure to include illustrations. Templates to record your learning are provided for you in the *Chemistry and Physics Notebooking Journal.*

Now you're going to make Matter Pockets for your notebooking journal. You'll label one pocket solids, one liquids, and one gases. On the outside of each pocket, write the correct definition for the state of matter labeled on the pocket. Then, with a parent's permission and guidance, search through magazines, newspapers, and the Internet for pictures of solid matter, liquid matter, and gas matter. Cut out or print the pictures and put them in the correct pocket. The *Chemistry and Physics Notebooking Journal* has templates for you to make your pockets.

Experiment
Earth's Water Cycle

Let's create a water cycle jar to represent the common states of matter that keep the earth alive and well.

You will need:

- a large, clear plastic container or jar with a tight-fitting lid
- rocks
- sand
- topsoil
- a plant from a plant store
- a plastic cup of water

1. To represent the layers of earth, put a layer of rocks on the bottom of the jar.
2. Place a layer of sand on top of the rocks.
3. Put a layer of topsoil on top of the sand. You've just created your earth model.
4. Dig a hole in your soil and plant your plant in that layer.
5. Take your cup of water and push it into the soil so that it stays upright.
6. Put the lid on the jar and place the jar in the sunshine.
7. Come back in a few hours and you will see the water cycle that is much like the one God created on the earth.

The water will evaporate and move as a gas out of the cup. The gas will then hit the top of the jar, condensing (turning back from a gas into a liquid) down the side of the jar and into the soil. That's your rain! Now you understand better how God created the states of matter to care for the earth.

Building Blocks of Creation

My favorite toy as a child was Lincoln Logs. I spent hours building small cities with these special logs. My children, however, preferred Legos. What do you like to build with? Well, God has a favorite building block as well—atoms!

You remember from the last lesson that God used atoms to make every single thing in the universe. This includes every star, every planet, every asteroid, and every comet—as well as every mountain, every ocean, every flower, and every creature on earth. All matter is made up of atoms. Do you remember how small an atom is? This lesson focuses on this tiny building block of creation.

What exactly is an atom? An **atom** is the smallest particle of an element that still keeps the properties of that element.

Think of it like this: Let's say that at the end of your physics study you decide to build a shrinking machine. To test it out, you come up with the brilliant idea of reducing one of your siblings to a tiny size. It works! After a while though, your very little brother or sister gets hungry, and all you can find to feed him or her is a cookie. But he or she needs tiny food! So you begin to break the cookie into smaller and smaller pieces. However, you find that every piece is still too large to be eaten by your shrunken sibling. So you get out a magnifying glass and work very carefully to break the cookie down to the smallest pieces possible. Finally, you have a tiny piece that still has all the parts of the cookie—the flour, sugar, butter, and salt—in all the right amounts. It's still a real cookie—just a really small piece of one. If you broke down the cookie even more, you would separate out its parts. You might get a piece of sugar, a grain of

salt, or some flour, but you wouldn't have the whole cookie. I don't think your small sibling would want to eat a grain of salt, do you?

That's kind of like an atom. An atom is the smallest part of a particular material that still has the same traits of that material. Do you understand now?

Sulfur, one of the naturally occurring elements, is a soft, yellow mineral.

Think of it this way: An atom of gold, though it's too small for your eyes to see, would still be gold. If you had a pile of gold atoms, you would then be able to see the gold. When we have a group of one kind of atom, we call it an element. If you had a group of gold atoms all together, you would have the element gold. If you had a group of mercury atoms all together, you would have the element mercury.

As far as we know, when God made the earth, He created about 94 different elements (that means 94 different kinds of atoms). We call these elements **naturally occurring elements** because they can be found in nature and were *made* by God. There are about 25 more elements God has helped man to create in science labs. Yes—man has made atoms! Remember that we are made in God's image. Because God is creative, we have the ability to be creative too. I bet you are very creative. I'm sure you imagine all kinds of things you would like to create. Well, because of the creativity that God gave to humans, we can create some pretty amazing things—including atoms! That's pretty awesome. We call man-made elements **synthetic elements**. "Synthetic" means man-made. Of course, these elements aren't as good as the elements God created because they eventually decay or die out.

Mercury is an element that is liquid at room temperature. It's poisonous if swallowed, yet it was once used in thermometers and tooth fillings.

Jupiter's moon, Io, is made up of a great amount of sulfur. That's why it's yellow.

Variety of Atoms

As I mentioned, God created atoms and their elements to be used in building the heavens and the earth. Although each element may *look* different to our eyes (gold doesn't look anything like oxygen), would you be surprised to learn that every single atom has the same basic structure and form?

It's kind of like working with Legos. All the Legos are built similarly, but there are so many different sizes and colors that you can build almost anything with the right mixture of Legos. Because of the way Legos are designed, each piece can fit together with almost every other piece to make just about anything.

Legos come in a variety of shapes and colors, but they all have the same basic structure.

Well, that's just like atoms! They all have a similar structure which helps them fit together to make everything you see around you. What's really interesting is that when atoms combine, unlike Legos, they can change into something totally different. For example, if you take two atoms of the gas hydrogen and one atom of the gas oxygen, you no longer have a gas. Those two gases connect to make a wet substance. Can you guess what they make? Water, or H_2O as it's sometimes called. H_2O is a molecule. When two or more different atoms are combined, they form a molecule.

Here's another example of atoms combining to make interesting molecules. The element carbon usually exists as a black, chalky substance. Many, many things on earth have carbon atoms in them, including all living creatures.

Take a look at the picture of a piece of the element carbon. In the element form, carbon is often called graphite. The only atoms found in that piece of graphite are carbon atoms.

Yet carbon combines with many different elements to create all kinds of amazing things—even plants, animals, and you! Yes—most of your body is made up of different combinations of carbon atoms! In fact, every single living thing is made of carbon. Yet when we take the black, chalky carbon atom and fit it with one single oxygen atom, we don't get something as lovely as you. Instead, we end up with a really bad gas called carbon monoxide. It's a dangerous gas that's deadly to breathe.

This family was built entirely out of Legos. They're found at Legoland in Germany.

If you fit several carbon atoms with several oxygen atoms and throw in several hydrogen atoms, you get a molecule that's altogether different. In fact, you get one of your favorite things—sugar!

Isn't that amazing? Together, carbon and oxygen can make a terrible gas or a wonderful, tasty treat—or even a wonderful person, like you! It all depends on how you combine atoms. Yes—it's all in how they're put together.

As you know, a molecule is formed when two or more atoms join together. But a **compound** contains at least two different elements combined. All compounds are molecules, but not all molecules are compounds. Let me explain: Some molecules have two atoms of the same element. For example, two hydrogen atoms can combine to make H_2. That's not a compound even though two atoms are connected. Water (H_2O) is a compound because it combines more than one element. The very smallest bit of water would be referred to as a molecule.

This is graphite, which is made up of carbon atoms. Carbon is found in all living things.

Attaching Atoms

God knew exactly which elements to connect to make everything He desired, whether it was an ocean, pineapples, polar bears, porcupines, or people! Although God knew from the beginning, scientists have just recently learned how atoms connect. Later, we'll be doing an experiment to connect the atoms in different substances in order to create new compounds and substances.

When we connect atoms, we have to be careful. Before we connect different atoms or elements, we should know *exactly* what will happen—otherwise we could get in real trouble. Let me explain why. You see, oxygen isn't a dangerous gas. Carbon isn't a dangerous element. But you remember that these two atoms together can be dangerous. That's why when we work with chemicals, we have to use great care. You never know what toxic substance you might come up with when mixing two perfectly nice chemicals together. You should always wear safety goggles and follow instructions very carefully so you don't end up with a dangerous gas or an explosion.

In fact, back in the olden days—way back before science was an important part of people's education—there were individuals who mixed lots of stuff together to make new things. They were usually called **alchemists**. People thought they were a little nutty, mixing all those chemicals together all the time. Most alchemists were hoping to find a way to make gold out of other chemicals. Sometimes they

This image depicts a famous alchemist in Europe, mixing chemicals in a strangely designed contraption.

thought they could develop cures for diseases. You see, alchemists didn't really understand atoms and how they fit together. Many of these alchemists believed that the strange reactions of chemicals (like smoking or exploding) were produced by magic or by chanting a spell over the chemicals. This is why alchemy was linked to witchcraft.

Sadly, many of these early chemists ended up harming themselves. They had no knowledge of dangerous gases and the energy that could be released when some elements were mixed with others. In fact, when some chemicals are combined or heated, they release a huge amount of energy—enough energy to explode an entire building! So you can see how alchemists lived a very dangerous life. Today, chemists know a lot more about atoms and understand what will happen when they mix chemicals together.

However, part of the fun of learning about chemistry is mixing substances together so you can create a big reaction. Let's mix a couple of innocent ingredients to see if we can cause a big chemical reaction!

Before doing the experiment below, explain what you've learned so far about atoms, elements, molecules, and compounds.

Try This!

You will need: A adult's supervision, gloves, safety goggles, a small empty soda bottle, 1 tablespoon of yeast (or potassium iodide for a stronger reaction), 4 tablespoons of very warm water, dishwashing liquid, food coloring, a cup, a stirring spoon, a deep-sided dish, and hydrogen peroxide. (The kind you get from the beauty supply store makes a bigger, more fun reaction.)

First, put on your gloves and safety goggles. (Although this is a safe experiment, it's a good habit to always wear protective gear when working with chemicals.) Next, mix the yeast and warm water together in a cup and put it aside. Pour ½ cup of hydrogen peroxide into the soda bottle. Then pour ¼ cup of dishwashing liquid into the soda bottle. Now squirt some food coloring into the soda bottle. Set the bottle in a sink or inside a large, deep sided dish. Finally, quickly pour the yeast solution into the bottle and stand back. The liquid it produces is perfectly harmless but quite abundant!

I'll explain why this chemical reaction happened on page 56. In the meantime, let's study the inner features of atoms to learn how they're built to connect with other atoms. This will help you understand how atoms form chemical reactions and new substances. This will also help you understand why the chemicals in this experiment acted the way they did when they mixed together.

Atom Anatomy

As you well know, atoms are small—but believe it or not, there are three things inside the atom that are even smaller. These three things are important to know about, so pay close attention. This information will come up again and again in this book and in science classes all throughout high school and college. The three things inside atoms are protons, neutrons and electrons.

Look at the picture of an atom on this page. Do you see the protons, neutrons, and electrons in the picture? You may have already noticed the protons have a plus sign on them, and the electrons have a minus sign on them. That's something called charge—positive charge and negative charge—which we'll talk about in a moment. Do you also see a faint line surrounding the atom? The line does not really exist; it's drawn in most illustrations of atoms to show that the electron travels around the proton and neutron.

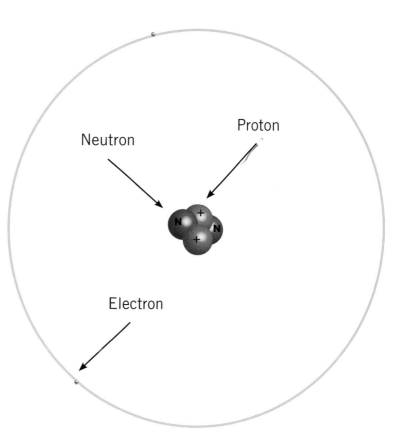

Neutron

Proton

Electron

Because you're made of atoms, you have an electrical charge. That's why the energy streams from this plasma globe are affected by your touch.

Charged Up

Let's talk about a strange thing scientists discovered about atoms. Some atoms are *attracted* to each other, and other atoms are *repelled* by each other. In other words, some atoms want to join together, and other atoms want to move away from each other. Scientists decided to call this strange occurrence **charge**—electron charge or electrical charge. Charge is a weird physics concept. It turns out that all atoms have electric energy. That means if everything is made up of atoms, and all atoms are electrical, absolutely every single thing on earth is electrical. The chair under you has an electrical charge. This book has an electrical charge. Even you are charged with electricity! Is that shocking to you? Well, God made an electrical world! We'll devote a whole chapter in this book to electricity. Now *that* will be an electrifying chapter, won't it?

Pluses and Minuses

Here's what we know: There are two kinds of electrical charges. We call one positive and one negative. It's not really that one has plus signs on it and acts positively and the other has minus signs on it and acts negatively. It's just that one is opposite of the other.

What exactly *is* charge? Frankly, scientists aren't sure what it is. It's not energy, but it can be used to produce energy. It's not anything we can clearly define. It's like asking, "What is time?" That's hard to explain, isn't it? There are so many things yet to discover about God's world and all He made. At this time, we can't really define what charge is. But we can say charge is something electrical that God built into all substances, and it's what makes all substances behave like they do. I hope you'll be happy with that definition. For now, that's all we know. You'll learn a lot in this book about how charge behaves. That will help you understand what it is.

As you may have figured out already, all atoms have positively charged and negatively charged particles inside of them. The positively charged particles are the **protons**, and the negatively charged particles are the **electrons**. They're

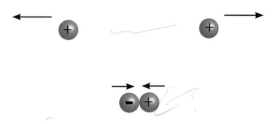

Particles with the same charge are repelled by one another. Particles with the opposite charge are attracted to one another. This is where we get the saying "opposites attract."

oppositely charged.

Normal atoms have the same number of protons and electrons, so we say the atom is neutrally charged. Neutral means neither positive nor negative. The positive and negative cancel each other out. That's basic math. If I add two and subtract two, I get zero. That's how normal atoms are. They have a charge of zero.

Positively charged particles are attracted to negatively charged particles. Particles with the same charge are repelled by each other. That means they aren't attracted to one another and actually move away from each other.

Primary Positives

Let's get back to how this affects atoms. As I said earlier, inside the atom are three little bitty particles. Can you name them? Great! Let's talk about these protons, neutrons, and electrons. Look at the picture of the atom while you read.

In the center of each atom, you'll find two kinds of tiny particles bundled together: neutrons and protons. Protons are the pluses you see in the picture. That's easy to remember since "plus," "positive," and "proton" all start with the letter P. The word "primary," which means first, also starts with P. The word "proton" comes from the Greek word that means first. That's because protons are the first or primary particle in an atom. In fact, the number of protons each atom has actually tells us which atom it is. Every atom has a different number of protons. If we count the protons in an atom, we know which atom we have! The number of protons an atom has is so important that it has a name: the **atomic number**.

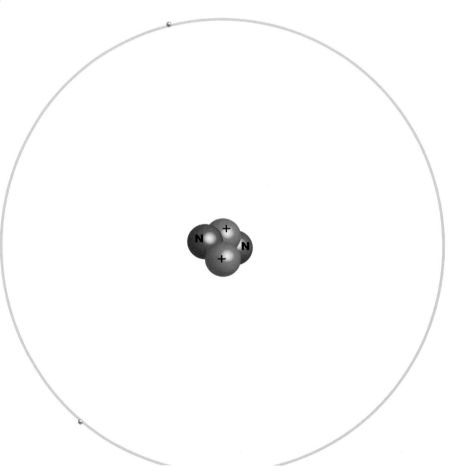

Can you identify the protons in this atom? They're the primary particles in the atom and are positively charged.

Speaking of atomic, this is a good time to start building an atomic model! To do this, you're going to build hydrogen and oxygen atoms using two kinds of candy. I think this will be a fun way to help you understand atoms better. Let's get started.

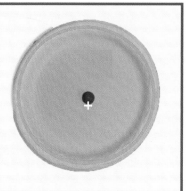

Try This!

You will need: An adult's supervision, small and large paper plates, a marker, glue, small candy (like Nerds), and large candy (like Peanut M&M'S or Gobstoppers).

First, choose one large candy to be your proton. Draw a plus sign on it with your marker and glue it to the center of a small paper plate. The plate represents the whole atom. Of course, real atoms are not flat like your paper plate; they're more spherically shaped like a ball.

You've just created the nucleus of the atom hydrogen. How do we know it's the atom hydrogen? Because it has only one proton! If it had more protons, it would be a totally different atom. Remember, the primary protons tell us *exactly* which atom it is.

Neutral News

In the middle of most atoms—snuggled in tight next to the protons—is another particle called the neutron. **Neutrons** are neutrally charged, meaning they have no charge at all. That's how they got their name—neutral, neutron. Makes sense, huh? They don't add any charge to the atom, but they're pretty big, so they do add mass.

Neutrons are about as big as protons but are just a bit heavier. So they have almost the same mass as protons, but just slightly more. We'll talk about the mass of an atom in a moment.

You won't be adding any neutrons to your hydrogen atom because the number of neutrons in hydrogen can naturally vary between none and two.

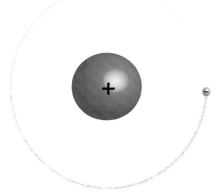

This hydrogen atom has one proton, one electron, and no neutrons. It's neutrally charged.

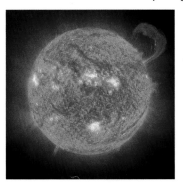

Hydrogen is a gas found in the sun. It gives the sun light and heat.

Protons and any neutrons are always found in the nucleus of the atom. The word "nucleus" means the central or core part of something that has other parts gathered around it. As you may have guessed, the **nucleus** is the center of an atom that contains the protons and neutrons. The nucleus is also the heaviest part of the atom because the protons and neutrons are the heaviest particles *inside* an atom. Together, protons and neutrons are called **nucleons**. So instead of saying protons and neutrons, we can just say nucleons. The number of nucleons an atom has is so important that it has a name: **mass number**. It's called the mass number because the nucleons make up almost all of the mass of the atom.

Before studying electrons, tell someone what you've learned about charge, protons, and neutrons.

Electric Electrons

Now let's get to the busy little bees of each atom—the electrons! The teeny, tiny electrical electrons are the life of the party—the action of the atom—the whirling, swirling activity that makes sure everything on earth is in constant motion. Yes! Even things that are sitting still—like this book—are really in constant motion because they have electrons in them. The electrons are constantly buzzing in speedy circles around the nucleus.

Electrons are tiny. I mean *really* tiny. In fact, while protons and neutrons have about the same mass, they're each almost 2,000 times more massive than an electron. As I mentioned earlier, almost all the mass (and weight) of an atom is in the nucleus. However, the atom's size (its volume or how much space it takes up) is mostly due to the busy little electrons. Do you know why? It's because they need and use a lot of space while they're moving around the nucleus.

Believe it or not, even though it's just a tiny little particle, an electron has exactly the same amount of charge as a proton. It's not the same charge, but it's the same *amount* of charge. The electron's charge is negative instead of positive. Again, you may remember that a normal atom has the same number of protons and electrons. When you add them together, they add up to zero, or neutral charge.

So now you know that all neutral atoms have the same number of protons and electrons inside of them! That's pretty easy to remember.

Let's complete our atomic model by finishing our hydrogen and oxygen atoms.

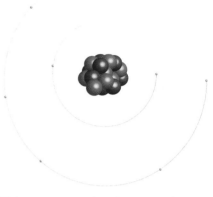

This oxygen atom has 8 protons, 8 neutrons, and 8 electrons. Its atomic number is 8. Its mass number is 16.

Try This!

Draw a circle along the outer edge of your atom to represent the path of the electron. Try to keep your marker as close to the edge of the plate as possible. Now glue one small piece of candy somewhere on the circle to be your electron. With the marker, draw a minus sign next to it. You've just completed one hydrogen atom! Write the letter H inside your atom; H stands for hydrogen. Now make another atom exactly like it so you have two hydrogen atoms.

Try This!

Oxygen has eight of everything: eight protons, eight neutrons, and eight electrons. Oxygen is a lot bigger than hydrogen, so you'll need a large paper plate. Gather your protons and neutrons and glue them in a pile in the center of your plate. Next, draw a circle around the outer edge of the plate, then draw another circle an inch or so inside the outer circle. You'll have two circles surrounding the nucleus. These two circles are the electron energy levels; oxygen has two electron energy levels. The first energy level of an atom can have only two electrons. Go ahead and glue two small candies on the circle closest to the nucleus. Now glue the remaining six candy electrons on the outer circle. Finally, place your hydrogen atoms on either side of your oxygen atom. You've just finished your candy atomic model!

Electron Energy

As you learned, electrons are busily moving around the nucleus of each atom. They never sit still. Every atom has electrons, and electrons are always moving. Whether the atoms are found in a solid, liquid, or gas, they're filled with moving electrons. Even a block of ice is filled with moving electrons. Of course, the atoms in a block of ice don't move as much as the atoms in a glass of water because they're very cold—but they are definitely moving. Here on earth, every electron—no matter how frozen or solid the substance may be—is always moving. Electrons never stop moving! The walls of your house may seem solid and still, but the truth is, the walls are moving. That's because they're filled with electrons. Down under the earth where the roots of trees are found, there are billions and billions of busy electrons. Up in the sky where the clouds exist, there are millions and millions of moving electrons.

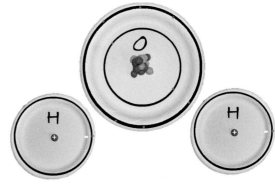

Your completed atomic model of water should look like this.

If the nucleus were the ball in the center of the field, the atom would be the size of the whole stadium. The black dot in the center represents the nucleus-ball. The atom is mostly empty space.

What's even more strange is the fact that atoms are mostly empty space. They have an enormous amount of empty space between the nucleus and electrons. In fact, some people say if the nucleus were the size of a football, the whole atom would be the size of a football stadium—and the nearest electron would be a mile away. In math terms, the atom is about 100,000 times wider than the nucleus—or a quadrillion times its volume.

It's hard to picture all of this, but it's important for you to understand that within an atom there's a lot of space. In fact, there's so much space that even solid objects are mostly empty space! The wall in front of you is mostly just empty space. This may not seem possible, but it's the truth. In fact, there's a whole field of science dedicated to studying where electrons may be at any moment. It's called quantum physics. Maybe you'll study quantum physics when you get older.

Clouds, Shells, and Orbitals

Those energy levels you created—the circles you drew around the nucleus—are really, really important.

You see, each electron is assigned to a particular **energy level**. Sometimes we call them **orbitals** or **electron shells**. You'll study the differences in high school chemistry. So just remember, if I say energy level, orbital, or electron shell, I'm talking about the same thing—the level where the electron spends its time buzzing around the atom.

Let's try to understand these orbits. First, since the atom isn't flat like your plate, electrons don't move in a flat circle around the nucleus the way the earth moves around the sun. The atoms are more spherical or ball-shaped, so the energy level is more like a cloud that surrounds the atom. The electrons can move anywhere around the atom, but they spend more of their time at their level.

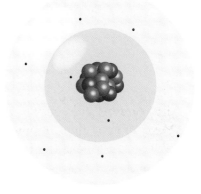

The electrons are located in their energy levels. The energy level is like a sphere or cloud that surrounds the atom. Each electron can be found anywhere inside its energy level, zipping around the atom.

51

Look at the atoms below. Count how many energy levels each has around the nucleus. Count how many electrons are in each energy level.

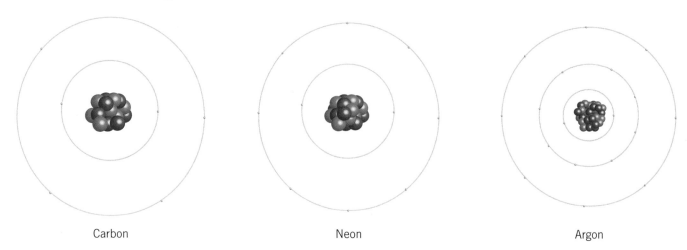

| Carbon | Neon | Argon |

There are more than two energy levels in most types of atoms. Every energy level can fit a certain number of electrons. The first electron shell can only fit two electrons. That's why you put only two electrons in your oxygen atom's first level. Some atoms only have one or two electrons in them, so they only have one energy level. That's like your hydrogen atoms.

If an atom has more than two electrons, the next electrons are placed in the second energy level. That's why you put the six electrons in the outer level of the oxygen atom. This second energy level can take up to eight electrons total. Once it has eight, it's full. Once it's full, if an element has any more electrons, they're placed in the next level up. On and on it goes. Every level can take more electrons than the level below it.

Atoms really prefer to have their outer shells full. A happy atom is an atom with a full outer shell! The oxygen atom has only six atoms in its outer shell, but ideally it should have eight. So it isn't happy unless it gets two more. Most atoms are *not* happy atoms. They're constantly connecting to other atoms to fill up their energy levels. This is how molecules are formed—atoms connecting to other atoms to fill their energy levels.

Valence Valor

You can see that the outside shells of each atom holding those outside electrons are really important. They're so important that we've given the electrons in the outer shell a special name: **valence electrons**. All the electrons in the very outside energy level are valence electrons.

Now look at the paper-plate hydrogen and oxygen atoms you made. As you know, the outer shell of your hydrogen atom could only fit two electrons. How many valence electrons does it have? It has one. The outer shell of your oxygen atom can fit eight electrons. How many valence electrons does it have? It has six. How many more electrons does the oxygen atom need to be full? Yes! Two more electrons is all the oxygen atom needs to be happy. If you could connect the atoms like Legos,

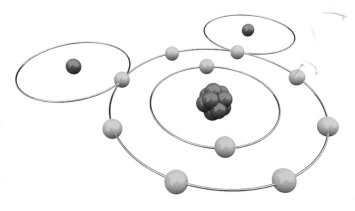

Two hydrogen atoms and one oxygen atom are a perfect match to fill up all the empty spaces in the energy levels.

how many hydrogen atoms would it take to fill up that second level of your oxygen atom? Exactly! It takes two hydrogen atoms to make one oxygen atom complete. It also takes one oxygen atom to make two hydrogen atoms complete.

Now you know why there's so much water on the earth! God created these two atoms to bond together. It's a match made in heaven—a perfect connection of three atoms that makes life possible on earth. Without water, we'd all be in trouble!

When two atoms share electrons, they bond together to make a molecule. It's very similar to how you fit pieces of a Lego structure together. Every Lego has a certain number of notches that can fit together with other Legos. The atom's "notches" are the empty spaces in its outer shell.

Now you know how all the atoms around you fit together to make molecules. Molecules combine to make all the things you see around you! Before we discuss the different ways and reasons atoms bond, let's look at little closer at all the elements found on the earth. Then we can better understand atomic bonding!

What have you learned about electrons? If you're taking a break for the day, be sure to write down in your notebooking journal the fascinating facts you've learned.

The Periodic Table of Elements

Did you know scientists love to organize information into charts? They've even placed all the elements God made into a wonderful chart called the periodic table of elements.

Look at the periodic table. As you can see, each element has a special name and symbol. Do you see the numbers inside the boxes? The number in the top corner is the atomic number. That's the number of protons the atom has. It's an important number. Although atoms can change the number of electrons and neutrons they have, they can't change the number of protons they have. The number of protons tells us which atom it is.

Look at the number in the box below the symbol. That number is how much mass those particular atoms have or how heavy those atoms are (if you're weighing them here on earth). It's really the weight of a huge number of those particular atoms put together. (It's impossible to weigh just one single atom.) We call it the atomic weight or the atomic mass. In simple terms, it's the number of protons and neutrons—or nucleons—the atom has. Sometimes the number is a bit smaller than you would expect. That's because some of the matter inside the atom is turned into energy needed to keep the protons together. But sometimes the number is a little larger than you would expect. That's because some atoms have a different number of neutrons than protons. We call those atoms with a different number

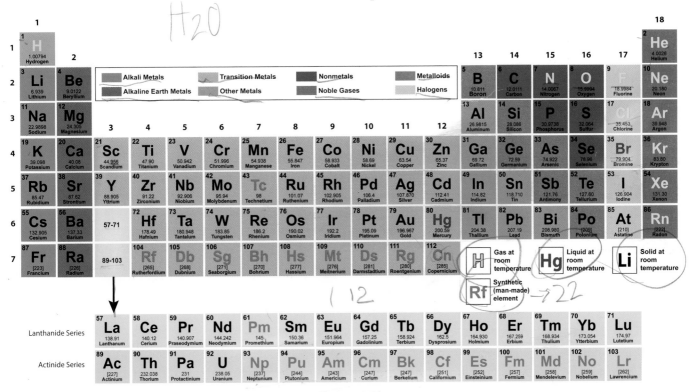

of neutrons **isotopes**. You'll learn more about atomic mass and isotopes in high school.

Do you see the letters in each box? Those are the symbols for each element or atom. Let's talk about how the element gets its symbol. Sometimes it's rather simple: Carbon is called C, which stands for carbon. Oxygen is O, which stands for oxygen. Can you guess what the symbol for hydrogen is? That's right—H.

Unfortunately, not all the elements are that easy to guess. That's because many of the symbols are based on the element's Latin name. Latin was once the language all the scientists and alchemists spoke back in the Middle Ages in Europe. Because they all spoke Latin, they were able to communicate with each other even though they lived in different countries. Since it's now considered a dead language (meaning people no longer use the Latin language to speak to each other), Latin is a good language to use for science because the meanings of the words won't change. In our English language, the meanings of words can change after 100 years or so. For example, the word "awful" once meant full of awe. Hundreds of years ago, if something was considered awful, it was wonderful and amazing, causing great awe. Now it means just the opposite! You can see why scientists prefer to use a language that doesn't change.

For example, the element gold has the symbol Au from its Latin name *aurum*. Can you find that element on the periodic table?

Can you describe gold? Look at the element above gold on the periodic table. What element is that? It's the element silver. It has the symbol Ag because its Latin name is *argentum*. Do you see how scientists used the first and third letter of the name to create the symbol? Do you think gold and silver are more similar to each other than gold and helium? (Helium is the gas that makes your balloons float.) Well, here's a little secret about the periodic table: Scientists put elements that have similar features in a column.

This Roman warrior would have spoken Latin to communicate with others.

The location of the element on the periodic table can tell you a lot about that element. It can tell you what it might look like and how well it combines with other elements to create new substances.

Try This!

We've talked a lot about relating atoms to Legos. Here's a fun activity you can do with your periodic

table and Legos. Now that you understand how to find the atomic number, gather all the Legos you have and separate them into stacks based on the number of bumps each Lego has. Then go through the periodic table and decide which Lego would represent which element based on the number of bumps matched to the atomic number. For example, a small Lego with two bumps would be helium. A Lego with one bump would be hydrogen. Do this for all your Legos. Then connect them into atoms and make up names for your atoms based on all that you've learned in this lesson!

The Key to Remember

You already know that elements similar to one another are put in a column. Look at the table on the previous page again. Do you see how some element boxes are colored? Do you notice the symbols have different colors as well? Color is another way elements with similar properties are coded in the chart. If you look at the key near the top, you can see that each color tells us something about the elements in that group or column. How many of the elements are considered metals? Actually, most of the elements God created are metals! Look around you. What do you see that's made of metal? I see some picture frames. Nails holding wood together. The frame of my television. The knobs on my cabinets. Even the computer I'm using to write this book. So much metal! Almost everything I mentioned was a different *kind* of metal. There's a lot of metal in and on the earth. God designed all the metals to make many different things. Even our bodies need some of these metals inside them to survive! You need iron, magnesium, potassium, sodium, calcium, and many other metals for your body to function properly. You also need nonmetals like hydrogen, carbon, nitrogen, oxygen, phosphorus, and sulfur. Without the elements, you simply couldn't survive!

Notice that the key on the periodic table also tells us which elements are solid, liquid, or gas at room temperature. Would you say that most of the earth's elements are solid, liquid, or gas? You probably noticed that most elements are found in the solid form; most things on the earth are solid. How many elements are a gas at room temperature? Which elements are they? How many are liquid at room temperature?

Try This!

Let's do a seek and find using the periodic table to find out how much you've learned about atoms!

First, find the element iron. It has the symbol Fe (from Latin, *ferrum*). How many protons does it have? How many protons does helium have? Its symbol is He. How many energy levels does helium have? Which element has 87 protons? Which has 10 protons? How many energy levels does that element have? Which element has an atomic mass that's a little below 56? What's the atomic mass of tin?

*You can find the answers to these questions in the answer key in the back of this book.

Explain in your own words what you've learned about the periodic table of elements.

Bonding Basics

We're going to take some time now to learn more about atomic bonding. That's just a fancy word for atoms connecting with other atoms.

Noble Gentlemen

You've learned a little about how atoms fit together to make molecules and how molecules make compounds. But not all atoms do this. Some atoms are more stable and choose not to combine with other atoms. A stable atom has all the electrons it needs in its outer shell.

There aren't very many stable atoms, but the ones that are stable are all gases. We call them noble gases. The word "noble" means dignified and having high morals. However, it also means nonreactive. Sometimes these noble gases are called inert gases. "Inert" also means nonreactive. When we say someone is noble, we mean that person is calm and not easily bothered; they don't react. That may help you remember that noble gases have the same nonreactive characteristic. They're gentlemen!

Are you aware there's a noble gas nearby? Take a deep breath. You just breathed in a noble gas! You might not be able to see the gas argon, but you breathe it in and out every single day. It's one of the gases that make up our atmosphere.

All the noble gases except for helium have eight electrons in their outer shell. They could technically hold more, but having eight electrons in the outer shell makes them happy atoms! This is called the rule of eight or the octet rule. Hydrogen and helium are exceptions to the octet rule. Their outer shells only hold two electrons. The **octet rule** teaches that when an atom has eight electrons in its outer shell, it becomes stable and less reactive. Just remember that eight is enough!

Neon and argon are elements used to create glowing signs. They're both in the noble gases group on the periodic table.

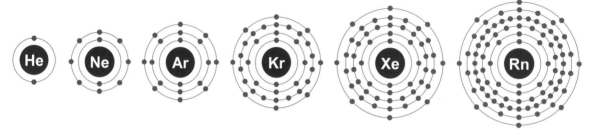

These are the noble gases. They are stable atoms.

Reactive Reactions

If having a full shell makes an atom the most stable, what do you suppose makes an atom the *least* stable? When you feel full, you usually feel satisfied and happy. But when your stomach is empty, you can be rather unstable. You may get grumpy or feel like you want to cry. You may even throw a big fit! Well, the more empty slots in the outer energy level, the more unstable the atom is. When these unstable atoms combine with other atoms to form a compound, they usually do so with a big reaction.

Once these atoms combine with other atoms, they're hard to separate. In fact, it takes just as big a reaction to separate the compounds as it does to combine them. Once an unstable atom has found another atom to bond with, it's hard to break them apart. Breaking up atoms that have bonded together is a fun part of chemistry. At the end of this lesson, we're going to break up the bond that makes water, separating water molecules into hydrogen gas and oxygen gas.

Dynamite is made in science laboratories by combining substances such as carbon, nitrogen, and oxygen to make nitroglycerine. When lit, it can explode violently. Dynamite has been used for over 100 years to blast open mines, remove boulders, and destroy buildings, such as the ones above.

Experiment Explained

Now that you understand how atoms combine with one another, let's take a moment to discuss the chemical reaction you created with hydrogen peroxide in the "Try This!" experiment on page 46. Hydrogen peroxide is written H_2O_2. It looks a lot like H_2O, except hydrogen peroxide has an extra oxygen atom. It needs to get rid of this extra atom, so it's not very stable. It's always trying to combine with whatever it can to release the extra oxygen atom. Hydrogen peroxide is always seeking to break down, but it usually happens very slowly. When you added the yeast solution to it, you sped up the reaction, and the hydrogen peroxide quickly reacted to release its extra oxygen atom.

Busy Bonds

Here's what you should know about atomic bonding: If an atom doesn't have enough valence electrons in its outer shell, it needs to either give up the electrons it has, share its electrons with another atom, or steal electrons from another atom. In fact, this sharing, stealing, or giving up of electrons is happening all around you all the time! Bonding atoms are busy sharing, taking, or releasing those tiny little electrons. Let's discuss these ways that atoms bond.

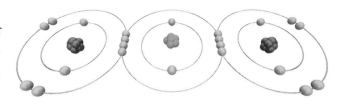

Carbon dioxide (CO_2) is a molecule with sharing (or covalent) bonds. The oxygen atoms share electrons with the carbon atom to form a bond. Carbon dioxide is the gas we breathe out of our mouths when we exhale.

Valence Bonding

When hydrogen and oxygen combine to form water, they cooperate with one another by *sharing* their valence electrons. When you share, you're being cooperative. We call a sharing bond a **covalent bond**. Whenever atoms are sharing electrons equally, they're bonding with a covalent bond. You can see the first letters of the word "cooperate" in the word "covalent." What other word do you see? That's right—"valent"! The valence electrons are cooperating and bonding—covalent bonding. Look at the picture of carbon dioxide above. This molecule contains two covalent bonds.

Do you remember the octet rule? When an atom has eight valence electrons, it's stable and happy! Atoms can obtain an octet of electrons by sharing them with others. A pair of oxygen atoms can form an O_2 molecule, and a pair of fluorine atoms can form an F_2 molecule by sharing their valence electron. When they do this, they feel complete with their eight valence electrons.

Try This!

You will need: An adult's supervision, a partner, 2 wire coat hangers (straightened), and 12 small fruits (blueberries, grapes, cherry tomatoes, or any other small, roundish fruit).

First, bend one of the coat hangers to make a circle. Thread six fruits through the circle. Now make a tiny hook at each end of the circle. Step into the circle and hold the coat hanger around your waist, then secure the ends of the coat hanger together at the hooks. Have your partner do the same. You are now two oxygen atoms with your six valence electrons each. (We're not including the inside electron shells because chemists typically draw only the valence electrons in their diagrams.) Now you and your partner move close to each other and move two of the fruits together at one section. Get your two fruits close to the two fruits on your partner's outer shell so it appears you're sharing two electrons to complete your outer circle, making eight!

You've just created a covalent bond! If you have a group of students, you can make several coat-hanger atoms and create these covalently bonded molecules: F_2, H_2O, H_2, CO_2, and CF_4. Remember that hydrogen is complete with only two electrons in its outer shell.

Now that you understand covalent bonding, let's look at the atoms that gain or lose electrons when bonding with other atoms.

Ionic Bonding

The last kind of atomic bond we'll study in this lesson is the ionic bond. When an atom steals an electron from another atom, it gains an extra electron. This atom is now called an ion. An **ion** does not have the right number of electrons. There's another kind of ion: an atom that loses an electron. Typically, it's been stolen by another atom. So any atom that does not have the normal number of electrons is called an ion. When an atom becomes an ion, it forms bonds with other ions. We call this **ionic bonding**.

Let's explore how ionic bonding works. Do you remember what charge is? Electrons have a charge. Do you know whether electrons are positive or negative? Yes! They have a negative charge. Also, you might remember that normal atoms have a neutral charge. That means they have the same number of positive particles and negative particles. What happens when an atom loses one of its negative particles? That's right—it becomes positively charged. But what if an atom gets an extra electron, giving it an extra negative particle? Correct! The atom becomes negatively charged. We call all atoms that have a charge ions.

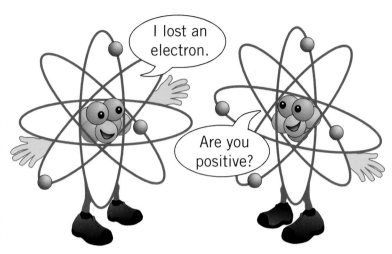

Atoms form ionic bonds because opposite charges are attracted to each other. Negatively charged atoms are attracted or drawn to positively charged atoms. When an atom has a charge, it attracts atoms of the opposite charge.

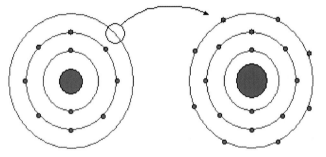

Which ion is the cation and which is the anion?

If the atom has gained electrons we call the ion an **anion**, simply pronounced "an ion." These negatively charged particles are looking for positively charged particles to form a bond. If an atom loses electrons, we call it a **cation**, pronounced "cat ion." Since it has lost some of the negatively charged particles, it's positively charged. Anions are attracted to cations.

A common ionic bond we see every day is the bond between sodium and chloride. Sodium is a shiny, silver metal (a very soft one). It has only one electron in its third energy level. As you might imagine, it's extremely unstable because that energy level needs a lot of electrons to be happy. Sodium decided it's easier to just get rid of the lone electron than try to gather seven more. Remember, if an energy level has a completed outer shell or eight electrons in the outer shell, it's happy! Do you remember the name of that rule of eight? That's right! The octet rule.

Sodium loses this spare electron very easily, making sodium quite unstable. In fact, sodium is so unstable that if you throw it into water, it reacts violently with water, liberating highly flammable hydrogen gas. If you go to www.apologia.com/bookextras, you'll see videos of people throwing sodium into water. It's very interesting. But don't do this at home! It can be very dangerous.

Look at the chlorine atom shown with the sodium atom. How many electrons does it need in its outer shell to be full? Well, it could technically hold up to ten more, but if it fills up to eight, it will be satisfied. Remember the octet rule!

The sodium atom gives up its lone electron. But it stays close to the chlorine atom as they are now attracted to one another's opposite charge.

So chlorine needs only one electron to find happiness. When sodium loses its electron and chlorine gains an electron, chlorine becomes a negatively charged anion, and sodium becomes a positively charged cation. Suddenly, these two ions are extremely attracted to each other, so they form a bond—an ionic bond!

Chlorine and sodium bond to form a very familiar substance—table salt!

When a giving/taking bond is formed, one gives its electron and one takes. That's how we sum up ionic bonding. So what do you get when you combine this dangerous green gas called chlorine with the reactive, shiny metal called sodium? Well, when these two elements bond, they make white crystals with a very familiar taste. In fact, that green gas and shiny metal together make everything on the dinner table taste a lot better. We call this mixture of elements table salt! Yes, that white stuff in your salt shaker is an ionic bond in action called sodium chloride! Next time you want your parents to pass the salt, be sure to say, "Can you please pass the sodium chloride?" Then they'll know you're learning a lot in science!

Sodium is a highly reactive silver metal.

You can use your coat hangers from the previous activity to form some ionic bonds. Let's do that now!

Try This!

You're going to simulate the bond between sodium and chloride.

You will need: An adult's supervision, the coat hangers and fruit from the last experiment, your partner, a marker, masking tape, and 2 pieces of copy paper.

First, make two signs with the paper and marker. One sign should read, "I am negatively charged." The other sign should read, "I am positively charged." Attach a piece of tape to the back of each sign. Decide which one of you will be sodium and which one will be chlorine. Now give and take electrons to form a bond. When you give away an electron, put on the sign that says you're positively charged. When you steal an electron, put on the sign that says you're negatively charged. Some other bonds you can create are MgO (magnesium loses two electrons, and oxygen gains two electrons) and $CaCl_2$ (calcium loses two electrons, and each of the chlorine atoms gains one electron).

You may wonder why you need to know all of this stuff. Believe it or not, many, many topics in this book discuss atoms and electrons and positive and negative charges. We'll discuss them when we learn about motion, sound, light, electricity, and magnetism. Throughout your life, you'll be able to understand how and why things happen because you understand how atoms work. We call this *foundational knowledge* because it's like putting a strong foundation on the house of knowledge you're building in your brain.

Final Matters

Now that you understand the building blocks God used to create the world, you're ready to really dive into the study of chemistry and physics. It all starts with the atom, and you'll understand science better because of what you've learned in this lesson. Now let's finish up with some activities and experiments!

What Do You Remember?

What is an atom? What is an element? What is the charge of a proton? What is the charge of a neutron? What is the charge of an electron? What is the nucleus of an atom made of? What are electron shells? How many electrons can fit in the first energy level or electron shell? How many electrons fit in the second energy level of an atom? What are valence electrons? When is an atom stable? When is an atom unstable? What is the difference between a covalent bond and an ionic bond? What is an ion? What is a cation? What is an anion? What do the numbers inside the box of an element on the periodic table of elements represent?

Notebooking Activities

You may have already been recording the fascinating facts you've learned in this lesson. If you haven't done so already, spend some time writing down some of the interesting things you learned. Then make an illustration of an atom and label its parts. If you have the *Chemistry and Physics Notebooking Journal,* templates for these activities are provided for you.

Next, I want you to create two different comic strips about atom bonding. Create the first comic strip with two atoms forming a covalent bond and the second with two atoms forming an ionic bond. Be sure your comics reflect the information you learned about how and why atoms bond together to form new substances.

Project
Sugar Cookie Periodic Table

Let's create your own periodic table of elements using sugar cookies! You'll need to make 110 square sugar cookies using the recipe below. After they cool, organize them into the chart, then spread icing on them. You do not have to match the colors in the chart. But do choose seven different colors to represent the seven different kinds of elements. Afterward, use a pastry tube of icing to write the correct symbol on each cookie. Take a picture for your notebooking journal before you eat them!

You will need for the cookies:

- 3 cups of butter, softened
- 4 cups of white sugar
- 8 eggs
- 2 teaspoons of vanilla extract
- 10 cups of all-purpose flour
- 4 teaspoons of baking powder
- 2 teaspoons of salt

1. In a large bowl, mix together the butter and sugar until it's creamy and smooth.
2. Beat in the eggs and vanilla.
3. Stir in the flour, baking soda, and salt.
4. Cover the dough and chill in the refrigerator for at least an hour (or overnight).
5. Preheat the oven to 400°F (200°C).
6. Roll out the dough on a floured surface ¼ to ½ inch thick.
7. Cut the dough into square shapes using a cookie cutter. (You can make a square cookie cutter by bending a round one into a square.)
8. Place the cookies 1 inch apart on ungreased cookie sheets.
9. Bake the cookies for 6 to 8 minutes and let them cool completely.

You will need for the icing:

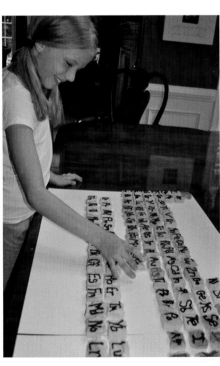

- 2 cups of powdered sugar
- 4 teaspoons of milk
- 4 teaspoons of light corn syrup
- 7 colors of food coloring
- pastry tube

1. Combine the powdered sugar, milk, and corn syrup in a large mixing bowl until smooth.
2. Divide the icing into seven separate containers.
3. Add a different color of food coloring to the containers of icing and mix well.

Compound Chemistry

What do we call a substance made up of only *one* kind of atom? An element. What do we have when an atom is connected with another atom? A molecule! Do you remember what a compound is? You may remember an element is a group of the same kind of atom. A compound is made up of two or more different elements combined. If you have one H_2O molecule, you have a molecule of water. It would be too small to see. If you have a group of H_2O molecules, you have the compound water. Compounds are everywhere. You use them; you eat them; you enjoy them. Hydrogen peroxide is a compound. Salt is a compound. Sugar is also a compound. There are many different kinds of compounds! In fact, there are so many that it would be impossible to cover all of them in this book.

In this lesson, we're going to closely study a few different kinds of compounds. We'll begin with crystals, then examine polymers. We'll look at acidic and basic

This crystal is called an amethyst and is often used to make jewelry.

compounds, then explore chemical reactions with compounds. So put on your chemistry coat, and let's get down to business!

Crystallized Creations

Crystals are curious compounds in creation. They bring geometry to life! Have you studied geometry in math? Crystals are solids that have formed into geometric shapes. Scientists say that a **crystal** is a solid that has a regular, repeating arrangement of atoms. These repeating arrangements are geometric shapes! As you study the crystals in this lesson, see if you can identify the geometric shapes in them.

Many substances form crystal patterns. Both elements and compounds can make crystals. Elements like carbon, silicon, aluminum, oxygen,

Do you see the many geometric shapes making up these beautiful crystals?

The repeating geometric patterns in these crystals all point toward the center of the rock.

magnesium, iron, and calcium are a few of the many, many elements that form crystals.

Some of the compounds that form crystals are salt, sugar, iron sulfide (which makes iron pyrite), and water. Yes—water! Water forms ice crystals. In fact, the most beautiful crystals on earth are probably snowflakes. We'll look at those special crystals and their delicate designs in just a moment.

You may wonder how crystals form. Crystals often form when a liquid is hardening into a solid. Look at the crystallized rock on this page. As the substance hardens, the atoms move around and structure themselves in specific patterns, making interesting three-dimensional shapes. The same pattern usually repeats itself over and over again, but some of the shapes are larger and some are smaller. When an element or compound does this, we say it crystallizes.

Let's study crystals up close with this experiment.

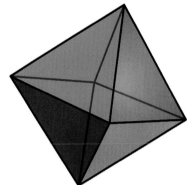

This geometric shape is called an octahedron. Many crystals with this shape can be found.

Try This!

You will need: An adult's supervision, a magnifying glass or microscope, ½ cup of salt, 1 cup of water, a pan, a stove, your notebooking journal, and a pencil.

First, study the salt crystals with the magnifying glass or microscope. Draw the shape you see in your notebooking journal. Now boil the water and pour the salt in the pan. Let the water completely evaporate, leaving only the salt in the bottom. Flake off a few of the crystals and study them under the microscope. Did the salt crystals retain their original shape? You may have noticed the crystals were different sizes, but they kept the same shape as the original crystals. Draw in your notebooking journal what you see, and record what you've learned so far about crystals.

Common Crystals

Although salt may seem like a common crystal compared to the rock crystals pictured in this lesson, common crystals like salt and sugar are still quite important. We definitely enjoy having these crystals around. I once made a cake and forgot to add salt to the batter. No one in the family could eat the saltless cake! That's when I discovered the importance of salt. Maybe that's why God tells Christians, "You are the salt of the earth" (Matthew 5:13, ESV). Just as salt makes food taste better, the love and joy we bring to others enhances their lives. The more time you spend reading God's Word and praying, the saltier you'll be!

As I mentioned earlier, although water is an extremely common substance, it makes some amazing crystals. When water begins to freeze, changing from liquid water to solid water, it forms crystals known as ice. In fact, the word "crystal" comes from the Greek word *kryos*, which means frozen. This name was given because the beautiful crystals looked like they were frozen, just like ice. Snowflakes are the best example of crystallized water. Since no two snowflakes are alike, every snowflake crystallizes differently, creating different patterns and structures. The first person to photograph

Sand is composed of quartz crystals containing the element silicon. We extract the silicon to make things like solar cells and microchips used in electronic devices.

Wilson "Snowflake" Bentley photographed thousands of snowflakes. Indeed, no two are alike!

snowflakes, Wilson "Snowflake" Bentley, captured them on velvet and photographed each before they melted. Look at the photos taken by Snowflake Bentley. The beauty of these snowflakes is a picture of God's beauty and creative handiwork. Yet even as beautiful as these are, God considers *you* even more beautiful!

Common crystals are important to our lives. But let's take a look at some other interesting crystals.

Precious Gemstones

Some crystals are considered more valuable than others. We call these crystals **gemstones**. People have treasured gemstone crystals for many years, often using them in jewelry. There are *many* different gemstones people use to make jewelry. Once our family went to a gemstone mine in search of these treasured crystals. It was exciting to dig through the sand and go home with an assortment of beautiful, crystallized minerals!

Although a lot of substances make gemstones that are shiny and pretty, there are four special gemstones that are considered precious gemstones, making them the most valuable of all: sapphires, rubies, emeralds, and diamonds.

When we find these precious gemstones, they're usually attached to crystallized rocks. In this state, we say they are "in the rough." That's because they haven't been cut out, chiseled to a pretty shape, and shined to be put in jewelry.

These precious gemstones are "in the rough." Do you see how the sapphire, emerald, ruby, and diamond are attached to the rocks?

Next time you go to the mall, stop by a jewelry store to look at the rubies, sapphires, and emeralds they have there.

Diamonds are very well-known gemstones. Let's take a closer look at them.

Diamonds

Do you remember discussing carbon in the last lesson? Carbon is usually a black, chalky substance called graphite. Graphite is actually carbon crystallized into a geometric shape that absorbs the light. That's what makes it black. When something absorbs all the light that hits it, that object becomes very dark. Look around you. How many black things can you see? Those things are absorbing most of the light. Yet when carbon is put under intense pressure and heat, then cooled quickly, it changes. It goes from the graphite crystal pattern to a more beautiful crystal pattern that hardly absorbs any light. Instead, it reflects the light. It becomes a diamond! The pressure and heat change the geometric shape of the carbon. What's really interesting is that graphite is a very soft substance that's extremely brittle and crumbles easily— which makes it a great pencil lead. Yet diamonds are the hardest

Diamonds are carbon atoms structured in a way that reflects light.

substance on earth! In fact, the word "diamond" comes from the Greek word *adamas*, which means unconquerable and indestructible. Because diamonds are the hardest substance in nature, they're used by machines to cut metals and other materials that are almost impossible to cut with any other item.

It's amazing what pressure and heat can do to a substance!

Pressure and Perseverance

In the same way that carbon becomes more beautiful when put under intense pressure, the Bible tells us *we* become better and more like Jesus when we experience pressure in our lives. Sometimes things don't go our way, or bad things happen in our lives. Although we never *want* these things to happen, if we have the right attitude when we go through the difficulties, God will use these hard things to make us stronger, more beautiful people. We'll develop perseverance and become more mature. Like a diamond reflecting light, we'll be able to reflect God's light to others.

James 1:2–4 tells us, "Consider it pure joy, my brothers and sisters, whenever you face trials of many kinds, because you know that the testing of your faith produces perseverance. Let perseverance finish its work so that you may be mature and complete, not lacking anything."

These people are digging for diamonds at Crater of Diamonds State Park in Arkansas.

Diamond Mines

Have you ever wondered where you might find a diamond in nature? They're usually found deep in the earth. People have to dig big holes, called mines, to find them. These holes usually look like a crater that an asteroid might leave behind, but they're actually the entrance to a volcanic pipe. You'll learn all about volcanoes when you study geology. Diamonds are mined throughout the world. Russia produces

Diamond mines are usually created by digging a crater-like hole in the ground.

the most diamonds. In the United States, Arkansas is home to a very famous diamond mine that's open to the public, Crater of Diamonds State Park. You can actually dig for diamonds for a small fee! On their website is a list of the latest diamond finds and the size of the diamonds found. Some of these diamonds are very valuable; others are not so much.

The Four Cs

What makes one diamond more precious and expensive than another? Just like your schoolwork might get graded, diamonds get graded too. They're graded on four Cs: cut, color, clarity, and carat. Let's learn a little bit about these four Cs.

Diamonds are *cut* by jewelers to bring out the brilliance of God's creation. In nature, diamonds form in an octagon or octahedral shape, which is a crystal with eight sides. We call each side a face, so a diamond has eight faces. Look at the image of the various shapes of diamonds to see the different ways diamonds are cut.

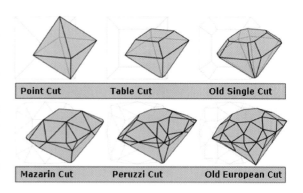

Point Cut   Table Cut   Old Single Cut
Mazarin Cut   Peruzzi Cut   Old European Cut

Diamonds come in all *colors* of the rainbow, but pure diamonds are clear and are very rare. Colored diamonds have other elements mixed with the carbon to give them their color. The price of the diamond depends on its color. The Hope Diamond, a blue diamond pictured to the left, is one of the most valuable diamonds in the world. It's an enormous diamond that was worn by several French kings.

Of course, *clarity* refers to how clear the diamond is. Some diamonds are crystal clear, while others are cloudy on the inside. A clear diamond gets a higher grade than a cloudy one.

The last thing a diamond gets graded on is its weight. We weigh diamonds in *carats*. The ring image below is of a one-carat diamond ring. That's not a small diamond—but diamonds can even be a lot bigger than that!

The Hope Diamond, a famous diamond worn by French kings, is on display in the Smithsonian Institution National Museum of Natural History. It was once 115 carats but is now a 45.5-carat blue diamond. The blue color is the result of a small amount of boron mixed with the carbon.

It's traditional for men to give women rings when they plan to be married. This diamond ring is about one carat or 0.2 grams.

One of the largest diamonds in the rough ever found is the Cullinan diamond, which is 3,106.75 carats. It was found in South Africa and is called the Great Star of Africa. It was later cut into several smaller diamonds.

If your mother or grandmother has a diamond, study it under a magnifying glass and look for the four Cs of the diamond! You can also go to a jewelry store and ask the owner if you can study the diamonds there.

Now you know a lot about one of the compounds found everywhere in nature—crystals. At the end of this lesson, you'll make your own crystals from household items.

**Explain to someone all that you've learned so far about crystals.
Be sure to include what you learned about grading diamonds.**

Putty, Plastics, and Pencil Erasers

Did you know that when Christopher Columbus arrived in the strange land now known as South America, he saw children playing with round rubber balls? People in Europe had never seen rubber balls before. It was later discovered that these balls came from the sap of a particular tree. The natives collected the sap and formed it into balls while it was drying. By adding more and more sap, they could make larger balls. The balls could bounce and were fun to catch and throw! Have you ever played with a bouncy ball? You aren't the first child in history to do that!

The sap that Christopher Columbus found was taken back to Europe. It was discovered that it could rub pencil marks off paper, so everyone began calling it rubber. Today, pencil erasers in England are still called rubbers.

A polymer called latex is being tapped from a rubber tree.

Rubber is created from a special kind of molecule called a polymer. The word "polymer" comes from the Greek roots *poly* meaning many and *meros* meaning part. Polymers are many repeating parts. **Polymer** molecules are arranged in long chains of lots and lots of repeating small molecules over and over again. Sound familiar? It should! Instead of forming crystals, the rubber polymer forms bouncy balls, rubber bands, and pencil erasers. In fact, the way the compound is structured makes most polymers stretchy.

Many substances God created on the earth are made up of polymers, and many of them are important in our everyday lives. The fibers in wood, cotton, wool, and silk are made from polymers. There are even polymer chains inside our bodies! The collagen in our skin, which makes our skin stretchy, is a polymer. When we get older, we lose some of that collagen and our skin doesn't bounce back into place as easily. The less collagen we have, the more wrinkled we get. Feel the skin on your arm. Pull on it. Does it bounce back into place easily? Now feel the skin on your parent's or grandparent's arm. Does it bounce back as easily? Probably not as quickly.

As we get older, our skin loses some of its elastic qualities. This results in wrinkles. The polymers in our skin make it elastic.

Not all polymers are stretchy like bouncy balls and skin, though. Silk and wool aren't really stretchy, but they *are* soft and pliable. Nylon is another fabric that man created using polymers. It's usually very stretchy. Take a moment to feel the differences among wool, silk, and nylon fabrics in your house or at a fabric store.

As you can see, not all polymers are found in nature. This is where chemistry gets really interesting! With a simple knowledge of chemistry, people have created man-made polymers, like nylon and many types of plastics. Today, plastics are used to make millions of items. **Plastics** are great polymers. They're light. They're hard to break. They're practically permanent because they

This lady is stretching wool into thin strings, or thread, to weave it into fabric. Wool is a polymer.

don't fall apart very easily. Plastics can also be recycled and made into new items over and over and over again. They're super easy to form into shapes and very inexpensive to make. Some plastics are the perfect compound to use for making or packaging almost anything. Look around you. Do you see anything made from plastic? If not, go into the kitchen, and you might find some polymer plastics there! Now you see how chemistry contributes to our daily lives. It's an important field of science, don't you think?

Would you like to play the part of a chemist and make a polymer that can be formed into a bouncy ball, much like the Native American children played with? Let's try that now!

Try This!

You will need: An adult's supervision, safety goggles, borax, cornstarch, white or clear school glue, warm water, food coloring, 2 small plastic cups, a spoon, a timer, and a zippered plastic bag.

First, mix 2 tablespoons of warm water, a few drops of food coloring, and ½ teaspoon of borax powder in one cup. Stir the mixture until the borax is dissolved. In the other cup, pour in 1 tablespoon of glue, then add ½ teaspoon of the borax solution. Next, add 1 tablespoon of cornstarch to the borax/glue solution, but do not stir yet. Allow the solution to sit for exactly 15 seconds, then stir until the solution is fully mixed. Once the mixture becomes impossible to stir, take it out of the cup and form it into a ball with your hands. You've just made your own bouncy ball! Keep the ball in the zippered plastic bag when you're not playing with it. Have fun bouncing your ball!

Try This!

You will need: An adult's supervision, a rubber band, a string, and a friend.

Stretch the rubber band out, then release it. Now stretch the string. How are these two things different? Let's do something different with the string to make it behave a little more like the rubber band. This will help you understand how the molecules in a polymer are organized.

Have a friend hold one end of the string. Begin twisting the string over and over again the same direction. Do you see how the string begins to bend and twist? Keep twisting the string until it's folded over on itself quite a lot. Now pull the string apart. It stretches out now, much like a rubber band!

Now that you've made a polymer ball, let's explore more about how polymers actually work.

Believe it or not, this is somewhat how a rubber band works, except it's happening on the molecular level. The long strings of molecules that make up a rubber band are twisted and kinked up just like the string was when you twisted it. That's what polymers do when they attach to each other. When you stretch out the rubber band, you're straightening out the twists and bends of the molecules in the rubber band.

Look at the image of the squiggly lines. The structure on the left is an example of a polymer in its natural state. When stretched out, it looks like the structure on the right.

It will always return to the original shape on the left when not under stress, just like your rubber band did.

Now let's explore some interesting ways polymer molecules behave. You can actually force objects between the polymer chains without breaking the chain. Let's try that now!

Try This!

You will need: An adult's supervision, a balloon, and a bamboo skewer.

To begin, blow up the balloon. Now find the end of the balloon that is opposite the end that is tied. This end is slightly darker than the rest of the balloon. Carefully and slowly insert the bamboo skewer into that small section of the balloon. You must go very, very slowly, using your strength to push the skewer into the balloon. Could you do it without popping the balloon? If it pops, try again.

What happened? Why didn't the balloon pop when you stuck the skewer in? Well, because of the structure of the polymer molecules in the balloon. Remember, these molecules are all twisted around each other. When you began inserting the skewer, the molecules began to twist around the skewer, creating an airtight seal. The polymer molecules in the balloon wrapped around and stuck to the skewer, encapsulating the skewer inside the polymer molecules, creating an airtight seal. So you can stick the skewer through, and the balloon won't leak or pop!

Silly Surprise!

Wouldn't it be fun to be a scientist in a lab who discovered a new substance? Well, in the 1940s, while playing around with different chemicals, some scientists discovered an interesting polymer. This polymer could be stretched, tied, twisted, flattened, rolled, and shaped over and over again. It was very unusual because it could bounce when thrown on the floor, but it could also break in half. Still, it could flow like a very thick liquid when played with. The scientists tried to get other chemists interested in this new substance, thinking it could be used for important purposes. However, no one thought it was very amazing. In fact, it almost went into the trash can— until one person realized it would be a great children's toy. So they packaged it and sold it as Silly Putty. It was a huge hit with children for many years. You can still buy Silly Putty today, more than 70 years later!

Most man-made polymers are safe and nontoxic. That's why so many things today are made out of plastic: water bottles, plates, cups, toys, and much more. By choosing the right polymers, you can make almost anything you want! Polymers can be hardened into a Lego. They can also be soft like a balloon and made into most any shape. In fact, we can even use man-made polymers called polyester and nylon to make clothing. We eat food packaged in polymer plastic containers. We drink water that comes through plastic piping in our homes. We sleep on mattresses made of polymer-based foam. We walk on polymer fibers in our carpet. Even cars today are manufactured using polymers for many of their parts. What a polymer world!

The Bad News

Plastic is an amazing and wonderful invention. As you learned, it's easy and inexpensive to make and can be made into almost any form. It's long lasting and can replace more breakable items like glass and wood. After all, a plastic army man, chess piece, or doll is less likely to break than a glass or wooden one. Imagine a world without plastic! Look around you now. What do you see that would not be there if plastics were never discovered? What do you think would replace that item?

Although there are many wonderful things about plastics and polymers, there are some negative things about them as well. Because they don't break down very easily, man-made plastics can become a problem when thrown into the garbage. Wood, paper, food, and almost everything else breaks down into particles in the landfill where all the trash is dumped. In time, all these items become part of the elements in the soil, returning to nature. When all the trash is broken down, the landfills can be made into usable land with grass, trees, and parks for people to enjoy. But if the trash doesn't break down, potentially beautiful land goes to waste.

Exposure to sun, wind, and rain helps items decompose. Often, when trash is thrown into the landfill, it's immediately buried.

Everything you throw away is dumped on a large plot of land called a landfill. Many of the items dumped won't decompose for thousands or even millions of years.

Try This!

Below are some items people throw away. Make a guess about how long it takes for these items to break down. Then look at the answer key in the back of this book to see if your guesses were close to the estimates scientists have made about each item. You can make a contest by having everyone in the family guess.

paper towel	wool sock	foamed plastic buoy
orange peel	glass bottle	aluminum soda can
banana peel	plastic bag	disposable diaper
paper bag	plastic film canister	plastic bottle
newspaper	nylon fabric	rubber boot sole
apple core	leather	plywood
milk carton	tin soup or vegetable can	Styrofoam container

This girl is recycling plastics in a recycling bin. The triangle with three arrows is the symbol for recycling. It tells us an item can be used over and over and over again.

The Good News

You're probably like me: you don't like to hear bad news. Thankfully, with plastics, there *is* some good news in all this bad news. The good news is that plastics, like all polymers, can be melted and remade into different items. They don't ever have to be thrown into a landfill. They can be recycled! Almost every polymer can be melted and refashioned into something else that's useful for man. Plastics can be recycled over and over again!

If your family doesn't recycle, today would be a great day to start. Instead of throwing away toys, plastic bottles, milk containers, and other plastics, put them in a special container for recycling. Most trash companies will send a truck to your house to pick up the recyclable items. Glass, cans, and paper can also be recycled, so it's a good idea to recycle those items as well.

Plastic Codes

Search around your house and see how many plastics you can locate. Look on the bottom of the plastic and find the number inside the recycle symbol. That number represents a specific kind of plastic that can be recycled. Rumors were once spread that the number on the plastic told how recyclable it was. That isn't so. The numbers were randomly assigned to the different plastics.

These recycling bins show that anything made of paper, glass, plastic, or metal can be recycled.

Study the plastic recycling chart below to see if you can answer these questions. Which code might you find on a baby toy? If you have a baby toy, check and see if that's the code on it. Which code might you find on a milk jug? Which code might you find on a cola bottle? What about a plastic chair or your recycling bin?

Society of the Plastics Industry Resin Codes

Symbol	Acronym	Full Name and Uses
♳ PETE	PETE or PET	Polyethylene terephthalate: polyester fibers, thermoformed sheet, strapping, and soft drink bottles
♴ HDPE	HDPE	High-density polyethylene: bottles, grocery bags, milk jugs, recycling bins, agricultural pipe, base cups, car stops, playground equipment, and plastic lumber
♵ V	PVC or V	Polyvinyl chloride: pipe, fencing, shower curtains, lawn chairs, and nonfood bottles
♶ LDPE	LDPE	Low-density polyethylene: plastic bags, six-pack rings, various containers, dispensing bottles, wash bottles, tubing, and various molded laboratory equipment
♷ PP	PP	Polypropylene: auto parts, industrial fibers, food containers, and dishware
♸ PS	PS	Polystyrene: desk accessories, cafeteria trays, plastic utensils, toys, video cassettes and cases, clamshell containers, packaging peanuts, insulation board, and other expanded polystyrene products (such as Styrofoam)
♹ OTHER	OTHER or O	Other plastics: acrylic, fiberglass, nylon, polycarbonate, and polylactic acid (a bioplastic). Multilayer combinations of different plastics: bottles, plastic lumber applications, headlight lenses, and safety shields/glasses

This stuffed bear will arrive safely to its destination because it's packed in Styrofoam.

Find the code for polystyrene. Polystyrene, also called Styrofoam, is considered a huge problem for landfills. Not only does it take up a lot of space, but it doesn't decompose for millions of years. Styrofoam also doesn't compress very easily. You can't crush it like you can a milk jug or water bottle. This makes it a great packing material because it adds volume without weight. It's very light and helps keep

Unlike Styrofoam, these water bottles made of plastic are easily compressed.

fragile items protected when they're being shipped.

Let's learn a little more about Styrofoam by conducting an experiment to make this polymer break down more quickly.

Try This!

You will need: An adult's supervision, safety goggles, several Styrofoam cups, a glass bowl or casserole dish, and ¼ cup of pure acetone from a beauty supply store (sold as nail polish remover). You can also use nail polish remover sold at the grocery store, but the results will not be as dramatic.

For this experiment, it's a good idea to work outside as acetone will remove the paint or finish from your furniture. It's also flammable, so keep it away from any flame or burning ember.

First, make a tower with your cups, stacking them inside one another inside the bowl or dish. Now have an adult carefully pour a small amount of acetone on the tower and watch what happens. Add more acetone to complete the reaction. What happened?

The Styrofoam appeared to melt and almost disappear, didn't it? Styrofoam is the polymer polystyrene, which has lots of air bubbles trapped inside it. In the experiment, the acetone dissolved the polymer and released the trapped air. Gasoline would dissolve the polymer just as well. We'll do more chemical reactions later in this lesson. In the meantime, let's recite what we know about polymers.

Explain to someone what you've learned so far. If you're pausing for the day, write down what you wish to remember in your notebooking journal. You might also want to record what you learned during the interesting experiments and projects.

Acidic Acid

Have you ever tasted vinegar? Have you ever tasted a lemon? If you never have, do that now! What makes your mouth pucker up when you taste these items? It's something called acid that's found in the vinegar and lemon. A lot of substances we eat and use have acid in them. Some are wet, like vinegar. But there are also acidic solids and acidic gases! The word "acid" comes from the Latin word *acetum*, which means vinegar. Long ago, chemists put every substance that behaved like vinegar into the vinegar, or acetum, group. So how do acids behave? An **acid** tastes sour, conducts electricity, ruins metal, and donates hydrogen ions. Can you think of any foods that are sour when you taste them? Grapefruits, lemons, and pickles are a few. Many acids are too powerful to taste. In fact, some could burn a hole through your mouth. So don't ever taste something just to find out if it's an acid!

The acid in the lemon tastes sour to this boy, causing his mouth to pucker.

Acids are said to be electrical because they can carry electric currents through them. That just means they can transmit electricity from one place to another. In fact, you can actually light a small light bulb with lemon juice! It takes a lot of lemons and two different types of metals to do it, but it can be done.

Have you ever heard of someone cleaning things with vinegar? Although a lot of people use vinegar to clean items, you should never use vinegar to clean your cars or any other steel items. Why? Well, when an acid comes in contact with a metal, it will often break down the metal—causing it to rust, corrode, and fall apart. Let's do an experiment to see this in action!

Try This!

You will need: An adult's supervision, safety goggles, a saucer, a paper towel, vinegar, and 3 to 5 pennies made before 1981 (copper pennies).

To begin, fold the paper towel in half twice, making a square. Now place the folded towel in the saucer and pour enough vinegar into the saucer to wet the towel. Place the pennies on top of the paper towel and wait 4 hours. What do you think will happen to the pennies?

Metals often rust when left outdoors.

Now you see why you shouldn't clean metal with vinegar! Do you remember that most of the elements God created are metals? Acids can dissolve and corrode a lot of the elements God made. This can create a real problem when the acid content in the air is heavy. Have you ever heard of acid rain? It's a term we use to describe rain that has strong acid in it. You see, there are acidic chemicals in our environment floating in the air. When it rains, these acidic chemicals get caught in the raindrops and fall to earth. They land on buildings, cars, statues, and everything else on the earth. As you may have guessed, some buildings, cars, and statues are made of metal. Acid rain causes these things to rust and corrode.

In addition to being sour, carrying electricity, and corroding metal, there's another thing all acids have in common. It goes back to atoms. Do you remember what an ion is? An ion is an atom that has lost or gained an electron. Well, acids donate hydrogen ions to other substances. A hydrogen ion is a hydrogen atom that's missing an electron. Basically, all acids give away hydrogen ions when they're mixed with other substances. In an acidic liquid, there are a bunch of charged particles—all those hydrogen ions—running around. A base is just the opposite. A base accepts hydrogen ions. So while acids give away ions, bases gather them! We'll talk about bases in just a moment.

Explain what you've learned so far about acids.

Strong and Weak

You may not drink vinegar, but you probably drink acids quite a bit. If you like seltzer water or soda, then you enjoy drinking acid—carbonic acid. We call these beverages carbonated drinks; they're liquids with acid added. Citric acid, which is found in many fruits, is also used to make beverages. Have you ever made lemonade? It's rather easy to make. Simply squeeze the juice from half a lemon into a glass of hot water and add 2 tablespoons of sugar. Stir it to melt the sugar, and then add ice. Yum! You have a delicious acidic treat!

Most of the time, the acids in vinegar, fruit juice, and carbonated drinks are not harmful to your body. But as I mentioned earlier, some acids are too strong to even touch, much less drink. There are strong acids and weak acids. On the chemistry level, strong acids are made of molecules that easily release hydrogen ions. Weak acids are made of molecules that don't release hydrogen ions very easily. The sourness of lemons and other citrus fruits is caused by citric acid. Some fruits have more citric acid than others, making them more sour. But citric acid is a weak acid—not many citric acid molecules release hydrogen ions. Some acids are much stronger than citric acid, though.

Lemons are citrus fruits, containing lots of citric acid.

For example, sulfuric acid, which is used in car batteries, is a strong acid. Sulfuric acid is used to make paints, plastics, and fertilizers for your yard. Although sulfuric acid is a really strong acid, one of the most corrosive acids in the entire world resides right inside your belly. It's the hydrochloric acid God placed in your stomach! This acid is so strong that if you didn't have a specially designed lining in your stomach protected by special chemicals, your stomach acid would burn a hole right through your body! You should be very glad God put this powerful acid in your stomach because it kills almost every single germ you eat. It also helps break down the food you eat so your body can use it to make you strong and healthy. You probably don't realize how many germs you eat. But that's okay—God has taken care of that problem with acid! As you may have guessed, strong acids corrode metals a lot faster than weak ones of the same concentration. You could easily conduct a science experiment to test the strengths of different acids by seeing how quickly they corrode a metal nail. But there are also strips you can buy at aquarium stores to test the acid content of liquids.

How acidic something is depends not only on the strength of the acid but also on how concentrated the acid is in the substance. When we say an acid solution is really concentrated, that means there's more acid in the solution. Other times an acid is really diluted, meaning there's less acid in the solution. It's like the difference between drinking lemon juice and lemonade.

One of the strongest acids known is the acid in your stomach. It's necessary to break down food and kill germs. It's so strong it could burn a hole through your body! However, God designed your stomach to protect you from this acid that is so important to your digestion.

Basic Bases

The chemical opposite of an acid is a **base**. In fact, if you've ever had an upset stomach, your mom may have given you an "antacid," like Tums or Maalox. An **antacid** is a base that works against the acid upsetting your stomach. You can see the prefix "anti-" (meaning against) in the word antacid, can't you?

If you could taste a base, it would taste chalky or bitter instead of sour. However, just as with an acid, you should never taste a substance that isn't food to determine whether it's an acid or a base.

Besides being bitter, bases also have a slippery feel, especially when they're wet. Soap, Maalox, and deodorants are bases—and so is baking soda. Many people add baking soda to their pool to make the water feel soft and smooth.

Just like there are strong and weak acids, there are also strong and weak bases. The kinds of bases you eat to neutralize the acid in your stomach are weak bases. Soap and deodorant are also weak. Strong bases can burn your skin just as strong acids can. One of the properties of a base is the ability to break down fats and oils. This is why bases are

The slippery feel of soap tells you it's a base.

often used to make soap and household cleaners. Oil is cleaned off our skin using soap, and oil is cleaned off our kitchen counters using cleaning products that contain a base, such as ammonia. One of the strongest bases is lye, a base found in some drain cleaners. Chemists usually call it sodium hydroxide (NaOH). It's so powerful it can break down all the matter in your drain without harming the metal.

Neutral News

As I mentioned, bases are often used to neutralize acids. That means they take away the effect of the acid. Essentially, when you combine an acid and a base, they cancel each other out, forming a neutral substance. Something is neutral if it's not an acid or a base. For example, water is neutral.

The acidic venom from a bee sting might be neutralized by applying a basic solution, such as baking soda.

Neutralizing acids and bases can be really important when you're stung by an ant or a bee. The sting is filled with acid. Making a paste of baking soda and water and rubbing it into the sting might neutralize the acid and reduce the pain and swelling. The opposite can be done when you're stung by a jellyfish in the ocean. Jellyfish release a toxic base from their tentacles. Vinegar may neutralize the toxic base of a jellyfish's stinger. See how important it is to understand chemistry!

The toxic base from a jellyfish sting can be neutralized by applying an acid, such as vinegar.

Potential pH

It's time to learn about pH. This is an important chemistry concept with acids and bases. Scientists use the pH scale to determine whether a substance is an acid or base. **pH** means potential for hydrogen. That makes sense doesn't it? All acids contain hydrogen ions. So, the pH scale determines which substances have more hydrogen ions and are thus more acidic.

The pH scale is a series of numbers usually from 0 to 14. A substance is neutral when it has a pH value of 7 (at 25°C or 77°F). Water is neutral. Most plants and animals survive best in soil and water that has a neutral pH of 7. We had a pond in our backyard with fish in it. In autumn, when the leaves would fall from the trees and into our pond, the pH of the water would change, causing our fish to die. This is why pond supply stores sell pH indicators. It's important to keep water as close as possible to a neutral pH of 7. If the solution is lower than 7 on the pH scale, it's an acid. If it's above 7, it's a base.

Look at the pH scale on this page. Which is the most acidic substance on the pH scale? Which is the most basic? Did you notice that the substances on either end of the scale burn the skin?

You can determine whether a substance is an acid or base by using an indicator. An indicator is a substance that changes color when mixed with an acid or a base. Litmus paper is the easiest indicator to use. It turns red when it touches an acid and turns blue when it touches a base. A universal indicator is much like litmus paper but turns specific shades to indicate the pH number from 1 to 14. It comes with a chart for matching the pH. You can also make litmus paper using coffee filters and cabbage juice. Or you can create your own indicator. Go to www.apologia.com/bookextras to find instructions.

1/10,000,000	14	liquid drain cleaner caustic soda
1/1,000,000	13	bleaches oven cleaner
1/100,000	12	soapy water
1/10,000	11	ammonia
1/1,000	10	Milk of Magnesia
1/100	9	toothpaste
1/10	8	baking soda seawater, eggs
0	7	pure water
10	6	milk urine
100	5	acid rain coffee
1,000	4	tomato juice
10,000	3	orange juice soft drink
100,000	2	lemon juice vinegar
1,000,000	1	acid from stomach lining
10,000,000	0	battery acid

Math It!

Look at the pH scale. It's what mathematicians call logarithmic. In simple terms, each step in the pH scale is a factor of 10, so a solution of pH 2 is 10 times more acidic than one of pH 3 and 100 times more than one of pH 4.

Let's test some substances now for an acid or base reaction!

Try This!

You can use litmus paper purchased at a pet store or drugstore to test your substances. Remember, blue litmus paper turns red under acidic conditions, and red litmus paper turns blue under basic (alkaline) conditions. The shade will depend on how acidic or basic the substance is.

You will need: An adult's supervision; safety goggles; plastic cups; and different household items to test, such as water, milk, lemon juice, Milk of Magnesia, baking soda mixed with water, vinegar, ammonia-based glass cleaner, and any other food or substance you wish to test. You may even want to test the dirt in your yard!

First, pour a small amount of each liquid into a different cup. Make a hypothesis about what color you think the litmus paper will turn for each substance. Now dip a strip of litmus paper into each substance. Was your guess about the acidity of the substances correct?

Explain to someone all that you've learned about acids and bases. Before moving on to chemical reactions, record some of this information in your notebooking journal.

Chemical Chaos

You've studied some interesting compounds so far in this lesson. Remember that compounds are pure substances made from more than one type of element. It's possible to change an element into a compound. It's also possible to change a compound back into an element. To do this, you would need a chemical reaction. A **chemical reaction** occurs when two or more chemical substances interact with each other and change into different chemical substances. Often, a compound will join with or separate from the original compound. When compounds do this, they sometimes produce evidence that a reaction is taking place. This evidence could be heat, fire, bubbles, light, or some other reaction.

Can you see evidence of a chemical reaction taking place in the experiment above?

This candle is experiencing both a chemical and a physical reaction. The burning wick is a chemical change. The melting wax and the gas it's releasing are both physical changes.

Chemical or Physical Reactions

In chemical reactions, elements change on the atomic level. That means atoms are changing around somehow. You actually see chemical reactions all the time. When you cook, sometimes the atoms combine to form new substances. When you bake bread, the yeast causes the sugar to break down chemically to form gases that help the bread to rise. As you noticed, when a metal rusts, a chemical reaction is taking place. As you learned, the metal atoms combine with the oxygen molecules. This causes the metal to corrode. The changing of iron to rust is a chemical change. It actually changes the metal into something different. Eventually, if the entire metal item rusted, it would deteriorate to the point of breaking down completely into dust.

If you simply heated up the metal to form it into a different shape, a physical change would occur. A chemical change actually changes the molecules. A physical change does *not* change the molecules; it only changes the way things look, and sometimes it changes the state of the chemical substance. We call this kind of change a **physical reaction**.

A physical change in a substance doesn't change what the substance *is*. Let's say you were to cut a piece of paper into tiny squares. That would be a physical reaction. But if you burned that paper, it would become something other than paper—releasing some substances as gas and leaving behind charred carbon. That would be a chemical reaction.

Let's explore chemical and physical reactions with some fun experiments.

Try This!

You will need: An adult's supervision, safety goggles, a 2-liter bottle of Diet Coke, a package of regular mint

Mentos, and a hot glue gun.

First, remove the Mentos from the package. Next, have an adult glue 8 Mentos together in the same way they were stacked up in the package. Now take your Diet Coke and stack of Mentos outdoors to a wide open area you don't mind getting messy. Open the Diet Coke and drop the Mentos stack into the bottle. Stand back immediately!

That, my friend, was a fun physical reaction! The Diet Coke reacted with the Mentos, but it did not change on the chemical level.

Can you explain what happened? The Diet Coke is full of a dissolved gas called carbon dioxide. If you were to study a Mentos candy under a magnifying glass, you'd see that it had a rough surface with lots of small pores. When you drop the candy into the bottle, the tiny pores become sites for the dissolved gas to form bubbles. These bubbles expand, then detach and float to the surface. This happens so quickly that the gas—along with the soda—forces itself out of the bottle in a fountain! This is a physical reaction; no chemical change occurred.

Try This!

You will need: An adult's supervision, safety goggles, 2 glass jars (with lids), a bowl of vinegar, 2 pads of steel wool, 2 thermometers, a sink, a bowl of water, and a pencil.

First, put the thermometers in the jars and close the lids. After 5 minutes, take out the thermometers and read the temperatures. Write down the temperatures. Next, soak 1 pad of steel wool in a bowl of vinegar and 1 in a bowl of water for about 1 minute. Standing over a sink, squeeze the vinegar and water out of the steel wool pads. Now wrap the steel wool around the bulbs of the thermometers. Place the thermometers and steel wool pads back into the jars and close the lids. After 5 minutes, take out the thermometers and read the temperatures. Write down the results.

What happened? The vinegar caused the iron in the steel to rust at a much faster rate than if it were simply wet with water. It created a chemical reaction. Remember, rust occurs when the electrons in the iron combine with oxygen and water molecules. As rusting occurs, heat energy is released. In your experiment, you were able to detect the heat of this reaction with your thermometer because it was happening at a much faster rate in the vinegar-soaked wool. Leave the lid off both the vinegar wool and the water wool. Let them sit for a day. Notice which one has more rust on it after one day.

Explain what you've learned so far about chemical and physical reactions.

Heat from the hair dryer will speed up the evaporation of water from this boy's hair, causing it to dry faster.

Reactants Releasing and Retaining

One thing you can be sure of is that whenever a chemical or physical reaction occurs, molecules are moving. Sometimes they move very fast; other times they don't move quite as fast. When iron that's left outdoors rusts, it takes a while for the chemical reaction to occur. The molecules are moving, combining and changing, but it happens slowly. However, you can speed up a chemical reaction by using a catalyst. A **catalyst** is a substance that speeds up a chemical reaction without being used up in the process.

Heat also speeds up the reaction rate, which is how fast a chemical reaction occurs. Can you think of times when you've added heat to speed up the rate of a reaction? Think of when you cook something. Heat speeds up and even causes the reaction. What about when you need to dry your hair? Using a hair dryer speeds up the evaporation of the water molecules from your hair. Can you think of any other examples of heat being used to speed up a reaction?

Once in a while, you can increase the reaction rate by increasing the concentration of the compounds that are being combined. If you add a lot of extra molecules to the same volume, it might increase the rate of reaction because there are more molecules to react. If you drop one Mentos into a bottle of Diet Coke, the cola will spew out the top. If you drop five Mentos at one time into a bottle of Diet Coke, the rate of reaction will speed up—as will the spewing cola!

In a chemical reaction, the substances you start with are called the **reactants**. What were the reactants in the experiments you conducted in this lesson? Some of the reactants were borax, glue, water, vinegar, steel wool, litmus paper, and the different acids and bases you tested. The substances these reactants make are called the **products**. In a chemical reaction, the products created are different from the reactants used. In a physical reaction, the products are the same, but they may be in a different form. For example, melting ice is reacting to the heat, but the frozen ice is in a different form than the water it produced.

Do you remember in your vinegar and steel wool experiment that the reaction caused heat to be released? In every single reaction, energy is either released or absorbed (taken in). When the reactants absorb energy, we say it's an **endothermic reaction**. As you know, many chemical terms come from the Greek language, and this is yet another one. "Endo" comes from *endon*, meaning within; "therm" comes from *thermotēta*, meaning heat. So "endothermic" means that heat energy goes into the product. Endothermic reactions store heat energy in the molecules. Heat is not released; it's absorbed. Ice cubes melting is an endothermic physical reaction. The H_2O molecules are taking in heat, causing them to change states. When you cook an egg, you're also creating an endothermic chemical reaction. Heat is absorbed into the egg, changing it from the wet sticky glob to a firm edible substance.

When energy is released during a chemical reaction, we call that an **exothermic reaction**. "Exo" comes from the Greek word *exō*, which means outside. So heat energy gets outside the molecules in an exothermic reaction. When this happens, things heat up!

As I mentioned, when you measured the temperature of the vinegar and steel wool, you noticed the temperature was increasing. That was energy

being released. When you light a candle, the flame is an exothermic reaction—releasing heat energy (and light) into the environment. You'll do a fun experiment at the end of this lesson that will release a lot of heat energy and smoke into the environment. You'll also make crystals—which is another exothermic reaction. (Heat is being released to transform a liquid salt into a solid salt.) Before we do these experiments and projects, let's spend some time reviewing and recording what we've learned by doing some fun notebooking activities!

Can you explain what type of chemical reaction is taking place in the images above?

Final Matters

Exploring science can be so much fun. I hope you've enjoyed learning about all the exciting things God created and how they fit together. From the beautiful snowflakes—each individually different and lovely—to the amazing plastics and the reactions when mixing chemicals, God made a wonderfully exciting world!

What Do You Remember?

What is a compound? What is a crystal? Name some crystals you have in your house. What is a polymer? Name some natural polymers. Name some man-made polymers. What is a chemical reaction? What is a physical reaction? What are some physical changes? What is a reactant? What is the product of a chemical reaction? What is an endothermic reaction? What is an exothermic reaction? What factors can influence the rate of reaction? Name some acids you know about. Name some bases in your home. What is the pH of pure water?

Notebooking Activities

After you've written down the fascinating facts you've learned and have recorded the experiments you conducted, do the following notebooking activity.

Write a story about the life of a plastic object. Begin with the object's life as a polymer. Then describe it being shaped, sold, used, and recycled. Be sure to tell how the plastic is remolded to become something different. You can make the story a nonfiction (true) story, or you can animate your piece of plastic and make it a fictional tale of a talking, thinking, feeling piece of plastic!

Experiment
Make a Smoke Bomb

The mixture you'll make is made from safe, nontoxic ingredients and is not dangerous. The smoke produced is not harmful; it's made up of carbon dioxide and water. However, there *is* a great deal of smoke, so make sure you light your smoke bomb outside in an area that cars will not be driving through. Do **not** light your smoke bomb inside your house, or your smoke alarm will go off, and it will appear that your house is on fire! Making a smoke bomb is a safe experiment if you carefully follow the safety instructions and have an adult help you.

You will need:

- an adult
- ½ cup of potassium nitrate (stump remover)
- aluminum foil
- ⅓ cup of sugar
- 1–2 teaspoons of water
- a wick
- an empty toilet paper tube
- safety goggles
- duct tape
- protective gloves

1. In a mixing bowl, mix ½ cup of potassium nitrate with ⅓ cup of sugar.
2. Now measure the temperature of this dry mixture.
3. Next, add 1 or 2 teaspoons of water until the mixture becomes like a very, very thick paste. If you add too much water, your smoke bomb will take more than 48 hours to dry. Measure the temperature of the mixture. (An endothermic reaction happens when you mix these ingredients.)
4. Line the inside of the toilet paper tube with aluminum foil. Then wrap enough duct tape over one end so that the mixture cannot escape. Now fill the tube with your mixture.
5. Place the wick in the center of the mixture with the tip of the wick sticking out.
6. Put your tube in a safe place to dry, making sure it isn't near any flames. Also, make sure it's out of the way of younger siblings, as ingesting the mixture can make you sick. Allow the tube of mixture to dry for a few days. Once it's dry, you'll explore the exothermic part of this experiment.
7. Take your smoke bomb outside and place it on a concrete area that does not have leaves or dry brush nearby. (Sparks from your smoke bomb can cause a fire!) Have an adult light the wick with a long match or lighter.
8. Immediately move back and watch huge billows of smoke fill the air!

The energy of this reaction comes from the burning of the fuel (sugar) to form mainly carbon dioxide and water vapor. Burning is a type of exothermic chemical change where a substance is combined with oxygen. In this case, potassium nitrate (KNO_3) provides the oxygen for the burning to occur. Usually when things burn, the oxygen comes from the air. However, the potassium nitrate provided the oxygen in this reaction.

Project
Grow Crystals

You may remember that rubies, sapphires, and many other gemstones are made from the elements aluminum and oxygen. A special compound called alum (which you can get at the grocery store in the spice aisle) is made from aluminum, oxygen, potassium, and sulfur. Under the right conditions, alum can grow beautiful, hard, and sizable crystals. Let's see if we can make this happen.

You will need:

- an adult
- a box of alum
- a glass measuring cup or bowl
- a large drinking glass
- thread or nylon fishing line
- a skewer or pencil
- a magnifying glass
- 1 cup of water

1. Fill the glass measuring bowl with 1 cup of water.
2. Have an adult help you heat the water in the microwave for about 3–4 minutes. Now have an adult help you remove the hot water from the microwave.
3. Carefully pour the entire box of alum into the bowl of water and stir. Let it sit for an entire day.
4. Next, pour the alum water into the drinking glass without allowing the crystals to fall in (as much as possible).
5. At the bottom of the glass measuring bowl will be several crystal chunks. Examine each of them under a magnifying glass.
6. Take the largest crystal chunk (or your favorite structure) and tie the thread or fishing line around it.
7. Attach the chunk to the center of the pencil or skewer.
8. Now submerge your crystal into the glass filled with the alum by placing the skewer across the glass and allowing the string and crystal to fall into the glass. Make sure the string is the right length so the crystal does not touch the bottom of the glass; the higher it hangs, the better. Also, make sure it doesn't touch the sides of the glass.
9. Keep checking your crystal growth over the course of the day.
10. Examine your crystal under a magnifying glass and illustrate in your notebooking journal the structure you see.

Multitude of Mixtures

Today you're going to finish your last lesson on chemistry. The rest of the book will focus on physics. So let's get started. Do you remember in the last lesson when we discussed the difference between physical reactions and chemical reactions? Can you describe the difference? A chemical reaction changes a substance on the molecular level—the molecules change. The substance becomes something different. That happened when you combined yeast and hydrogen peroxide in lesson 3. It also happened when you made bouncy balls out of borax, corn starch, and glue. Can you think of any other experiments you did that created a chemical reaction?

Not so in a physical reaction. The substances are the same substance, even if they look different. Do you remember growing crystals? That was a physical change. The substance did not change into something different.

This leads us to an important chemistry concept. Many things you see are mixtures of substances that don't combine on the chemical level. **Mixtures** are two or more substances that have been combined. However, each substance keeps its own chemical identity. Its original properties stay the same.

Most of the things around you are mixtures. Some mixtures are obvious, like salsa and salad dressing. You can look at these items and see that there are different substances in the mixtures. When we can actually *see* the different substances, we call the mixture **heterogeneous**. *Hetero* is a Greek word that basically means different. You can see the different things in a heterogeneous mixture.

This bowl of Italian dressing is a mixture of many substances. However, the substances do not combine chemically.

Some mixtures are so well mixed that they look like they are one substance. Milk is an example of this. If you've ever had the unfortunate experience of leaving a glass of milk out for a while, you know that the different parts of the milk separate after sitting for a long time at room temperature. That's because milk itself is a mixture. So

is saltwater. Neither the water nor the salt change on the chemical level when you combine them. Though they are mixed, you still have water, and you still have salt. Milk and saltwater are very well-mixed kinds of mixtures. They're called **homogeneous** mixtures. *Homo* is a Greek word that basically means same or like. In a homogeneous mixture, the substances are so well mixed that they look the same.

Heterogeneous Mixtures

Did you know that most of the things you eat are heterogeneous mixtures? When you pour a bowl of cereal, then add milk, you've made a heterogeneous mixture. Macaroni and cheese is also a heterogeneous mixture. Can you think of any others?

Heterogeneous mixtures are easy to tell apart from compounds or homogeneous mixtures. Remember, compounds are pure substances made from the same molecules, and homogeneous mixtures are so well mixed that they look like one substance. Look at the images below. Can you identify which ones are heterogeneous mixtures, which are compounds, and which are homogeneous mixtures? The answers can be found in the answer key in the back of this book.

Let's create a heterogeneous solid mixture from things you have in the kitchen. I think you'll find it rather tasty!

Try This!

You will need: An adult's supervision, ½ cup of flour, ½ cup of sugar, ½ cup of melted butter, ½ cup of old-fashioned oats, ½ cup of chocolate chips, a greased baking sheet, a mixing bowl, a mixing spoon, and an oven.

First, preheat the oven to 350°. Now mix all your ingredients to make dough. Separate your doughy mixture into small chunks, whatever size you prefer. Place your chunks on a greased baking sheet and bake them for about 15–20 minutes. Allow them to cool, then enjoy eating your heterogeneous treat!

Note: Baking your cookies caused *some* chemical change, but your cookies are mostly a heterogeneous mixture.

Suspensions and Emulsions

Have you ever seen a swamp? If you dipped a glass into a swamp and pulled out some water, do you think it would look like a pure substance or a heterogeneous mixture? Suspended in the water might be all kinds of different substances—some living and some not—such as mud, algae, plants, rocks, and microscopic creatures. When we have a liquid heterogeneous mixture with visible, solid things suspended in a fluid, we call it a suspension. That's easy. Things are suspended in a suspension.

A lot of heterogeneous mixtures are suspensions. A **suspension** is a mixture where larger particles are mixed into smaller particles—with the larger particles suspended throughout the mixture. Eventually, particles in a suspension will separate from each other. They'll either float to the top or settle to the bottom, depending on their density.

This swamp water is a heterogeneous suspension. It's easy to see it's not a pure substance.

Do you remember I asked you to save the lava lamp you made in lesson 1 for lesson 5? Get your lava lamp now and shake it vigorously until the entire thing is mixed together. Set it down and keep an eye on it for the rest of today's lesson.

Usually, in a suspension, you see things settle to the bottom. However, in some suspensions the visible substances suspended in the water move up and out of the mixture. Can you think of what that suspension would be? Carbonated drinks! The carbon dioxide gas in the carbonated drink is a separate substance that's visible in the liquid. This makes it a heterogeneous mixture and a suspension. When the carbon dioxide escapes the liquid, it rises to the top and enters the air.

Try This!

doit

You will need: An adult's supervision, a clear carbonated drink (carbonated water or Sprite will do), a glass, and 8 raisins.

First, fill the glass with the carbonated drink. Now drop the raisins into the glass. Watch the raisins. What's happening? Do the raisins sink or float? Keep watching the raisins for several minutes.

The raisins are obviously denser than the carbonated water, so at first they sink to the bottom of the glass. Because carbon dioxide is suspended in the liquid, it begins to rise to the top. Carbon dioxide gas is less dense than the liquid. Remember what gases do—they expand, escaping their container. When these rising gas bubbles come upon the rough surface of a raisin, they attach to the raisin. The raisin is then lifted because of all the gas bubbles surrounding it. It becomes more buoyant or floatable. When the raisin reaches the surface, the bubbles pop, and the carbon dioxide gas escapes into the air. The raisin then loses buoyancy and sinks. This continues until most of the carbon dioxide has escaped. After a while, the raisin gets soggy and becomes too heavy to rise to the surface. This is very much like the Mentos experiment in the last lesson. The bumpy surface provides places for the carbon dioxide to attach. When enough gases attach, up and out they go together!

Explain what you've learned so far about mixtures.

Homogeneous Mixtures

As I told you earlier, a homogeneous mixture is a very well-mixed mixture—so well mixed that you can't easily see the individual parts. These can often be confused with compounds because they *seem* to be so well mixed that they appear as one kind of substance. However, they aren't. They're mixtures of different substances that can be separated from one another without using a chemical reaction.

We sometimes call a homogeneous mixture a solution. I know you've always heard that solutions are the answers to your math problems, but they're also homogeneous mixtures! In a solution, all the compounds are equally and completely spread out and mixed in—so you can't see the individual parts.

Stainless steel is a homogeneous mixture of different metals, such as iron and chromium.

Salute the Solute

Let's discuss solutions a bit more. A **solution** (which is a homogeneous mixture) is made up of one substance that's dissolved into another substance. Think of saltwater. What's the substance dissolved in the water? Salt. All solutions have a **solute** (something being dissolved) and also a **solvent** (something doing the dissolving). We would say the salt is the solute, and the water is the solvent. In other words, the solute dissolves, and the solvent does the dissolving. There's almost always more of the solvent than the solute.

Look at the images above. Tell someone which substance is the solvent and which is the solute.

As I mentioned, air is a solution—a rather important one, at that. It's a solution of oxygen, nitrogen, and other gases. Nitrogen is the most abundant chemical, so it's the gas every other gas, including oxygen, is dissolved in. Which is the solute and which is the solvent? Oxygen is the solute, while nitrogen is the solvent.

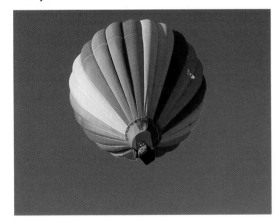
The air inside and outside this hot air balloon is a homogeneous solution. It's a mixture of oxygen, nitrogen, argon, and a few other gases.

Scientists usually use water as the solvent when they make solutions. That's because water is sometimes considered the closest thing to a **universal solvent**. What does that mean? Many other substances on earth are able to dissolve in water because of its chemical properties. Let's learn about these chemical properties. You'll have to put on your thinking cap because this stuff is really complicated. Are you ready? Let's learn!

Scientists often use water as the solvent in many solutions. Can you explain why?

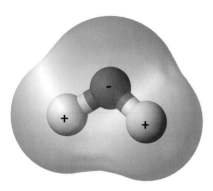

Water molecules have two positive charges on each end and a negative charge in the center. This is why water is such a great solvent.

Polar Bonds in Water

Water is such a good solvent because of how the hydrogen and oxygen atoms bond together. Because it needs to fill its empty valence shells, the oxygen overpowers all the electrons and pulls on them. So the electrons are pulled more toward the oxygen atoms than they are to the hydrogen atoms. This makes the water molecule's charge lopsided. Look at the image on the left. The oxygen atom has a pull on all the negative electrons, so the oxygen side of the atom is negatively charged. At the same time, the two hydrogen sides of the water molecule have a positive charge. The overall molecule is neutral, but parts of the molecule are positive and negative. Essentially, one side of the atom is positively charged, and one side is negatively charged.

We call a lopsided molecule a polar molecule. Just like a magnet, it has two different poles. One pole of the molecule is positive; one pole is negative. Water is a polar molecule.

How does this affect solutes that are added to water? Here's what happens: When a solute is added to water, the water molecules surround parts of the solute. If the solute has a positively charged part, the negative side of the water molecule is attracted to and attaches to the solute molecule. If the solute has a negatively charged part, the positive side of the molecule does the attracting and attaching. When it attaches, it helps to dissolve the solute into the water. This is why so many substances dissolve in water. Positively charged substances and negatively charged substances can both dissolve in water because water is polar.

But what if the substance you put into the water doesn't have a charged part at all? What if it's totally neutral? It won't dissolve in water! We call those substances nonpolar substances since they have no charges or poles. The molecules in those substances are sharing electrons evenly and are quite content to stay together. A **nonpolar molecule** won't dissolve in water at all.

Oil is nonpolar. What happens when you mix oil and water? Do you know *why* that happens? Listen carefully because this is an important scientific truth: It's because like dissolves like. A nonpolar substance added to a nonpolar substance will often dissolve into that substance. A polar substance added to another polar substance will also dissolve. That's what I mean when I say like dissolves like. That will be important for you to know as you go throughout your life.

This is especially useful to know if you like to cook. For example, the flavor molecules in onion, garlic, and many other spices are nonpolar. If you cook onion and garlic in water, they don't add much flavor to the water because they don't dissolve well. They're best added to oil or fat so they can dissolve and spread the flavor.

Another place this becomes important is at the sink!

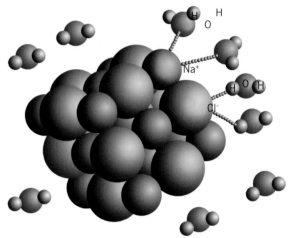

Salt crystal dissolving

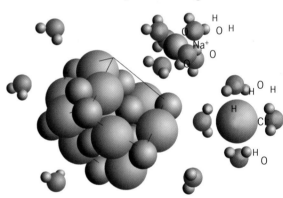

Salt after dissolving

When salt is placed in water, it begins to dissolve. At first, the positive and negative ions of the salt crystal are attracted only to each other. But for the salt to dissolve, these ionic bonds need to be broken. Otherwise, the salt will be floating around in the water undissolved.

What happens is this: The negative chloride ions become somewhat attracted to the positive hydrogen atom. At the same time, the positive sodium ions are attracted to the negative oxygen atom. But sodium and chloride are still attracted to each other.

So it's a pulling competition between the salt and water molecules. In this case, the water always wins the pulling contest.

Soon the chloride and sodium ions are completely surrounded by water molecules. Each part of the water molecule is pointing toward the oppositely charged sodium or chloride ions of the sodium chloride.

Soapy Solutions

Did you know most of the germs and dirt you pick up during the day are nonpolar and stick to the oils of your hands and body? Well, oil doesn't dissolve when you wash your hands. If you've ever tried to wash oil off your hands with just water, you know this. Let's try that now!

Try This!

You will need: An adult's supervision, cooking oil, running water, and soap.

First, rub some cooking oil all over your hands. Now try to wash it off with water. As you wash, consider that the oil is nonpolar and the water is polar. Why won't the oil wash off? Oil and water aren't like substances; therefore, they won't dissolve each other. Now add some soap to your hands and rub the soap all around, being sure to scrub well. Finally, wash off the soap and see what happens!

Can you see now why you shouldn't use just water to wash the germs and dirt off your hands? Your hands don't get clean using only water. How does soap help get the oil off? Well, soap and other cleaners are unique because they're both nonpolar and polar. They have a very big nonpolar tail attached to one end. They also have a small polar head at the other end. Look at the image below to see what they look like. When the nonpolar tail is mixed with a nonpolar substance, it sticks to the surface of that substance. So the nonpolar tail of the soap you used stuck to the oil. But the little polar head on your soap molecule protruded above and out of the oil. It stuck so far out that it made contact with the water flowing from the sink. This caused the polar ends of the soap molecules to attach to the water. So one end of the soap molecules was attached to the oil, while the other end was attached to the water. As the water flowed over your skin, it took the oil with it! The more you scrub, the better it works! This is because the soap molecules can reach more of the oil on the surface and lift it off your hands. Pretty cool, huh?

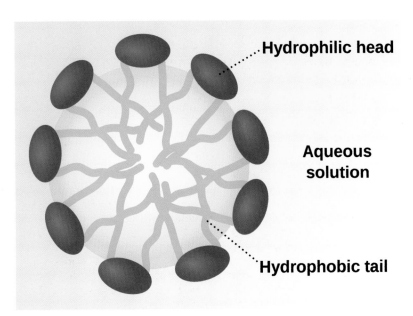

Hydrophilic head

Aqueous solution

Hydrophobic tail

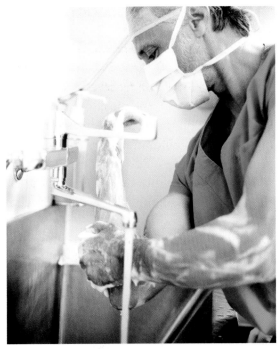

There's a special name for soapy substances: "amphiphilic," from Greek *amphis*, meaning both, and *philia*, meaning love and friendship. These substances got this name because they have ends that love both oil and water. The polar end is called hydrophilic (water-loving), and the nonpolar end is called hydrophobic (water-fearing) or lipophilic (fat-loving). Amphiphilic substances are also called surfactants because they like to be on the surfaces between oil and water.

It's important for this surgeon to wash his hands and arms with a special soap before performing surgery. The soap will remove any germs on his skin that could cause his patients to become infected.

8 7

Try This!

You will need: An adult's supervision, a bowl or plate that has a high lip (a pie plate works well), ½ cup of milk, food coloring (red, green, blue, and yellow), a cotton swab, and dishwashing liquid.

First, pour about ¼ inch of milk into the bowl. Once the milk has stopped moving, add one drop of several different colors of food coloring into the center of the bowl. With the cotton swab, touch the milk in the center of the bowl. What happens? Now put dishwashing liquid on the tip of the cotton swab and predict what will happen when you touch the milk in the center of the bowl this time. Go ahead and touch the milk with the tip of the cotton swab. Hold it there for 15 seconds. You can continue to add dishwashing liquid to the swab and touch the milk again and again.

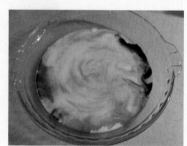

What happened? Dishwashing liquid is bipolar (nonpolar on one end and polar on the other). This breaks down protein and fat bonds in the milk. The dishwashing liquid's nonpolar hydrophilic (water-loving) end dissolves in water, while at the same time its hydrophobic (water-fearing) end attaches to a fat particle in the milk.

The molecules of fat move in every direction as the dishwashing liquid molecules swirl about to join the fat molecules. With all this activity, the food coloring is moved and shoved around until the soap is mixed well with the milk.

That was some pretty tough science! See how much of it you can explain to someone else before you move on.

Alloys

For many thousands of years, even before the great Flood of Noah, man mixed metals to make different, more useful metals. When we mix metals together, we have what is called an alloy. **Alloys** are metals that have been dissolved into other metals to form a metal solution. Scientists and metal workers have been experimenting with alloys for thousands of years. They've combined just about every metal on earth in different combinations and amounts—seeking to discover the perfect alloy for just about everything. Brass is an alloy made of zinc and copper. Bronze is copper plus tin. Steel is made from iron mixed usually with carbon. Sometimes it's mixed with other metals, such as manganese, vanadium, chromium, or tungsten. Because of the alloying elements, steel is 1,000 times stronger than pure iron.

The Golden Gate Bridge in San Francisco, California, is almost two miles long. It's constructed of steel and is painted orange.

The Bible mentions several alloys, including brass and steel. It was early in the history of mankind that man discovered these alloys. In fact, steel was found at an archaeological site about 4,000 years old. It was mostly used to make strong weapons. The steel industry in America is huge. In fact, steel has always been used to create many products, including bridges, automobiles, ships, rockets and space ships, buildings, tanks, rails, and fences—as well as stoves and pans.

One of the most important discoveries in our time has been stainless steel. Stainless steel is an alloy made of iron with some chromium added in. Stainless steel is special because it doesn't corrode easily. It's extremely hard and can be used for a variety of purposes. Silverware, pots and pans, and many other items in your house are probably made of stainless steel.

When was the last time you drank out of an aluminum can? The alloy that makes aluminum cans is another amazing invention. Before aluminum cans were used by drink companies, all drinks were sold in glass bottles. Bottles are heavier and can break easily. Scientists mixed aluminum with about 1% magnesium and 1% manganese to create the perfect can for sodas and other beverages. Not only is the

These steel and aluminum cans are being recycled. They will be melted down and remade into new cans.

aluminum can lightweight and easy to mold, but it also resists rust and corrosion and is strong enough to contain the pressure in a carbonated beverage. It's also easy to stamp graphics and designs on an aluminum can. Soon after aluminum cans became popular, manufacturers realized something. If they could get the cans back after they were used, they could be melted and remade into new cans. So the manufacturers decided to offer money for the return of cans. People could return cans to recycling centers for five cents a can. This is how recycling got its start! Instead of having to dig up new aluminum every time they wanted to make a new can, manufacturers had a ready supply of aluminum from the recycling centers. This helped save money and a natural resource—aluminum!

Mixing metals is the job of chemical engineers. It's an important job that helps to create many new products and inventions. Many inventions we have today were created by chemical engineers with NASA, the National Aeronautics and Space Administration. These engineers were seeking to find good materials for space travel. The titanium alloy is one of those amazing inventions created by NASA engineers looking for a strong, lightweight metal. Titanium is very lightweight. It's as strong as steel but almost half as dense. Like aluminium, titanium resists corrosion—even by seawater and dilute acids. When mixed with small amounts of aluminum and other metals like vanadium, titanium is incredibly durable and hard. It was initially used to make the bodies of planes

This titanium crystal bar is made from an alloy created by NASA engineers.

and rockets. However, because titanium's so light, it's now used to make golf clubs, baby strollers, and expensive watches. Chemistry can bring lots of improvements to our lives!

During the 2011 earthquake in Japan, there were certain buildings made of materials that allowed the buildings to bend and sway but not fall during the earthquake. These buildings and the people inside them were not harmed when the earthquake hit Japan. Today, scientists are seeking to create more alloys that can be used to construct buildings in places where earthquakes are common.

Most jewelry, even gold or silver jewelry, is actually an alloy. Most gold jewelry is an alloy made of mainly gold mixed with copper or nickel. Which is the solute and which is the solvent in gold jewelry? Since it's mostly gold, the other metals are dissolved in the gold. Therefore, gold is the solvent, and the other metals are the solute. The reason jewelry makers combine copper and nickel with gold is that small amounts of these other metals make the gold much harder. Why do you think people choose not to make rings out of pure gold? Let's do an experiment to find out!

Try This!

You will need: An adult's supervision and aluminum foil.

First, tear off a small strip of aluminum foil. Now form the piece of foil into a ring that will fit on your finger. Squeeze your hand tightly, then look at your ring. What happened to it? Try a few other activities that involve putting pressure on your ring. How does your ring look now? Pure gold is about as soft as your aluminum-foil ring!

Most metals you see around you are actually mixtures of metals. Some metals are not even considered alloys but are simply plated. That means the metal surface is coated with another metal, making the surface a different color. This makes it *appear* the metal is an entirely different metal. A lot of jewelry is gold- or silver-plated. You discover this when the gold or silver begins to wear off after a while. If the jewelry remains gold or silver for a long time, even after getting wet, it might be made of real gold or silver.

Explain what you've learned about alloys before moving on to the rest of the lesson.

Colloids

Another homogeneous mixture we should take a look at is colloids. The particles in a **colloid** are larger than the particles in a solution but smaller than the particles in a suspension. So a colloid is somewhere between a solution and a suspension. Colloids may look homogeneous to the naked eye, but the particles are actually big enough to be seen with a microscope. You can't see atoms and molecules with a microscope, but you can see the particles in a colloid. One example of a colloid is milk. Milk is made up of about 85% water with a lot of different fat proteins and globules mixed in. If you were to look at milk under a strong microscope, you'd see the fat globules as separate from the liquid. If you leave milk standing for a long time, the fat globules eventually rise to the top, and what's left underneath is the watery skim milk. If you looked at skim milk under the microscope, it would look like a pure solution. Skim milk has had the fat removed or skimmed from the milk.

Have you ever milked a cow? If so, you may remember that when the milk came out of the cow, it wasn't well mixed. When you looked in the pail, you probably noticed the fat was on top, while the watery part of the milk was below it. Fat is less dense than water, so it rises to the top. This is what milk looks like before it's been homogenized. The dairy farmer puts the milk through a process called homogenization. Does that word look familiar? Homogenization shakes up the milk so much that it mixes the milk particles really well. This breaks down the fat globules into smaller and smaller particles so that they distribute throughout the milk. We call it homogenized milk, but it's really still a colloid.

It's not always easy to tell a colloid from a pure homogeneous solution. All colloids have one particular property that can help you distinguish them from other solutions: The particles in a colloid scatter light. If a beam of light shines into a colloid, the light is scattered by the particles in the colloid. This causes the beam of light to be seen easily in that solution. This is called the **Tyndall**

The milk in this pail is not homogenized; the fat globules are floating on top of the watery milk below. It looks different from the milk you'll find in most grocery stores.

effect. When a beam of light passes through a true solution, the light cannot be seen because the particles are too small (molecule-sized).

You've probably seen this in your own home. The air in your house appears to be a pure solution of oxygen, nitrogen, argon, and whatever else is in the air. But if a beam of sunlight comes through the window, you'll see a vast number of dust particles. These particles make the air in your house a colloid. The Tyndall effect can also be seen when the sun's rays come through a hole in the clouds or when a car's headlight beams can be seen on a foggy night. Fog is a colloid.

Let's do an experiment to see if we can separate the fat globules from a homogeneous milk mixture. We'll separate the particles in this colloid to make butter and skim milk!

This image of the sun's rays coming through the trees in this forest is an example of the Tyndall effect.

Try This!

You will need: An adult's supervision, heavy whipping cream, and a small glass jar (like a baby food jar) with a lid.

First, let the cream come to room temperature. Now fill the jar half full of cream and put the lid on tightly. Get ready to shake it for a long, long time! You may need someone to take turns with you. Shake the jar in a slow, hard, repetitive motion. Make the motion somewhat like you're cracking a whip—hitting the cream against the sides of the jar over and over again. Eventually, the homogeneous milk mixture will begin separating into fat globules. These fat globules begin to find other fat globules and join with them to form one large fat globule! This results in phase separation: The fat part separates from the watery part. When you get the large fat globule, you can drain off the buttermilk liquid and sprinkle a bit of salt on your homemade butter. Spread it on some toast, and you've just made a yummy snack!

There are many different kinds of colloids. Here are some common ones: A **gel** is a colloid made of solid particles mixed in a liquid. An example of this is pudding. An **aerosol** is another colloid. One type of aerosol is a liquid mixed in a gas. Hairspray in a can with a nozzle you press down comes out as an aerosol. Another type is a solid mixed in a gas, such as dust in the air. **Foam** is another kind of colloid. Foam is made by mixing a gas in a liquid. It may seem like an aerosol, but it's not because the main ingredient is the liquid. Whipped cream is a foam of air and cream. The last kind of colloid is an **emulsion**. Droplets of liquids mixed with another liquid form an emulsion. Paint is an emulsion of dyes, oils, and other chemicals. When paint sits for a long time, these mixtures separate. That's why paint stores sell stirring sticks to remix the paint if it settles. Milk and salad dressings are also emulsions. Mayonnaise is an emulsion because it's a mixture of egg yolk and oil. These are just a few of the different kinds of colloids.

Let's study concentrates by making a concentrate!

Try This!

You will need: An adult's supervision, powdered chocolate drink mix, a spoon, and a large glass of milk.

To begin, put a tablespoon of the powdered chocolate drink mix in the milk and stir it well. Now taste it. How does it taste? Add another tablespoon of the powdered chocolate and taste the milk. Repeat this procedure again and again, continuing to add tablespoons of the mix until it no longer dissolves into the milk.

Diluted Versus Concentrated

Let's talk about diluted and concentrated solutions. You actually already know all about these chemistry concepts. In fact, when you made your chocolate milk, you were experimenting with them.

When you added one tablespoon of chocolate powder to your milk, it became a diluted solution. Did your chocolate milk taste very good when it was a diluted solution? As you continued to add the solute, you increased the concentration of the solute in the mixture. Once you added a lot of the solute, you had what we call a concentrated solution or a concentrate. A **concentrate** has a large amount of solute in the solvent. Did you prefer your chocolate milk when it was a concentrate? Everyone prefers a different amount of solute in their chocolate milk.

As you continued to add more solute, you eventually reached the saturation point. A **saturated solution** is a solution that has reached the point where no more solute can dissolve in the solvent. When you continued to add more solute after that point, you created a suspension. You could actually see particles of chocolate mix in the milk. This is a yummy way to learn about dilutes, concentrates, and saturated solutions, isn't it?

There's one more type of solution. Can you guess what it is? It's a **supersaturated solution**! This type dissolves *more* than a saturated solution—but it's very unstable. Soda is a supersaturated solution. That's because an oversupply of carbon dioxide gas is pumped into the solution. When the lid is on, the gas stays dissolved, but as soon as it's opened, the gas escapes, and the amount dissolved decreases to the saturated level.

The gas bubbles in this carbonated water make the drink a supersaturated solution. Once the gas escapes, it will be a saturated solution.

In the glass above, adding lemon to water makes a diluted solution. Lemonade, however, is a concentrated solution.

Separating Mixtures

Do you remember whether mixtures are chemically combined or physically combined? That's right—they're *physically* combined. Because they're combined in this way, they can be separated into their individual components using physical methods. We didn't use a chemical reaction to separate the fat from the milk; we did it with a physical process. We can use several physical processes to separate mixtures. Some of these processes are evaporation, filtration, sifting, magnetism, and chromatography. Let's learn about these methods, then do a chromatography experiment. If you'd like to experiment more, you can go to www.apologia.com/bookextras to find some ideas. You can also find extra experiments in the "Test It Out" section of your *Chemistry and Physics Notebooking Journal*.

Evaporation occurs when a liquid turns into a gas. This can separate a mixture combined with water because as the water evaporates, it leaves behind what was mixed in. You can speed evaporation by heating water. But water naturally evaporates on its own when the temperature is warm enough. You used the evaporation method to separate a mixture when you heated the saltwater until the water evaporated, leaving the salt crystals behind.

Filtration is used to allow a liquid to seep through a substance that traps larger particles, letting only the pure liquid through. Water filtration systems use substances that trap the elements often found in tap water so that you're drinking mostly pure water. The water that comes through your sink has most likely been through a process that purifies it for drinking. One of those processes is filtration. At the end of this lesson, we'll conduct an experiment to filter dirty water using processes similar to the ones water treatment plants use.

Sifting is another method used to separate large or important parts of a mixture. My children often sift through our trail mix and pick out the most delicious items (like M&M's), leaving the boring items behind in great numbers!

Magnetism is used to separate mixtures that have highly magnetic metals in them. The metal is attracted to the magnet, leaving the other substances behind.

Chromatography is another method of separating mixtures as they move across a certain material that attracts the components differently. The word "chromatography" literally means color writing (from Greek *chroma*, meaning color and *graphein,* meaning to write) because it was first used to separate strongly colored plant pigments.

Sifting is a good way to separate the yummy items in a nut mixture.

Let's conduct a separation of mixtures using chromatography!

Try This!

You will need: An adult's supervision, Crayola markers (original classic colors), 4 white Crayola sidewalk chalk sticks, 4 plastic cups, and water.

Using black, brown, violet, and green markers from your Crayola marker pack, draw one ring of color all the way around one chalk stick (about ½ to 1 inch up the stick) for each color marker. Now set each chalk stick in a cup with a small amount of water. Make sure the water level is below the mark you made. As the water creeps up the chalk, watch what happens!

You just separated a homogeneous mixture! What did you learn from this experiment? Record your findings in your notebooking journal. You may want to take a picture of the results and attach it to your journal page.

Final Matters

You've learned so much in chemistry. Give yourself a pat on the back and a big high five! The rest of the book will focus on the study of physics and the mysterious way God made the world work. It's now time to conclude with some writing, drawing, and another experiment.

What Do You Remember?

What is the difference between a mixture and a compound? What is a heterogeneous mixture? What is a homogeneous mixture? What are alloys? What is a concentrate? What is a saturated solution? What are some ways to separate the component parts of a mixture?

Notebooking Activities

Write down the fascinating facts you've learned about mixtures. After that, do the following notebooking activity.

Make a chart with two categories: heterogeneous and homogeneous. Go through your house and list items that fall under each category. The *Chemistry and Physics Notebooking Journal* has a chart for you to use.

Experiment
Filter Water

Rivers, lakes and streams are often the sources for the water that comes into your home. However, these sources contain impurities that make the water look and smell bad. It may also contain bacteria and other small organisms that can make you sick. So this water must be cleaned before it can be sent to your home for you to drink.

Water treatment plants clean the water using aeration, coagulation, sedimentation, filtration, and disinfection. This experiment will take you through the first four steps of water purification. You won't be using the harsh chemicals needed to disinfect the water and ensure all the bacteria are killed. So the water still won't be drinkable, but you'll see much cleaner water in the end.

You will need:

* ½ gallon of swamp water or muddy lake water
* a two-liter soda bottle with a cap
* a two-liter soda bottle with the top and bottom cut off (You'll need both the top and bottom.)
* a large glass beaker or a large glass vase with a wide mouth
* 2 teaspoons of alum
* ½ cup of fine white play sand or beach sand
* ½ cup of coarse or industrial sand
* ½ cup of small pebbles (Aquarium rocks work well.)
* a coffee filter
* a rubber band
* spoon
* a stopwatch
* scissors

Aeration
1. Pour some swamp water into the two-liter bottle and save some for the end of the experiment.
2. Smell it, describe it, and then cap it.
3. Shake the bottle vigorously for 30 seconds.
4. Cut off the top of the two-liter bottle to make a bigger spout. This will make it easier to transfer the water.
5. Pour the water back and forth 10 times between the vase and the bottle. You should have gotten all the gases out of the water by doing this. This is the first step in the purification process, called aeration. You aerated the water by adding air to it, thus releasing all the gases.

Coagulation
1. Pour the aerated water into the bottle with the top cut off.
2. Add 2 teaspoons of alum to the aerated water and slowly stir the mixture for 5 minutes. You'll see particles stick together to make larger clumps. This allows all the suspended particles (like dirt) to chemically stick together into a substance we call floc (clumps of alum and sediment). We do this to make the particles larger so they can be easily removed with a filter.

Sedimentation

1. Allow the water to stand for 20 minutes. Check it every 5 minutes and write down what you see. This is the process that happens when gravity pulls the now heavier/denser particles of floc to the bottom of the cylinder.

Filtration

1. Using a rubber band, attach a coffee filter to the outside neck of the top part of the cut two-liter bottle.
2. Turn it upside down into the vase or beaker.
3. Pour the fine sand into the bottle-top filter.
4. Now pour the coarse sand in.
5. Finally, pour the pebbles on top of the coarse sand.
6. Carefully pour about ¾ cup of the aerated swamp water into the filter. Continue to add more water as it filters through. Be aware it can take 3–4 hours for all your water to move through the filter.
7. Compare the newly filtered water to your original swamp water.

The last step at the treatment plant is to make sure all organisms like bacteria are removed from the water using chemicals that disinfect the water. Since you won't be doing this step, your water is **NOT** safe to drink. However, you now know how to purify water!

Mechanics in Motion

I hope you've had fun exploring chemistry with atoms, molecules, compounds, and mixtures. You've learned a lot of science already this year! It's pretty amazing that God created everything you see around you using fewer than 100 different kinds of atoms, isn't it? In the beginning, when God created the heavens and the earth, He made all those elements and designed each of them to behave in unique ways. Let's look at the Bible to find out what God did in the beginning. The Bible tells us that the Spirit of God was doing something important. Do you remember what that was?

Let's read Genesis 1:1–2 together: "In the beginning God created the heavens and the earth. Now the earth was formless and empty, darkness was over the surface of the deep, and the Spirit of God was hovering over the waters."

The Spirit of God was hovering (some translations say moving) over the waters. Now there's a physics concept we should explore—the science of moving or motion.

Understanding how all the parts of the car move and work together helps this mechanic fix the car.

Mechanical Mechanics

Did you know that a person who fixes machines is called a mechanic? The study of motion in physics is called mechanics. If you boil it down, a mechanic is someone who fixes a machine that's no longer moving properly. You could say a mechanic gets machines back in motion. That makes it easier to understand why **mechanics** is the study of motion.

Why is it so important to study motion? Without a good understanding of motion, we can't make machines that move properly—whether those machines are remote control cars, watches, automobiles, airplanes, or spaceships. We need to study and understand the way God created things to move. After all, He created the birds that fly and all the animals that move along the ground. He put the earth in motion around the sun and the moon in motion around the earth. He even put the electrons in motion around each atom. God is the master of mechanics!

Understanding how motion works will help us in many ways, so let's get going!

Always in Motion

Do you remember that every single thing in the universe is moving all the time? You might think you're sitting still while you read this book, but you aren't. Do you know why? Well, there are several reasons. One is that you are made of atoms. What are those atoms doing? They're moving, moving, moving! Which part of the atom is moving? You're right—the electrons. Those electrons that make up you are always zipping here and there and everywhere in their little energy shells. Even when you sit still, you're in motion!

God created all the planets to spin on their axes as they orbit the sun. The laws of motion keep the planets moving and moving and moving!

Another reason you're moving is that the earth is spinning on its axis very fast. A person on the equator is moving with the earth at 1,000 mph (1,600 km/h). Also, the earth is moving around the sun at about 66,500 mph (107,000 km/h). Let's say I was standing on a spaceship outside the earth looking at you through really powerful binoculars. Because you're moving so fast, I would have to keep adjusting my binoculars to keep you in focus. Let's face it: No matter how much you're told to sit still, you simply can't because you never stop moving. You're always in motion! Isn't that interesting?

Scientists have always been fascinated by motion. To learn more about it, they're constantly asking questions. What makes things move so quickly? Why do things move the way they do? What's causing the movement? What can stop the movement? What happens when the movement stops? Why does it happen that way? Does the same thing happen in space? Why or why not?

As you can imagine, this concept of mechanics has been a hot topic for scientists for many years. Do you remember who Isaac Newton is? We talked about him earlier in this book. Long ago, in the 1600s, Newton discovered some amazing truths about motion. Today we call these truths laws. There are only three of these laws of motion, so that makes it easy to learn them. We'll spend the rest of this lesson exploring these three laws. At the end of the lesson, we'll learn a little more about Newton, the man who discovered the laws of motion.

This boy can repair his bike because he understands the physics of how it moves.

Newton's First Law of Motion

The first law Isaac Newton discovered is often called the law of inertia. What does inertia mean? Well, let me ask you a question: When you ride a bike, it takes some effort to get the bike going, doesn't it? Once the bike is going fast, is it easier to stop the bike or keep it going?

It's harder to get the bike going from a stop and harder to get the bike to stop once it's going because of **Newton's first law of motion** or the law of inertia. This law tells us that something at rest prefers to stay at rest unless something forces it to move, and something in motion prefers to stay in motion unless something forces it to stop moving. This is **inertia** in a nutshell. Believe it or not, we have to deal with inertia every single day, all day long—both to

These bike racers are going fast down the hill. They have to use force to slow down.

start something moving and to stop something that is already moving.

Let's get back to your bike. Even if you've never ridden a bike, you can imagine how it works. When you're riding your bike at full speed, is it easier to go straight or turn the corner? If you want to turn, you typically need to slow the bike down. Here's the point: Inertia resists a change in direction. That means inertia likes objects to keep doing what they're doing in the direction they are doing it.

But is it really true that something in motion will keep moving unless something else forces it to stop? After all, my bike will stop eventually when I quit pedaling. That's because there are forces on this earth that stop the bike, like gravity and friction. Let me explain it this way: Imagine you're in a spaceship in outer space where there's no gravity or friction in the

air. You're traveling straight out of our solar system at 800 mph. Suddenly, you realize you're out of fuel—and you're unable to get more. How long do you think you can keep going? At what point will your spaceship completely stop? Amazingly, you would keep moving in the same direction at the same speed forever. Yes, forever and ever. You would *never* stop unless an outside force—maybe an asteroid, a comet, or another plane—got in your path and you hit it. But then you might start traveling in another direction forever and ever and ever. You could also get caught in the sun's or another planet's gravitational pull and become a satellite, circling around the sun or a planet forever and ever. You see, an object in motion will stay in motion unless acted upon by an outside force. Since there's no gravity or friction to stop you in space, you would just keep moving.

Let's explore inertia with some experiments.

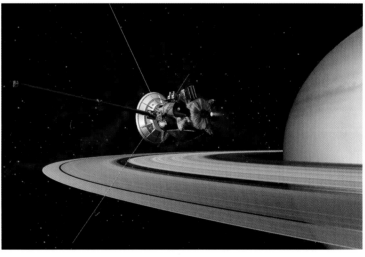

This is a drawing of the Cassini-Huygens spaceship near Saturn. Its mission is to study Saturn and Saturn's largest moon, Titan.

Try This!

You will need: An adult's supervision, 6 pennies, and a table.

First, stack 5 pennies in a neat stack on the table. Lay the sixth penny flat on the table near the stack. Now with a lot of force, slide it into the big stack.

What happened? Inertia happened! Did you notice only the bottom coin moved? It was *forced* to move. The other coins resisted movement; they preferred to stay at rest, right where they were. This is an example of Newton's first law of motion.

Try This!

You will need: An adult's supervision, your stack of 6 pennies, an index card, a table, and a glass full of water.

Place the glass of water on the table and place the index card on top of the glass of water. Now carefully place the stack of pennies on top of the index card and yank the card out!

Did the pennies come out with the card or fall into the glass? Did you notice the stack was suspended in midair for a moment? That's inertia!

Inertia in Motion

You just experimented with the part of the law that concerns objects at rest. But remember, objects in motion won't stop unless they're *forced* to stop. Newton's law states that an object in motion tends to stay in motion at the same speed and in the same direction unless some force acts upon it to stop it from motion. In other words, once an object starts moving, it will continue moving in a straight line unless something stops it. The object will be in perpetual (everlasting) motion. Forever. Unless it encounters a force. However, there are powerful forces that make perpetual motion nearly impossible here on the earth.

What is a force exactly? Well, a **force** is a push or a pull on an object. You *pushed* the penny into the stack, and you *pulled* the index card out from under the glass. You created force in both situations. The force of gravity here on earth causes the pull on things toward the earth. This slows us down and makes us feel heavy. It also makes us tired when we're in motion because we're always working against gravity to move. Gravity drags us down toward the earth; this slows and sometimes stops motion.

A force called friction also slows down movement. You'll learn a lot about gravity and friction in this and the next lesson. Just remember: Things start moving only when they're forced to, and things stop moving only when they encounter another force.

One child is pushing and one child is pulling in the images above. Both are applying force to the wagon.

It might be hard to believe that something will keep moving unless a force stops it. However, if you've ever been ice skating, you've experienced Newton's first law of motion in action. The ice has very little friction against the steel skate blades, so once you get moving on the ice, it's really hard to stop—especially if you're new to ice skating. In fact, you may have to bump into a wall to stop moving!

Here's a fact to consider: The more massive an object at rest, the more it resists movement. In other words, the harder it is to get moving. Think about how much harder it is to get a bowling ball rolling than a marble. In the same way, it's harder to stop a heavy moving object than a light moving object. Essentially, if there's a lot of mass, an object stays in motion even more. Which object would be easier to stop if it were rolling down a hill—a marble or a bowling ball? When summing up this part of Newton's first law, just remember that the more mass an object has, the more it resists change from whatever it's doing—

With very little friction to stop their motion, these ice skaters will keep moving on the ice until they fall, crash into something, or force themselves to stop.

100

whether it's moving or sitting still.

Also remember that when an object is in motion, it will keep going in the same direction at the same speed unless some force acts to stop or turn it. The bigger the object, the more force will be needed to change its acceleration (its speed and direction).

Consider a huge ocean liner—an enormous ship. This vessel travels through the water with a lot of power and speed. It takes a lot of energy to get this huge ship moving and out of the harbor where it's resting. But once it's moving, it keeps moving. If a little rowboat gets in its path, it's up to the rowboat to move out of the way since it's not easy to stop or turn the massive ocean liner. Think about what needs to happen if the boat captain wants to change the direction of the ship. It takes a lot of force to change the direction. This force is provided by huge rudders, which themselves require large forces to turn. Many machines located in the bottom of the ship have to turn huge cranks to turn huge wheels in order to move the enormous rudders!

Once this cruise ship gets going, it takes a lot of force to stop or turn it.

Inertia causes the ship to resist moving when it's still and to resist stopping once it's going. However, there are always forces here on earth that will eventually work on the ship to slow and eventually stop its movement.

It's the same for every object that's put into motion. If there were no gravity or friction, the object would keep moving in the same direction at the same speed at which it was launched.

Think of a gun shooting a bullet. If there were no gravity or friction against the air, the bullet would stay in motion going the same direction at the same speed forever—until it hit something to stop it from moving. But instead, the bullet slows down because of the friction of the air. Eventually, the bullet will curve downward and fall to the ground because of the pull of gravity.

If there were nothing to stop this bullet, it would continue to travel in a straight line forever—in perpetual motion.

Roller Coaster

A funny part of this law of inertia is what happens when a body is in motion, but that body is inside an object that's *also* in motion. When I was a child, my friends loved for my mom to take them places because she drove very fast and made sudden turns. It was like riding a roller coaster! Of course, that was back before there were seat belt laws, so we weren't belted in. My friends and I would be riding along in the back seat of my mom's enormous car, when suddenly the car would turn sharply to the right—without slowing down! Guess what happened to us? Our bodies kept going straight as the car turned. This caused us to slam against whatever was on the left side of the car. Our bodies *resisted* the change of direction because of inertia.

Have you ever been in a car that was moving forward then had to make a sudden stop? What happened? Your body kept moving forward when the car stopped. That's why you lurched forward in your seat and all the items on the seat flew forward! Your seat belt acted as a force on you to stop you, but the unbelted items kept moving forward. If you hadn't been wearing a seat belt, you could have flown to the front of the car and maybe even out the front window when the car stopped. That's because your body wants to stay moving at the same speed even though the car stops. Yes—bodies in motion tend to stay in motion unless an outside force stops them. It's because of inertia. So please wear your seat belt!

What would happen to you if the earth suddenly stopped spinning? Think about what happens to you when the car suddenly stops. Your car is going only a fraction of the speed of the earth; the earth is spinning at about 1,000 mph. It would be a very bad day if the earth stopped spinning, even for a second. You would keep moving, flying forward as if you were in a car accident. But you wouldn't fly off the earth because gravity would keep you grounded.

Here's a question for you now that you understand Newton's first law of motion so well: Why are you forced back against your seat when the car you're in suddenly accelerates? The answer is in the answer key in the back of this book. Look to see if you guessed correctly!

Spend some time explaining to someone all that you've learned so far about gravity, friction, and Newton's first law of motion. You also might want to write down in your notebooking journal any fascinating facts you learned.

The children on this roller coaster are forced to the sides as the roller coaster turns. This is because of inertia. Inertia resists a change in direction.

Newton's Second Law of Motion

You just learned about Newton's first law of motion. Scientifically speaking, you learned that objects at rest and objects in motion tend to stay that way unless acted on by a force. Exactly how much force is needed to affect objects in motion or at rest? That's where **Newton's second law of motion** comes in. This law is all about that force.

Essentially, this law says that force is what causes an object to change speed or direction. It also says this change of speed or direction is resisted by the mass of the object. So objects with greater mass resist change *more* than objects with lesser mass. What do you need to get that more massive object moving in a different direction? You need more force!

Is it easier to push an empty wagon or a wagon with a friend in it? Of course, the heavier or more massive the wagon, the more force you need to push it.

This can be explained with a math formula. In high school you'll get to play around with this formula, using lots of the math skills you'll learn between now and then. The formula is this: $F = m \times a$, which means Force = mass x acceleration. You could also say it like this: The amount of force is equal to the amount of mass multiplied by the amount of change in speed or direction.

You know what force and mass are. **Acceleration** means the change in speed and in the direction something is going. In our everyday language, accelerating means speeding up. But in physics, acceleration means *any* change in speed or direction. So even slowing down or driving around a curve counts as acceleration in physics.

Force is required for any type of acceleration. When we're driving and we need to slow down, we apply pressure on the brake pedal. Our foot on the brake is the force needed to change the acceleration. We can turn a car or bicycle by applying a sideways force using the steering wheel or handlebar.

Consider that math formula again: Force equals mass times acceleration. In simple terms, it means the force needed is equal to how heavy the object is and how fast the object is changing its speed or direction. You naturally already understand this. You know that if the object is bigger and moving faster, you'll need to apply more force to move or stop it.

Although it's hard to get this bowling ball in motion, once it's in motion, it's difficult to stop it. Even these bowling pins cannot stop the bowling ball from moving forward.

For example, if there's a tennis ball bouncing down the hill toward you, it won't take much force to accelerate it enough to stop

It would be difficult for one person to apply enough force to stop the acceleration of this tire.

it. But if a large car tire is rolling down the hill toward you, you probably won't have enough force to stop it by yourself. You'll have to gather the strength of a few friends to change the acceleration of the tire to stop it from rolling.

This law also explains why smaller cars get better gas mileage than bigger cars. If both cars speed up at the same rate, they're accelerating at the same rate. The force required to accelerate a small car is less than the force required to accelerate a big car (if everything else is equal). The bigger the car, the more force is needed. However, this same principle also explains why big cars are safer than small cars. Imagine a truck traveling 40 mph crashing into both cars. Which one will experience more damage?

Try This!

You will need: An adult's supervision; a tin pie pan; a glass of water; a raw egg; an empty toilet paper tube; and a smooth, flat surface.

First, put the glass of water on a smooth, flat surface. Now place the pie pan on top of the glass of water. Next, stand the toilet paper tube in the center of the pie pan. Now rest the egg on top of the toilet paper tube. Hold your hand about 12 inches away from the pie pan, then quickly hit the side of the pan with your hand, knocking the pan away from the top of the glass.

What happened? The pan and the toilet paper tube should have sailed away from the glass, while the egg should have stayed in place, falling into the glass. If this didn't happen, try again. You may need to line up your items more carefully.

Why did this happen? Inertia strikes yet again! But this time, we're seeing what happens when mass is involved. You see, the pan transferred its energy to the toilet paper tube and both went flying away when you hit the pan. Here's what this teaches us: The greater the mass of an object, the greater its inertia and the more force needed to change its acceleration. That means heavy things really resist moving more than light things. That's why the egg stayed where it was until gravity pulled it down into the glass of water.

Indeed, the more mass an object has, the more it resists moving or stopping. Scientifically speaking, we would say it resists acceleration—which is, as you know, any change in speed or direction.

Explain Newton's second law of motion to someone.

Newton's Third Law of Motion

Now it's time to explore **Newton's third law of motion**. The law essentially says this: For every action there's an equal and opposite reaction. You'll hear that a lot in science as you get older. Say it aloud to help your memory.

Let's do an experiment to see this law in action.

This device is called a Newton's Cradle. When the outer ball hits the line of other balls, one ball on the opposite end will have an equal and opposite reaction to the hit.

Try This!

You will need: A balloon.

Blow the balloon up, but don't tie it shut. Let your balloon go and watch it sail around the room. Try it several times and have fun!

As this rocket is launched, it pushes on the gas from its engine. The gas pushes back, forcing it up into space.

What happened in your experiment? As the air escaped, the balloon flew around the room in the opposite direction of the escaping air. Because the balloon is flexible, the "nozzle" moved around and the air escaped in different directions. For each direction change, the balloon went in the opposite direction. Just as Newton's law states: For every action, there's an equal and opposite reaction.

Newton's third law is very important when it comes to accomplishing many great and small feats. In fact, real rockets are launched using this same principle. If you've never seen a rocket launch, go to www.apologia.com/bookextras to watch one. A rocket launches as gas is expelled out of the engine with a huge amount of force. Once enough gas has been expelled, the rocket begins to lift off. A rocket can lift off *only* when it expels enough gas out of its engine to force the rocket upward. The rocket pushes on the gas, and the gas in an equal and opposite way pushes on the rocket, forcing it upward. The forces on any two objects pushing on each other are equally strong but in opposite directions.

One interesting fact about this particular law is that whenever you push on something, it's always pushing back with an equal amount of force. That's because for every action there is an equal and opposite *what*? Reaction! That's right. What about when you bump into a wall? Does the wall react by bumping you back? Indeed it does! It doesn't seem like it, but strangely, it's true. Everything on earth and in space reacts with an opposite reaction. When you throw a tennis ball against the wall, the wall actually pushes back against the ball. This happens even when we throw something toward the earth! The earth pushes back on that object that hit it with an equal force. The wall and earth may seem solid. But they do have the ability to stretch, somewhat like a rubber band, when something is forced against them. This all happens on the atomic level—involving all those atoms and molecules we discussed. We don't see the pushing when it's a solid, still object like the earth or a wall. But it *is* happening. The wall is pushing; the earth is pushing; everything is pushing back. It's a scientific fact!

Why don't the earth and wall respond as much as smaller objects? Because they're much more massive. Objects with greater mass resist movement more than objects with lesser mass. You remember this from your egg experiment earlier. It all boils down to inertia. The earth, the wall, and larger objects with more mass have more inertia.

Newton's Third Law in Space

Astronauts discovered how important Newton's third law of motion really is when they attempted to do work outside their space station in outer space. Without gravity to give them stability, everything the astronauts pushed against pushed back against them—propelling them in the other direction. If they pushed against the space station, it pushed back—sending them flying away from the space station. If they pulled on a cord, attempting to get back into the station, the cord pulled back. The astronauts had no control over their environment because gravity wasn't there to help.

Imagine if the astronauts became unhooked from the space station with nothing but an oxygen tank on their backs.

Without cords attaching the astronauts to the space station, they would not be able to do any work in space. This is because of Newton's third law of motion.

They would begin heading away from the space station, traveling forever and ever in the other direction—never to be seen again. They would be floating away from the station at a slow pace in a straight line—in perpetual motion. The astronauts would continue in the same direction. Do you know why? Because an object in motion will stay in motion at the same speed forever unless a force acts upon it! You remember Newton's first law, don't you?

You may wonder whether there is anything the astronauts could do to save themselves. Can you think of anything that would help them? Could the astronauts begin, somehow, to move in the opposite direction toward the space station? Think about it for a minute. What could the astronauts do to get going in the other direction, back toward the space station? The astronauts could use the same technique that satellites use to maneuver. Essentially, they would use the air in their breathing tanks as a propellant to push them back to the station. As you can see, knowing physics can sometimes save your life!

You can mimic being in space by attempting to do work in a swimming pool. Being underwater is the closest environment we have to the weightlessness of outer space. Next time you're in a pool, think of Newton's third law and test it out!

You've learned a lot about mechanics in this lesson. Let's finish our study with a look at the genius mind that gave us these interesting laws of physics: Sir Isaac Newton. But first, explain to someone what you've learned about Newton's third law of motion.

Sir Isaac Newton

So who was this Mr. Newton who gave us all these laws? Sir Isaac Newton was a strong Christian who loved studying the Bible even more than studying science. God gave him a great mind to understand scientific concepts. God also gave Mr. Newton a special job to do in this world, and he did it well! This job included exploring science, math, and the Bible. Newton effectively communicated the things he discovered to the world. He believed the Bible instructs Christians to understand the invisible things around us—invisible forces, invisible concepts, and even our invisible God!

Newton discovered amazing things about gravity, motion, light, and telescopes. There's a story you may have heard about Isaac Newton sitting under an apple tree thinking about gravity. Suddenly, an apple fell from the tree and hit him on the head! He then understood gravity—the invisible force that pulls everything toward the earth. I'm not sure if that story is true, but it's a great story to remind us about the man who discovered the laws of gravity. We'll study these laws in the next lesson.

All of Newton's writings about math and science include a lot of information about God and the Bible. Newton understood and taught that all the laws of the universe were laws God put in place. He wrote: "This most beautiful system of the sun, planets, and comets could only proceed from the counsel and dominion of an intelligent Being."

Because Newton spent more time studying the Bible than he did science, he was able to write about theology (the study of God). His devotion to God is probably why he was able to discover so many amazing truths. I hope you'll follow in Sir Isaac Newton's footsteps and study the Bible more than any other subject. It will give you a greater understanding of everything else you study.

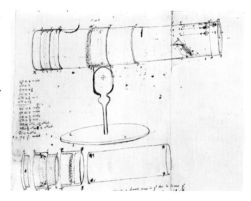

Newton kept a science notebook with everything he learned, thought, and discovered—just like you're doing!

Final Matters

Isn't it amazing that we can discover the laws of motion God created? He's the original scientist! He not only *put* everything in motion, but He also *keeps* everything in motion. That's what the Bible tells us: "The Son is the radiance of God's glory and the exact representation of his being, sustaining all things by his powerful word. After he had provided purification for sins, he sat down at the right hand of the Majesty in heaven" (Hebrews 1:3).

What Do You Remember?

The study of motion is called the study of _____. What is Newton's first law of motion? What is a force? If you were riding in your car with books on your lap, what would happen if your car suddenly stopped? Why? What is Newton's second law of motion? What is acceleration? What is Newton's third law of motion? Who was Isaac Newton?

Notebooking Activities

Write down what you learned in this lesson on your "Fascinating Facts" pages. I would also like for you to do a little more research on Sir Isaac Newton. Find books from the library or have a parent help you search the Internet. You can also go to www.apologia.com/bookextras to find some websites about Newton. Make notes about what you learn. After you've done that, write a biography of Newton or a story about his life. Templates are provided for these activities in the *Chemistry and Physics Notebooking Journal*.

After you finish your paper on Newton, cut out three sheets of paper, making them about 6 inches long and 3 inches wide. Write "First Law of Motion" on the first piece of paper, "Second Law of Motion" on the second piece, and "Third Law of Motion" on the last piece. Glue the top edges of the papers into your notebooking journal to create flaps you can lift up. Under each flap, write down the law in your own words. The *Chemistry and Physics Notebooking Journal* has templates for you to cut out and a page onto which you can paste your laws of motion flaps.

Game
Ringers

You can see Newton's laws in action by playing a fun game of Ringers! Ringers is a game played with marbles by boys and girls all over the world. Maybe you've played it with your friends. Even if you haven't, the rules are simple.

First, prepare your playing area. Draw a circle at least 3 feet in diameter but no bigger than 10 feet. The bigger the circle, the harder the game will be. If this is your first time playing Ringers, start with a small circle. Your circle should be drawn on a flat, smooth surface. It can be in dirt, on a driveway, or on a large piece of poster board that lies flat on the floor. It just needs to be in a place where marbles will roll easily.

Next, draw a line on either side of the circle so that the lines are parallel to each other like this:

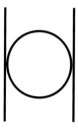

Decide who's going first by rolling or shooting a marble from one line across to the other. Whoever gets closest to the line goes first. The next closest player goes next, and so on. This is called lagging.

Begin playing by placing 13 marbles in the center of the circle in the shape of a plus sign. The object of the game is to knock the marbles out of the circle by hitting them with a slightly larger marble called a shooter. Place at least one knuckle on the ground and then shoot the larger marble toward the other marbles by rolling the larger marble with a quick flick of your finger. The first time you knuckle down, you must shoot from outside the circle. But after that, you can shoot from wherever your shooter lands. You get to keep each marble that you knock out of the circle. If you knock out a marble and your shooter stays inside of the circle, you continue to try to shoot other marbles out. If no marbles roll out of the circle or your shooter rolls outside of the circle, your turn is over and the next person gets a turn to shoot out as many marbles as possible. When all the marbles have been shot out of the circle, count your marbles to see who won.

There are many other rules that can make the game more challenging. You can even play in an official Ringers competition and win prizes. But for now, pay attention to the way the marbles roll around. See if you can observe any of Newton's laws at work.

Which law do you see when the marbles are all lined up, just sitting still before the game starts? Which law explains why the shooter rolls in a straight line? Why do marbles that are stationary suddenly start rolling when the shooter strikes them? You can find the answers to these questions in the answer key in the back of the book.

Dynamics of Motion

In the last lesson, we learned about Newton's laws of motion. In this lesson, we'll explore forces that can start and stop motion.

Do you remember what a force is? A force is a pull or push on something. Can you name one force that you live with every single day? That's right—gravity. Do you remember the name of another force we discussed in the last chapter? It's called friction. Gravity and friction are two well-known forces that affect the motion of an object. In this lesson we'll explore these forces with some fun activities and projects.

Rub your hands together back and forth for two minutes. What happens? Your hands get hot because of friction. The energy of the back-and-forth motion is converted to heat energy.

Eventually, if you continued rubbing your hands together, the friction between your hands would wear away your skin! If you've ever worn shoes that didn't fit quite right, you know what friction can do. In time, when the shoes rub against your skin over and over again, they cause blisters. The blisters are the result of friction!

Friction can really do some damage, can't it? Let's find out more about this amazing force.

Feeling the Friction

Have you ever been to a water park? As a child, I enjoyed going to water parks where I could slide down water slides into pools down below. Sometimes when I was going down a slide, my skin would suddenly hit a dry patch, and I would stop. It was a huge disappointment! I couldn't understand why my wonderful ride downward was interrupted. So what

The reason we rub our hands together when we're cold is to generate friction. This force converts our movement to heat energy.

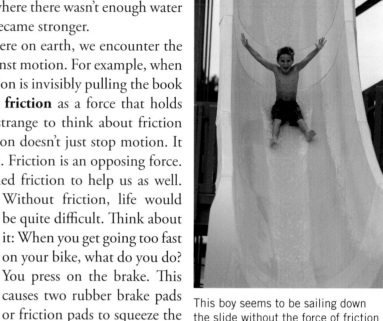

stopped me from that joyous journey down the slide? Well, friction was at work. At first, the water on the slide reduced the friction between the slide and me, allowing me to sail down with ease. But in spots where there wasn't enough water between the slide and me, friction's pull on me became stronger.

Whenever we try to get something moving here on earth, we encounter the force of friction. Friction is a force that works against motion. For example, when you push a book forward on a wooden table, friction is invisibly pulling the book back in the opposite direction. Scientists define **friction** as a force that holds back the movement of an object. It may seem strange to think about friction this way, but it's scientifically true. You see, friction doesn't just stop motion. It actually works in the *opposite* direction of motion. Friction is an opposing force.

Although it may slow us down, God designed friction to help us as well.

The brake pads pressing on this bicycle tire cause friction. This enables the rider to slow down or completely stop the bicycle's motion.

This boy seems to be sailing down the slide without the force of friction acting against him.

Without friction, life would be quite difficult. Think about it: When you get going too fast on your bike, what do you do? You press on the brake. This causes two rubber brake pads or friction pads to squeeze the tire rims. These brake pads are using the power of friction to pull the tires in the opposite direction in order to slow them down. In turn, the friction of the tires on the road slows the bike down. Thank goodness for friction! Without friction you would be in real trouble.

Try This!

You will need: An adult's supervision, a partner, and a bicycle with hand brakes.

You're going to study how the brakes on a bicycle work. First, study the mechanisms that make the bike stop and go. Now have a partner hold the back tire up off the ground. Using your hand, circle the pedal so that the wheel begins to move. Be very careful not to get your fingers stuck in the spokes or chain; keep your fingers away from the turning wheel. Now squeeze the hand brakes and watch the two brake pads on either side of the wheel. Do you see the pads apply pressure on the wheel? That's friction at work!

Friction is an important part of life. Without it, life as we know it would be a lot more difficult. Have you ever tried to grab an object that kept slipping and sliding out of your hands? If you've ever tried to grab a bar of wet soap in the bathtub, you know that it just slips right out of your grasp. However, a dry bar of soap doesn't do that. That's because the dry bar of soap has more friction against your hand than the wet one. Think about how this works on the atomic level. The molecules in a liquid move more freely than the molecules in a solid. On a wet surface, the molecules are free to slide past each other. Friction is more powerful when dry objects slide past each other.

Water and oil can reduce the power of friction on an object quite a lot. For example, I once lived in an area that almost never saw rain. The oil that dripped from the cars coated

WHEN WET

the streets for months and months without being washed away. What do you think happened when it rained? With all that oil and a little water, the streets became very slippery. There was less friction between the car tires and the road. That's why sometimes you'll see a sign on the side of the road that warns, "Slippery when wet." The road is the most slippery when the rainfall is just beginning. After the rain has been falling for a while, much of the oil is washed away.

You've probably figured out that friction is stronger on rough surfaces. Sandpaper has a lot more friction than copy paper. The street has a lot more friction than a slide. Carpeted steps have more friction than smooth, marble steps. But very few things on earth are so smooth that they completely resist the force of friction.

You can usually predict which objects will produce more friction. But some results may surprise you. Let's test some objects to find out!

Try This!

You will need: An adult's supervision, a small toy car (such as a Matchbox car), a glass or wooden table, water, and soap (or oil).

To begin, give the matchbox car a push across the table. Did it roll quickly? Now add a thin film of water to the surface of the table. Roll the car again. Did the water reduce or increase the friction? Now add soap or oil to some water and mix it up. Apply a thin film to the surface of the table. Try rolling the car again. Did it roll better on the dry surface, the surface with water, or the surface with water and soap (or oil)? You may have found that water is a poor lubricant. Its molecules tend to stick to surfaces. That's why soap or oil is often used to reduce friction.

Some objects didn't slide as easily because the surface of those objects grabbed the surface of the table. Sometimes this happens on a microscopic level with tiny indentions that can be seen only through a magnifying glass or microscope. When you added oil to the wooden surface, you decreased the friction between the board and the objects. This enabled them to slide more easily.

Having the right hiking gear can improve the threshold for friction so that you don't slip and fall on the rocks as easily.

Increasing Friction

Have you noticed that when objects push harder against one another, they produce more friction? You can see this in action when you feel the difference between lightly rubbing your hands together and rubbing your hands together at the same speed while pushing them harder against each other. Your hands get even hotter more quickly. Friction is increased. If you double the force used when objects are pressed together, you double the amount of friction.

Friction is something we often need to get along in the world. When my son went on a 10-day hiking trip in New Mexico, we bought him special hiking boots. The bottom surface of the boots had pits that were made of a special material that increased the friction. This design enabled his boots to grip the ground better when he was climbing up smooth rocks. Increasing friction in this way helps keep hikers safe.

When a car is stuck in the mud, we say it has no traction. **Traction** is the friction between two objects that keeps them from sliding across each other. What would be the best thing to do to get the car out of the mud? Gather a group of strong men to push the car while someone pushes the gas pedal? Or add dry sticks, rocks, and dirt around the wheel and give the car a small push up onto the sticks and rocks?

Actually, it would take a lot more effort to push the car out of the mud than it would to give the tires traction with the dry materials. Next time you see a car stuck in the mud, help out by gathering some dry materials to put under the wheels.

Ballerinas who dance on pointe shoes often face friction problems when they perform on stage. The stage floor can be slippery. Without traction, the ballerinas are unsafe turning and jumping on their toes. The stage crew will often pour a sticky, soda-like substance all over the floor to increase traction. The ballet dancers will also use a powder on their shoes to increase traction. This allows them to turn on their toes without stopping.

Football receivers (those catching the ball) often face similar problems. If it's wet outside, the traction needed to catch a ball is reduced. Friction can be increased by purchasing special gloves made with polymers. The gloves increase the traction between the football and the hand while catching. In dry weather, players depend on their fingerprints and handprints to help them grip and hold on to the ball. Without fingerprints, many items would simply slip out of your hands! It's the same with your footprints. The indentions on the bottom of your feet help give you traction when you walk around barefooted.

As you can see, there are many reasons to increase traction in our daily lives. Can you think of any others? Consider your car's wheels, your bathroom or shower floor, icy sidewalks, or other slippery surfaces.

Ballerinas need traction to safely turn and jump on their toes.

Football players wear special gloves to increase friction. This prevents the ball from easily slipping off their hands.

Explain everything you've learned about friction so far.

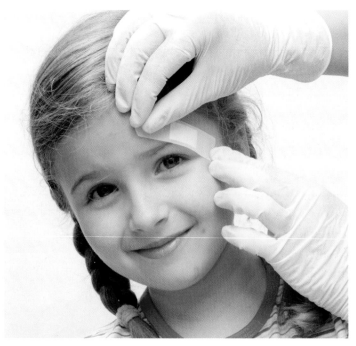

The bandages on this girl and her bear will remain in place because of the coating on the bandages.

Adhesion

Another form of friction is adhesion. When we talk about adhesion in chemistry, we aren't talking about the times when you're walking and your foot sticks to the floor for a moment. We're usually referring to sticky substances.

Adhesion is the sticking together of two different materials. Adhesion is a lot like cohesion. However, **cohesion** is the material sticking to itself. If you fold tape over and it sticks to itself, that's cohesion. The tape is sticking to the same surface.

We call tape, bandages, and other sticky items adhesives. Something is an adhesive when it's able to hold materials together by surface contact. Bandages are held to your skin by a layer of a sticky, glue-like substance between the bandage and your skin. Tape also has an adhesive layer. The paper part of the tape is coated with an adhesive material—sticky stuff. Double-sided tape has *two* layers of adhesive material—one on the top and one on the bottom. Because of this it's great tape to use when wrapping gifts. Adhesives use a certain type of glue to create the sticky surface. Glue is also an adhesive, but it's a lot thicker than the adhesive spread on the strips of tape or bandages.

Adhesion is like friction. It holds back movement. If it's a super strong adhesive—like Super Glue, epoxy, or Gorilla Glue—it stops movement fairly permanently. How do adhesives work? That's a great question—one that scientists are still exploring. Adhesives and glues have been used for thousands of years. Even Noah was told to cover his boat with pitch—a black, gluey substance.

This gecko has adhesive feet. They enable it to adhere to the window using van der Waals forces.

Most scientists believe that dispersive adhesion is caused by something called van der Waals forces. This force was discovered by a Dutch scientist named Johannes Diderik van der Waals. He taught that adhesion happens on the molecular level. Remember that polar molecules have a positive side and a negative side, so they can be attracted to almost any charged surface. This explains how geckos are able to walk up almost any surface and hang there, clinging with only one little toe. The gecko's adhesive feet use van der Waals forces. The molecules in the gecko's feet are strongly attracted to the molecules on the surface onto which it climbs. You now know why understanding atomic bonding was so important to learning physics!

Let's create some fun adhesives by doing the following activities.

Try This!

Did you know you can make a plain piece of paper adhere to a window? Can you guess how to do it? Let's find out how!

You will need: An adult's supervision, a piece of copy paper, a window, and some water.

First, try to adhere the dry piece of paper to the window. Does it stick? Now wet the piece of paper and try again to adhere it to the window. Did it stick this time? You just saw van der Waals forces in action!

Tell someone all you've learned about adhesion.

Reducing Friction

Sometimes you don't want to increase friction between two objects; instead you want to decrease it. Our family learned how to deal with the force of friction when we set up our Slip 'N Slide on a hill in our front yard. A Slip 'N Slide is a long plastic sheet that works like a water slide. We would set up the hose to stream water down the slide so the kids could sail down. We learned that if we added a lot of water and some dish soap to the slide, the children could slide down much faster. The soap worked as a lubricant to reduce friction and make the slide more slippery. It was a great way to stop the friction that was keeping our children from having an exciting ride down the hill!

Adding soap to the slide will reduce the friction, giving this girl a faster ride!

This man is applying oil to a machine. The oil will keep the parts from rubbing against each other and wearing out.

A **lubricant** is a substance that reduces friction. Once when a ring was stuck on my finger, I removed it with soapy water. Water and soap are great lubricants. Can you think of any other liquids we use as lubricants?

Oil is another important lubricant. Most machines require oil to operate properly. Oil reduces the friction between the moving parts of a machine. It also keeps the parts from rubbing against one another and protects them from wearing out. Do you have any doors in your home that squeak when you open them? They need oil! When a moving part is squeaking, it needs lubrication to stop the friction. When you add oil, the friction is reduced, and the squeaking stops.

The moving metal parts in a car need oil for the same reason. You see, the engine and other metal parts move against

each other to propel the car forward. The metal parts will wear out quickly without a friction-reducing oil. This oil needs to be changed regularly because it gets dirty. Eventually, the dirty oil won't be able to lubricate the moving parts, and the car's engine will wear out.

The Egyptians faced the power of friction when they tried to move huge stone blocks to build the pyramids. Adding oil was not an option. However, they discovered if they used logs as rollers on the bottoms of the stone blocks, they could reduce the friction pulling against those blocks. They could move the blocks hundreds of feet up the pyramid with much less effort! Let's see how that worked with a friction-reducing experiment.

These Egyptian pyramids were made with huge stone blocks. Logs used as rollers reduced the friction, enabling the stones to be moved up the pyramid with a lot less effort.

Try This!

You will need: An adult's supervision, a shoebox or other small box, a 20-inch string, a small rock, tape, a table, a few small toys or objects, and 15–20 pencils.

First, tie the string around the rock. Now tape the free end of the string to one end of the box. Place the toys or other objects in the box. Next, place the box on the end of the table with the small rock tied to the string hanging over the edge. What happened? Probably nothing. Now place the box with the rock near the end of the table like you did before. Line up the pencils next to one another and place them under the box toward the rear. What happens? You can experiment with different sized rocks at the end of the string to see how this might affect the experiment.

The pencils worked to reduce the friction between the box and the table, much like the rollers the Egyptians placed under the huge stone blocks.

Tell someone all you've learned about friction. Record and illustrate your learning in your notebooking journal. Be sure to include the projects and experiments you did.

Air and Water Friction

Friction not only affects solid objects; it affects gases and liquids as well. Gases and liquids are both fluids. The word "fluid" comes from the Latin word *fluo*, which means to flow. Fluids always flow over objects moved through the fluid. Have you ever walked around in a swimming pool? If so, you experienced the water flowing around you as you walked. It slowed your motion down, didn't it? That's because the water exerted the force of friction on you as you tried to move through it. You may not realize it, but you experience the same thing every day with air. The air around you exerts a frictional force on you in the same way that water does. It's a lot less friction because water is much denser than air, but it's still friction.

It's difficult for this boy to walk underwater because of the drag against his body.

Have you ever held your hand outside the window of a moving car? Like me, you were probably told not to do this because of what might hit your hand while it was out there. However, if you've done this, you probably noticed it was difficult to keep your hand level. It kept flying backward as if it were hitting a brick wall, didn't it? That was because of air friction. We sometimes call it air resistance or drag. **Drag** is the friction that slows an object as it moves forward through air or water.

Have you noticed you can position your hand outside the car window in a certain way to make it float easily through the air? You can change the shape and angle of your hand against the wind so it will sail through the air without a lot of resistance. Drag (air or fluid resistance) is affected by the size and shape of the object moving through the air or water. It's also affected by the type of fluid it's moving through. As you know, it's harder to move through water than air. It's also much harder to walk through thick mud than air.

When an object is shaped in a way that enables it to travel through the air much more easily, we call it **aerodynamic**. An aerodynamic shape also allows an object to move through fluids without as much drag. Think about how airplanes, submarines, birds, and fish are shaped. They're typically shaped so that the surface area heading into the air is the thinnest surface. The more surface area an object has facing the air, the more that object will experience air resistance.

Let's do an experiment to see air resistance in action!

Try This!

You will need: An adult's supervision, 2 pieces of paper, and a chair.

To begin, crumple one of the pieces of paper into a ball. Now stand on the chair and hold the crumpled and flat pieces of paper high up in the air. Release both pieces of paper at the same time. What happened?

Air resistance pushed up on the flat paper. That kept it from falling as quickly as the crumpled paper. Both papers weighed the exact same, but their size and shape affected how well they moved through the air.

Drag keeps objects from moving smoothly. If you can eliminate or reduce the object's drag, the object can move more quickly under the water or through the air.

Champion swimmers understand how important drag is. They choose clothing that reduces drag when swimming. Swimmers can win a competition by a fraction of a second. So anything that could slow them down—even a tiny bit—must be removed. Swimmers cover or remove every bit of hair on their bodies because it could slow them down. Every motion they complete in the water is designed to reduce drag. This helps them sail through the water with as little resistance as possible. Swimmers must correctly position their arms, hands, head, body, legs, and feet in order to get the fastest swimming time.

Aerospace engineers spend a great deal of time designing objects that can sail through the air with the least amount of air resistance. At the end of this lesson, you'll create an aerodynamic design for a car or airplane. You'll also make several different kinds of paper airplanes to see which one flies the farthest and the longest.

Swimmers rely on exact body positions to help them move through the water with greater speed.

Explain to someone all that you've learned so far.

Grasping Gravity

Picture yourself flying a kite way up in the sky. Now imagine there's another child flying a kite, but he's on the exact opposite side of the world from you. You're certain your kite is up. He's certain his kite is up. But his kite is flying in the opposite direction from your kite! From your perspective, his kite would seem like it's down. The truth is, both the kites are flying away from the center of the earth. When we say the kite is up, it's really *away* from the center of the earth. When things fall down, they aren't really falling down; they're actually falling toward the center of the earth. This is because of that amazing force God created called **gravity**.

As you know, the earth is a large round ball that's pulling everything toward its center with a powerful tug. Even things that come near the earth are pulled in toward it. Let's take a look at this amazing force that affects motion.

Gravity is all about attraction. God designed the whole universe to operate in such a way that every single object is attracted to every other object. It may not seem so, but all objects are constantly pulling on every other nearby

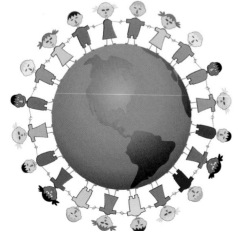

object. Heavier objects pull with more strength than lighter objects. This is especially obvious in space. But it's also occurring here on earth. It's a force that happens between all objects. It's even happening between the book you're holding and you!

Here's another thing you may already know: Objects that are closer pull with more strength than objects that are farther away. The closer the things are to one another, the more powerful the attraction. We call this the **law of universal gravitation**. Guess who discovered this law? Think about the last lesson. You got it—Sir Isaac Newton!

I bet you didn't realize you have a gravitational force around you pulling on everything that's nearby. We don't feel the force as much here on earth because of the earth's size. It's so big and heavy that its gravity pretty much overpowers all other gravitational pulls we may experience. Earth is by far the most massive object anywhere nearby. Its pull is more powerful than anything else on the earth. Thus, in every pulling contest, the earth wins; everything is pulled toward it.

Even though the earth wins every pulling competition, everything that exists is continuously pulling on everything else that exists. It's hard to see or feel this happening. But just remember this is what we mean when we talk about the law of universal gravitation.

As with most of Newton's laws, this concept of gravity is more easily seen in space. As you know, objects in space pull on each other. The objects with more mass pull with more force. This is what keeps our whole solar system in position. Every planet is

This image is not to scale because the sun is much more massive than shown. But it's clear that the sun's mass keeps all the planets revolving around it.

revolving around the huge massive sun, and almost every planet has a moon or a few moons orbiting around it. Everything is pulling on everything else. This keeps everything perfectly balanced in our solar system! Because of Newton's third law, the objects are pulling on each other with equal force. But because of Newton's second law, the more massive objects aren't affected as much by the force. This makes them accelerate or move toward the other objects less. The sun has over 99% of the mass of the solar system. This is why it hardly moves at all. Yet all the other planets, being so much smaller, accelerate or move in continual circles around the sun.

Let's take a look at how this works with the moon and the earth. You already know that the moon revolves around the earth, and the gravity from the earth's pull keeps the moon exactly in place. However, the moon is pulling in an equal and opposite way as well. The moon doesn't move the earth very much because the earth has 81 times the mass of the moon.

However, the moon's gravity does pull on our oceans. They move easily because they have less mass than the earth. This causes our oceans to swell upward toward the moon. As the earth spins, the oceans that are facing the moon are pulled up toward the moon. On the opposite side of the earth, the oceans pile up away from the moon's pull. The moon's pull on the side of the earth facing away from the moon is not very powerful because of its location. This causes high tides (high waters) on both the near and far sides of the earth. This happens because most of the oceans are concentrated in these two spots. We call the places where

This is an image taken from space of the earth and the earth's moon. It's night on one side of the earth and day on the other. Where do you think the sun is?

the ocean thins out low tide. As the earth turns and different parts face the moon, the areas with high tide and low tide change. Every day, because the earth is spinning on its axis, the ocean swells up, then retreats back down. It happens about every 25 hours. It's not every 24 hours because the moon is also orbiting around the earth, so it's changing its position too.

On those occasions when the moon and

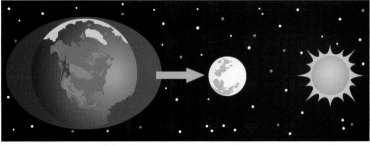

Spring tides occur when there's a full or new (shown) moon, and the sun and moon are in a line.

sun are in a line, the high tides are about 20% higher than average, and the low tides are about 20% lower than average. We call these spring tides because they "spring forth." This happens when there's a new moon and full moon. But during the quarter moons, the sun's pull is at a right angle to the moon's. So the pulls somewhat cancel each other out. This results in weak tides, which we call neap tides.

Isn't it interesting that the location of the sun and moon affect how big the ocean tides are! I want to assure you that nothing else in the solar system has anywhere near the effect of the sun or moon on the earth. So don't be worried by doom stories about planets lining up; they can't make the slightest noticeable difference.

The earth pulls, the moon pulls, and the sun pulls. Everything is pulling on everything else in order to keep the earth exactly where God designed it to be.

Neap tides occur when there's a quarter moon and the sun's pull is at a right angle to the moon's pull.

But what keeps us from flying right into the sun? Why doesn't the moon get pulled right into the earth, causing a huge tidal wave to flood all the land? Why do some objects, like meteorites and comets, get pulled into the earth and other planets? The answers to those questions have something to do with the laws you learned about in the last chapter. Let's take a look.

Distance Dynamics

Sometimes rocks in outer space pass too close to the earth and get pulled into it. You see, when a smaller object gets too close to a larger object out in space, the smaller object gets into the gravitational field of the larger object. That smaller object then gets yanked toward the larger object. Have you ever seen a shooting star? You can see a lot of them in August during the annual meteor shower. Meteor showers occur because as the earth travels through space, it encounters dirty patches with dust and debris. The dirt in those patches gets pulled into the earth. Because of the speed at which the dirt travels toward the earth, this dust and debris encounter an

These shooting stars are simply dirt and debris being powerfully pulled toward the earth by gravity.

enormous amount of friction. Remember, when friction is really powerful, it generates heat. This frictional force is so powerful that it causes the dirt and debris to heat up and eventually light on fire. We call these lit-up dirt particles shooting stars! They aren't stars at all, but you can learn more about that in *Exploring Creation with Astronomy*.

As you know, gravity is affected by distance. The farther away something is, the less gravity it feels from the larger object. Once a spaceship has left the earth's atmosphere, the farther away it travels, the less of a pull it experiences from the earth. In fact, at some point the spaceship isn't noticeably

This meteor crater in Arizona was caused by a 171-foot wide asteroid that collided with the earth. The crater is more than 500 feet deep and about 4,000 feet in diameter.

affected by the earth's gravity at all. However, if the spaceship were to get too close to another planet, what do you think would happen? That's right! It would get pulled into that planet. Why? Because it's so much smaller than the planet.

We know that mass doesn't necessarily have anything to do with size. A baseball would pull with more force than a tennis ball, even though they're the same size. In fact, a tiny marble might pull with more force than a big beach ball. This is because marbles can have more mass than beach balls. So in space, more massive objects—no matter how big or small—will pull in less massive objects that get too close.

As you may have guessed, every planet in our solar system has a different amount of gravitational pull based on how massive the planet is. On smaller planets, gravity does not pull with as much force. If you were on Mars, you could run a lot farther than you can on earth without getting tired. That's because when you run on earth, you're working to overcome the gravitational pull on you. The moon has even *less* of a gravitational pull. That's why you could jump extremely high on the moon. There are video clips of astronauts doing just that when they visited the moon.

With gravity, it's all about attraction, mass, and distance. That about sums it up. Everything is attracted to everything else. More massive objects have a stronger attraction than less massive objects. Heavier objects win the tug of war because they have more inertia. The closer the objects, the more powerful the pull. That's the universal law of gravitation.

Now you know what gravity does, but what exactly *is* gravity? It's another one of those mysteries that only God understands because He created it. We don't know exactly what gravity is, but we do know how it works. Everything is held in place by this amazing force. God created gravity to keep everything in motion and the world working just right.

Explain to someone what you've learned about the law of universal gravitation.

Accelerating Action

If you drop a baseball and a tennis ball from the same height, which object do you think will hit the ground first? Try this experiment to see if your prediction is correct.

Try This!

You will need: An adult's supervision, a partner, a video camera, a baseball, a tennis ball, and a ledge.

To begin, have your partner set up the video camera. Now set the balls on the ledge. Next, use your hands to push them off the ledge at the exact same time. Have your partner videotape the balls as they hit the ground. What was the result? Try this several times to be sure you get consistent results.

If you did the experiment correctly, you learned that heavier objects, no matter how heavy they are, accelerate at the same rate as lighter objects. It's been said that a scientist named Galileo did an experiment in the 1500s with two cannon balls of different weights. He dropped them both off a tall building in Italy called the Leaning Tower of Pisa. When Galileo dropped the balls, he discovered this interesting and important scientific truth about acceleration due to gravity. Let me explain why this happens.

It's true that heavier objects are pulled more strongly than lighter objects. It seems this would make the heavier object fall faster. However, heavier objects also have more inertia than lighter objects. You remember what inertia does. It resists movement. A heavier object with more inertia will naturally resist change more than a lighter object with less inertia. So if the heavier object is at rest, it resists being moved more than the lighter object. And if the heavier object is moving at a constant speed, it naturally resists forces that try to increase

Galileo discovered an important scientific truth about acceleration when he dropped two cannon balls off the Leaning Tower of Pisa.

this speed. Although gravity is pulling on the heavier object with more force, that object is also resisting that force with more inertia. The heavier object has more inertia to resist the earth's pull than does the lighter object. However, your initial thoughts were correct: The earth is pulling harder on the heavier object. So if there were no inertia, the heavier object would fall faster.

This difference between an object's inertia and the gravitational pull causes everything to fall to the earth at the same speed, even though one object is heavier than the other. Essentially, inertia and pull cause everything to cancel each other out, making the objects fall at the same acceleration. In simple terms, an object twice as massive has both twice the weight and twice the inertia. So it will have the same acceleration when being pulled by gravity.

Even if every jet is carrying a different sized bomb, when released, they will all hit the earth at the same time. This is because heavier bombs resist inertia more than lighter bombs.

Free Falling

As we studied, when you drop something, the object is being pulled down by gravity—but it's experiencing resisting forces as well. Can you name those two forces that resist motion? Air resistance and inertia. These two forces work against gravity. We might say they stop or hinder movement.

Did you know there's a speed limit for falling objects? It's true! Objects can fall really quickly or really slowly. However, if they continue falling they'll eventually hit the speed limit and won't be able to fall any faster. This speed limit is called terminal velocity. Imagine a person jumping out of an airplane. As he falls toward the earth, he continues to speed up. However, as the person's pull toward the earth increases, the friction also increases. So the faster an object moves, the more air friction (or air resistance) it will encounter. Eventually, the force of friction will become as strong as gravity. These forces will then cancel each other out. This means there's no unbalanced force on the object. The forces working for and against movement are equal. As a result, there will be no change of speed. The object will continue at the same velocity; it will not speed up or slow down. This is **terminal velocity**.

Although these divers weigh different amounts, they fall at the same acceleration. This is because the heavier divers resist acceleration because of inertia.

It's essentially the maximum speed you reach when you fall—the speed limit for falling. For an adult skydiver like those in the picture, terminal velocity is about 122 miles per hour (195 km/h or 54 m/s). That's pretty fast if you ask me—especially if you're falling toward the earth after having jumped out of an airplane!

Diving from the Sky

When people jump out of an airplane in flight, we say they're skydiving. These skydivers wear a special backpack that has a parachute inside of it. After they jump, they just fall for a while. Some people skydive for fun, to experience the fall. Other people, like those in the military, skydive to get from the air to the ground quickly. When something (or someone) is falling, we call the falling motion a free fall.

There are many videos of people doing amazing stunts while falling to the earth. I've even seen two people get married while falling. After falling for a while, they pull a string (called a rip cord), and out pops the parachute. The parachute increases the area that's encountering air resistance. This greatly increases the friction, slowing down the skydiver and giving him a safe—though somewhat bumpy—landing on the ground.

Now that you've learned so much about the physics of motion, let me ask you a question: After a skydiver jumps from the plane, how should he position his body to decrease the air resistance and get to the ground more quickly? How would *you* position your body if you were trying to slow down your fall? Here's the answer: To fall

A skydiver's parachute increases the air friction, slowing the diver down enough to land safely on the ground.

more quickly after jumping from the plane, you would point your feet downward. This reduces the surface area facing into the air. Special forces in the military do this in order to get from the plane to the ground more quickly so they can carry out their special mission. To fall more slowly, you would lay your body horizontally, with your stomach facing downward. This would give your body more surface area, which would encounter more air resistance (drag). If you were skydiving for fun, this would be your best body position in the air.

This skydiver's body position is creating more drag. This will enable her to enjoy a slower fall.

Before you move on, explain to someone the interesting things you've learned today.

Centripetal Force

Do you remember the story of David and Goliath from the Bible? Well, in his battle against Goliath, David used a physics concept called centripetal force. We're going to discuss centripetal force and learn how it showed up in David's confrontation with Goliath. Let's begin with an experiment.

Try This!

You will need: An adult's supervision, a penny, and a balloon.

First, place the penny inside the deflated balloon. Now blow up the balloon and seal it by tying it tightly. Next, spin the balloon in tight circles to get the penny moving around and around inside the balloon. Finally, stop spinning the balloon and watch what happens.

What happened? The penny stayed on the outside walls of the balloon, didn't it? Why is this? Well, the penny is being pulled away from the center of the balloon because of its inertia. The walls of the balloon apply centripetal force to the penny.

"Centripetal" means center seeking. Centripetal force is not really a new force. It's just a way of describing how forces, like gravity or friction, work together to make an object go in a circular direction rather than a straight line.

Let me explain. We know that an object in motion will travel in a straight direction unless some force acts upon it. So whenever an object is continuously moving in a circle around something else, some force must be acting upon the object to make it go in a circle instead of a straight line.

Here's the scientific definition of **centripetal force:** a force that acts on a body moving in a circular path and is directed toward the center around which the body is moving. That may sound complicated, but let's look at a familiar example: the moon and the earth.

Can you tell me a force that is acting on the moon? Right! Gravity. Let's see this in action with an experiment.

Try This!

You will need: An adult's supervision, a small pail with a handle, and some water.

First, go outside and pour some water into the pail. Now swing the pail back and forth in a steady motion. Continue swinging the pail higher and higher until it swings over your head in a circular motion. Make sure you're swinging the pail at a constant speed. Are you surprised by what happens?

What happened? The water stayed in the bucket! Why? The centripetal force caused the water to be held toward the center of the circle, which was you. It kept the water in the bucket as it swung around your head. What would have happened if you had released the bucket when it was circling around you? Inertia would have caused it to stay in motion, but it would have moved in a straight path away from you.

David and Goliath

Let's see how this relates to David and Goliath. When David was swinging his sling in a circular motion, what force was at work? It was centripetal force. David's hand spinning the sling was the center of the circle. The rock that killed Goliath was being held by David's slingshot and was going around and around in a fast orbit.

The centripetal force was provided by another special force holding the rock in place while it was traveling in that fast, circular motion. That force was tension. Tension is another force that surrounds an object to pull or push on it. The tension of the leather sling holding the rock in place kept the rock from traveling in a straight path. Remember, Newton's first law tells us that objects in motion will move in a straight path. But instead, it was moving in a circle, gaining speed as it was spinning. David's hand supplied centripetal force to the strap, and the strap supplied centripetal force to the rock. Around and around the sling spun. Centripetal force was at work preparing for Goliath's demise!

What happened when David let go of the rock? There was no longer any centripetal

David used centripetal force to defeat Goliath!

force or tension acting on the rock. Its inertia caused the rock to continue moving in a straight line, angling away from the place it was released. When something is circling around another object, there are forces that keep it circling. When those forces

Even today, shepherds use slings like David's to keep prey away from their flocks. This photo is of a Palestinian shepherd boy swinging his sling.

are released, the object will follow Newton's laws and inertia and will move in a straight line away from the object it was circling.

I'm sure David had to practice a lot with that leather strap to learn when to release the rock so it would hit its target.

Now you know the main forces affecting motion. Let's do some activities to help you remember all you've learned in this lesson.

Final Matters

You've discovered some important things about movement in this lesson. What was the most interesting thing you learned? As you continue your journey through physics, be sure to remember that God is the author of all that you're discovering. Give Him glory and thanks as you explore the amazing way He created the world to work!

What Do You Remember?

What is the force that resists movement between two objects? What is a lubricant? Name three lubricants mentioned in this lesson. What is adhesion? What is the law that tells us all objects are attracted to other objects according to their mass and distance? Which of the two objects would hit the ground first if pushed from the same height—a bowling ball or a basketball? What kind of resistant force does an object traveling through water encounter? What kind of resistant force does an object traveling through air on the earth encounter? How do people reduce air or water resistance? What is the speed limit of falling objects called? When an object is in free fall, what two resisting forces will the object encounter? What was the force that was in effect when David was twirling the sling?

Notebooking Activities

Record in your notebooking journal the fascinating facts you've learned in this lesson. In addition, write about some of the experiments you did. You can record this information on the pages provided in the *Chemistry and Physics Notebooking Journal*. Finally, complete the notebooking activity below.

Design a race car or airplane that would incorporate the best model for reducing the forces it encounters, giving it more speed. Be sure to diagram and label all the design aspects that help your car or plane travel faster.

Project
Paper Airplane Design

Creating efficient paper airplanes that fly well is a skill that takes thought and effort. You can do a project to determine which of the classic airplane designs creates the most aerodynamic paper airplane.

Follow the instructions for folding the paper airplanes found on this page and the next page. You'll create multiple airplane designs. Before you fly them, form a hypothesis about which plane you think is going to fly the best. Make sure you use heavy card stock paper. Also remember to measure and graph your results, testing each plane several times to make sure your results are consistent.

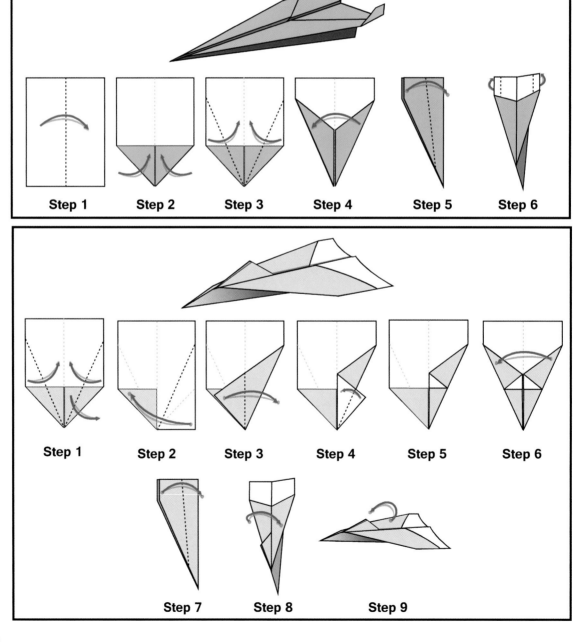

Step 1   Step 2   Step 3   Step 4   Step 5   Step 6

Step 1   Step 2   Step 3   Step 4   Step 5   Step 6

Step 7   Step 8   Step 9

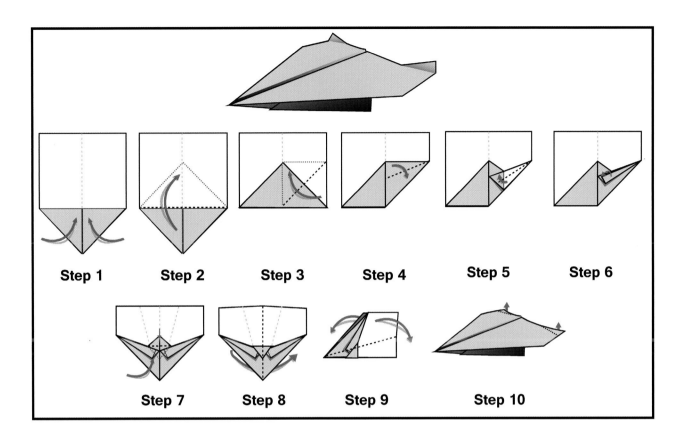

Step 1   Step 2   Step 3   Step 4   Step 5   Step 6

Step 7   Step 8   Step 9   Step 10

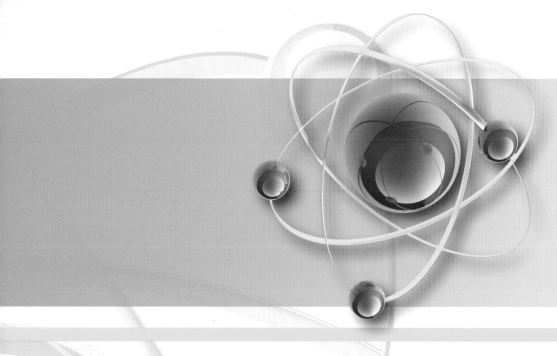

Work in the World

After reading that God's Spirit was moving over the surface of the water, we studied movement. Let's go back to that second verse in the Bible again. We aren't quite done with this verse yet. There's actually more physics to be explored in the very first chapter of the Bible.

Let's read Genesis 1:1–2 together again: "In the beginning God created the heavens and the earth. Now the earth was formless and empty, darkness was over the surface of the deep, and the Spirit of God was hovering over the waters."

What makes you able to move? Think about this for a minute. When your mother spends the day cooking, cleaning, teaching, driving, talking, and working, she's using something stored inside her to do all of these things. In fact, if you ask her to take you to the park at the end of the day, she might tell you she doesn't have any of this left. If she doesn't have any left, she won't be doing much of anything! Have you figured it out? We're talking about energy.

Scientists tell us that **energy** is the ability of someone or something to do work. What's work? Well, it's not just what you do to earn money. It's about making things move. When you throw a ball, you've done work. Your body did work, and the ball was forced to do work. When a dog pulls a sled, the dog and the sled are at work. When a flower blooms, it has done work. When a cannonball shoots across the field, that's work too. Even when a faucet turns, a book opens, a marble rolls, a stomach digests food, a cat yawns, and the sun heats up the field, it's all movement of molecules—and it's all work.

We know that energy is the ability to do work, but what exactly *is* energy? Energy is one of those really strange concepts, like charge and gravity. I can teach you

A lot of energy is being used in this picture. The children are using energy stored in their bodies. The ball is also using energy. Even the grass is using energy!

all about the different kinds and forms of energy. I can explain some scientific laws regarding energy. But I can't tell you what energy looks like or what it really is. It's not something you can hold or see. We don't know what energy is; we only know what energy does. Energy really is a mystery! Maybe all of these mysteries will be solved for us when we get to heaven.

Finding Energy

Energy is found everywhere on the earth. Let's look at the pictures on this page to learn about energy. First, the sun shines its light rays on the earth. Those light rays make the corn grow; the sun's light is a form of energy. The excitement the sun causes inside the corn is energy; the corn stores the sun's energy inside of it. People use energy to collect the corn. When someone eats the corn, he uses energy. The energy in the corn is transferred to the person as nutrients. These nutrients are stored in the body and are used to give the person more energy. The person then uses those stored nutrients as energy to work and play. There's so much energy everywhere, and it all began with the energy from the sun!

Kinds of Energy

There are two main kinds of energy: kinetic energy and potential energy. All energy—whether it's from the sun, in the corn plant, in your body, in a machine, or anywhere else—is either potential energy or kinetic energy. Let's learn about these two kinds of energy.

Connecting Kinetics

The word "kinetic" comes from a Greek word for movement. Some children are labeled kinesthetic learners, meaning they learn best when they're moving. When I was in college, I studied kinesiology. That's the study of movement, specifically the movement of the human body. Can you guess what kind of energy kinetic energy is? You're right—**kinetic energy** is energy in motion. It's on the move!

Can you think of some examples of kinetic energy? An ocean's crashing waves use kinetic energy. The sound that moves from the waves into your ears is kinetic energy. Machines also use kinetic energy; they have moving parts in them. When you speak, walk, think, or play, you're using kinetic energy. Remember, *anything* in motion is using kinetic energy.

Let's compare kinetic energy to the other kind of energy—potential energy.

Potential Power

Has anyone ever told you that you have great potential? If not, let me be the first to tell you that. You have a huge amount of potential! That means you have the potential to do great things and be very useful in this world. I know you have a lot of potential because the Bible says so. The Bible says you were created in Christ Jesus to do good works, which God prepared in advance for you to do (Ephesians 2:10). That means you have lots of potential! What does the word "potential" mean? In physics, **potential energy** means energy that is stored up, just waiting to be used.

Some things have more potential energy than others. That means some things have the possibility of creating more work (or more energy) than other things. One example involves motion. If I put a bouncy ball on a book that's sitting on the floor, there's the possibility it could roll off and maybe bounce a little as it rolls away. When it's sitting

on the book, the ball has a small amount of potential energy. But if I put the same bouncy ball on a high window sill, it has more potential energy than it did on the book. This type of potential energy is dependent on gravity. We sometimes call this kind of energy **gravitational energy**.

The banana sitting on my counter has a different kind of potential energy. What's the potential energy of a banana? Think about it. The banana has nutrients that can give me energy to write the rest of this book. Indeed, food has potential energy, called chemical energy.

After I eat the banana and it's digested, the energy from the banana is transferred from potential energy to kinetic energy. That's because I'll get moving once I fill my body with the chemicals it needs to keep my brain thinking and my fingers tapping on the keyboard.

Look at the pictures below and tell someone whether they represent potential energy or kinetic energy. You can find the answers in the answer key in the back of this book.

Do you remember I said a banana's potential energy could be used by my body to get me moving? That means potential energy can be changed into kinetic energy. Yes indeed! Energy can be transferred to different things. In fact, that's what energy is always doing—moving from thing to thing. Kinetic energy can be changed into potential energy. Pick up an unbreakable object (like a pencil) and hold it in the air. You used kinetic energy to do that. Now the object you're holding in the air has potential energy. Let the object fall. The potential energy turned back into kinetic energy as the object fell. You were transferring energy around, moving it from one kind of energy to another—and back to another!

Try This!

You will need: An adult's supervision and a rubber band.

Loop the rubber band around your thumb and pull back on it with your other hand as if you were going to let it fly. This pulling motion uses kinetic energy. While you hold the rubber band in a stretched position, the kinetic energy is stored as potential energy. But when you release the rubber band, you'll transfer that potential energy to kinetic energy!

Conserving Energy

All of this brings us to a very fascinating truth about energy. The truth is: Our world has a certain supply of energy, and that energy is always being transferred around from one thing to the next. That's easy to understand. But here's the amazing thing. Listen carefully. Even though we don't fully understand what energy is, we know that energy can now never be created nor can it be destroyed. It can only be transferred to other things or transformed into a different form of energy. That's a pretty awesome truth, isn't it? When God created the world, He put a specific amount of energy into the world; we can't get more, and we can't get less. It's always the same amount, being transferred from potential to kinetic (such as with the banana and me), or kinetic to potential (as with the sun and other matter making the banana grow), or kinetic to kinetic (as with the electricity making your light bulb glow), or potential to

This puppy is a bundle of potential energy. However, deep inside chemical energy is being used while the puppy's tummy digests food and its lungs take in oxygen. But when this puppy awakens, he'll become a bundle of kinetic energy!

While we sleep our bodies create more energy that's stored in our cells as potential energy. However, throughout the next day, that energy will be used as kinetic energy.

potential (such as when you put a dart in a dart gun and pull back on the trigger). We never create energy; it's just moved around. We call this the law of conservation of energy.

To conserve something means to protect and preserve it. The **law of conservation of energy** states that energy is protected and preserved. We can't run out of it, and we can't make new energy. If your mom doesn't have the energy she needs to take you to the park, you'll have to wait until she gets more energy. Usually, a good night's rest will allow her body to store up new energy for the next day.

Explain the law of conservation of energy in your own words.

Creation Confirmation

As we discussed, some people believe that everything in this world came from absolutely nothing—by accident. However, the law of conservation of energy is another example of a scientific law revealing God's hand in creation. If energy cannot be created or destroyed and the universe contains a certain amount of energy that can never be reduced or increased, then somehow all of that energy must have come from somewhere or *Someone*. You see, the law of conservation of energy tells us the world could not have come from nothing. Someone had to create the world and give it energy before it could be conserved. This law is evidence for a Creator.

Let's now have some fun with the transfer of energy!

Try This!

You will need: An adult's supervision, 2 pencils, and an object to use as a drum, such as a can with a plastic lid or a large cookie tin.

First, hit the drum with one of the pencils. Listen to the sound. Now hold one pencil (somewhat loosely) at an angle on the drum. With the other pencil, hit the pencil that's sitting on the drum. Does it make a similar sound?

You just experimented with the transfer of energy. The kinetic energy moved through the top stick into the bottom stick and onto the drum, making a similar sound. Energy was transferred.

Let's do another experiment.

Try This!

You will need: An adult's supervision, safety goggles, a wooden spool with a large hole, electrical or duct tape, a washer, a toothpick, a pencil, a thin rubber band, and scissors.

Feed the rubber band through the spool using an ice pick or pencil. Put the toothpick through the loop of the rubber band sticking out of the end of the spool. Tape it down in the middle. Break off the ends that stick out beyond the spool so it can roll freely. Place the loop of the rubber band through the washer on the other end of the spool. Put a pencil on top of the washer, feeding it through the rubber band loop. Now turn the pencil around and around, making the rubber band tighter and tighter as you wind the pencil. When the rubber band is quite tight, put your device down on the floor and let it go!

What happened? When you wound the pencil around and around you were creating a device with stored potential energy. When you put the device down, that potential energy transferred into kinetic energy!

Try This!

You will need: An adult's supervision, a tennis ball, and a basketball.

To begin, go to a place that has a hard floor and is clear of any item that could be broken by a bouncing ball. Now drop one ball at a time. Observe how high each ball bounces. Can you guess how many feet the balls bounced? Next, place the tennis ball on top of the basketball, making sure they're touching one another. Now drop the balls together on the floor. Be sure the balls are still touching when the larger ball on bottom hits the floor or this will not work. If the balls lose contact before they hit the floor, try again.

What happened? Do this again and note how high the basketball bounces. Did it bounce less than usual?

This happened because the larger ball's energy was transferred to the smaller ball. You noticed that the basketball didn't bounce much, but the tennis ball probably flew across the room!

Before you dropped the balls, did they have potential or kinetic energy? Potential. When they were falling, was the energy potential or kinetic? Kinetic.

This experiment also shows us another important scientific principle: Things with more mass have more energy at a given speed. The basketball was bigger, so it had a lot of energy to transfer to the bouncy ball. Scientists would say that energy is proportional to the mass of an object. Think about that for a minute. Can you explain it in your own words?

Be sure to tell someone all that you've learned so far before moving on. Explain the difference between potential and kinetic energy. Explain the law of conservation of energy again.

Forms of Energy

Kinetic and potential are two *kinds* of energy. But there are actually many different *forms* of energy. Some important forms of energy are chemical energy, nuclear energy, sound energy, light energy, heat energy, electrical energy, and mechanical energy. We're going to discover all these forms of energy with fun activities and experiments throughout the next few lessons. You'll get to explore electricity, build circuits, and make a rainbow and a solar heater. You'll also get to do many other fun projects and experiments as you learn. But let's finish this lesson by exploring two forms of energy: chemical and nuclear. We'll discuss an energy concept you'll hear a lot about in the news: renewable energy. It's important that you understand these forms of energy so you can really grasp what people are talking about when they discuss energy. Let's get started!

Chemical Energy

Most of the potential energy around you is in the form of **chemical energy**. The energy inside a grain of corn or a banana is chemical energy. That's because chemicals (molecules and atoms) are stored inside these foods. After we eat these foods, the same molecules and atoms are stored in our bodies to be used as kinetic and thermal energy. This gives us the ability to think, run, play, study, work, fight disease, and eat some more! Chemical energy fuels our bodies and many other things.

Have you ever heard the word "fuel"? What does that word make you think about? We put fuel in our cars to make them run. If you camp, you probably know that fires need fuel to keep burning. All fuel is chemical energy. In the same way, almost all chemical energy is used as fuel in one way or another. Here's an important science concept to know: Fuel is burned to make energy. When we burn fuel, it makes heat. Sometimes you can't see the fuel actually being burned. When your body transfers the chemicals you ate into warmth and activity, you don't see it. However, when you eat nutrients, your little cells are indeed burning the chemicals to release the energy in the food. Your cells have miniature fires going on to burn the fuel you eat!

The more calories our food has, the more potential and chemical energy it contains. Choose healthy food to give your body the energy it needs to accomplish all you need to do.

Food is not the only chemical energy or fuel that's burned for energy. We also burn the chemical energy in wood, natural gas, oil, and coal. When these fuels burn—or give off their heat—they're involved in a chemical reaction. What kind of chemical reaction releases heat: endothermic or exothermic? You're right—exothermic! The burning of chemical energy, used as fuel, produces an exothermic reaction, giving us heat and other kinds of energy. Isn't it amazing that there are exothermic reactions going on inside your cells right now as you use stored energy to learn about energy!

Energy over Time

Man has always used a lot of energy each day trying to find new ways to make life more comfortable. Even the earliest civilizations sought to make finding, cooking, and eating food easier. It was much more difficult in the early days of human history. Back then, most of the day was spent not only getting water and cutting wood for cooking, but also locating, hunting, growing, and preparing the food that was to be eaten that day. Indeed, a lot of energy was spent each day just trying to survive. It was exhausting, hard work.

Things became easier during the time of the Roman civilization. Marketplaces were filled with meat, bread, olives, and many other foods to buy. People didn't have to spend all their energy growing and hunting food for themselves. Waterwheels were used to grind flour; it was no longer done by hand.

The Romans even had heated public pools called baths. Wood was burned all day long to keep the public bath water hot. Every day, thousands of slaves cut and gathered the wood required to heat food, homes, baths, and anything else where heat energy was needed. As you can imagine, the hills and mountains around Rome were not very lush because all the trees were constantly cut down to be used as fuel.

Let's fast forward to the Middle Ages and the European cities. People living in this time period needed to heat their food as well. Although wood was still used, the main source of heat was coal. Coal has more energy than wood, so it is a better source for heat. People needed only a little coal

A lot of energy was used each day to keep these Roman baths hot.

compared to a lot of wood to make dinner. However, coal creates a lot of soot when it burns. Thus, entire towns were covered with gray soot from all the burning of coal. A fine, black powder covered everyone and everything.

Whale blubber provided the energy needed to light and heat many early American homes.

Let's speed ahead to the beginnings of America. Here we find individual homes with lanterns lighting the rooms. These lanterns were filled with another kind of chemical energy—oil. Where did people get the oil? From whale blubber! Whale oil was an extremely valuable fuel for many, many years. However, many whales had to be killed in order for people to have light and heat. It really hurt the whale population. In addition, whale oil stank horribly. Like coal, the soot it created coated everything in the house with a greasy residue. This left everyone and everything oily and gunky.

Consider how difficult it was just to get light and heat compared to today. Wow, have things changed! Children don't have to spend the entire day gathering food, water, and fuel. In fact, many simply throw something into the microwave and instantly find a satisfying meal. Children today can flip a switch, and light pours into the house without making everything black and sooty or stinky and greasy. They can turn on the TV, computer, or iPod for education or entertainment. But how did all this become possible? Because of advancements in the ways we use chemical energy.

The chemical energy we use in our homes comes from many sources, but the main ones are coal, oil, and natural gas. These fuels make up about 85% of the fuel used.

Let's explore these fuels a little more.

Fossil Fuels

Long ago (about 4,500 years according to the history recorded in the Bible) there was a worldwide Flood that covered the earth in a huge deluge of water. All that was once living was immediately and permanently buried. Billions of plants and animals packed with energy were covered with mud. These living things died and eventually became fossils. The energy from these fossils transferred to the ground around them and was converted into different forms of stored energy. These forms of energy remained under the mud—deep in the earth where they were covered. We call these fossilized forms of energy **fossil fuels** because they are a great source of fuel.

Although the Flood was an unhappy event, it gave us some amazing forms of energy. As a great theologian named Augustine once said, "God judged it better to bring good out of evil, than to suffer no evil to exist." God allowed the worldwide Flood—which wiped out everyone and everything except Noah, his family, and the animals on the ark—to bring good to us today. You see, all those buried remains of the beautiful plants and animals God made are now being used to print this book. These remains are also being used to light your home, power your car, and give you many important products you depend on every day.

This image shows what the worldwide Flood may have been like. God used this event to provide much of the energy we need.

Many dinosaurs were fully preserved acting out certain types of behavior, such as this mother dinosaur caring for her young. They were also preserved in groups. This is very unlike how you would find a dinosaur that had died a natural death and is further evidence for the worldwide Flood described in the Bible.

Let's explore the different fossil fuels that came from the buried plants and animals.

Oceans of Oil

Some of the fossils produced huge lakes of oil deep in the earth. These lakes of oil are called **oil reservoirs**. The oil found in these reservoirs, called crude oil, varies in color and is quite sticky. Oil companies are always searching for new oil reservoirs. Geologists locate the oil by surveying different land formations, testing the soil and rocks on the surface. They also use X-ray and radioactive measuring devices to look below the surface. When they think they've located an oil reservoir, workers use large machines to drill deep into the earth to get the oil.

When oil companies drill and drill but fail to find oil, they call it a dry hole. Sometimes they fail to find oil because the finding equipment is wrong. However, true dry holes do happen now and again. Because it costs about $100 million to drill one well, dry holes are a huge money loss.

Yet if a company strikes oil, it will make back all that money and a whole lot more from the sale of the oil. Today, the countries that have the most oil reservoirs are Saudi Arabia, Venezuela, Canada, and the United States. The leading oil-producing area in the U.S. is in the Gulf of Mexico. Oil is also found in Alaska, Texas, California, Oklahoma, and North Dakota.

There's also a lot of oil offshore under the floor of the ocean. To get the oil out,

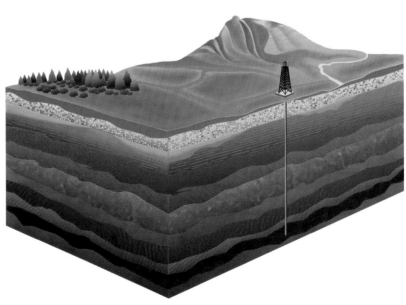

Buried plants and animals created huge lakes of oil under the earth. This oil well is drilling down through many layers of the earth. It will pump the oil out to be used for many different purposes.

enormous platforms are built right in the ocean. These platforms are called offshore oil rigs. The rigs have anchoring systems that keep them in position. Oil rigs are some of the strongest structures in the world. They can stand up against hurricane winds and enormously powerful, crashing waves. The drills on these rigs bore far, far down into the rocks of the sea floor. The oil is then either sent to land through huge pipes or held in a floating tank that's taken to land by large ships.

This offshore oil rig has drills that bore far down into the ocean floor. It's strong enough to withstand hurricane winds and crashing waves.

After the oil is brought up from these oil reservoirs, it's refined. That means it's cleaned and separated into different parts, including gasoline, kerosene, and other oils. Many products you use and love are made from this oil, such as ink, crayons, DVDs, tires, eyeglasses, deodorant, and dishwashing liquid.

When the companies first drill into an oil reservoir, the oil sometimes spews up from the hole because it's under so much pressure under the ground. The pressure is built because millions of tons of rock and earth are lying on the oil. Also, the earth's natural heat builds up the pressure in the reservoir. When the well strikes the reservoir, this pressure is released, much like air escaping from a balloon. Years ago, when the equipment wasn't as good as it is today, the oil would spurt hundreds of feet out of the ground! It was called a gusher. Today, however, oil companies install special equipment on their wells that prevents gushers and helps control the pressure inside the well. This helps protect from oil spills, which are bad for the environment.

This famous gusher was located in Spindletop, Texas. Today, oil companies don't allow the oil to spew out of the wells.

Let's do an experiment to explore how and why oil comes out of the reservoir on its own and why it occasionally needs help coming out.

Try This!

You will need: An adult's supervision, a zippered plastic bag, water, a kitchen counter near the sink, and 2 straws cut at an angle to make a sharp point.

First, fill the bag with water, closing it with as little air left in the bag as possible. Lay the bag on the counter. Now insert the sharp point of the straw into the corner on one side of the bag. If water leaks out the side, try again or use tape to seal it. Keep the straw upright so the water doesn't spill out. Now press down on the bag for a second, then release. The water should squirt out like a gusher!

The millions of pounds of rock lying above the oil reservoir are pressing down on the lake of oil. This pressure, combined with the heat of the earth, causes the oil and gases to explode from the reservoir when a hole is made in the lake. While holding the straw upright, insert another straw into the opposite corner on the same side. Both straws should be held upright. Now blow into one of the straws. What happens?

You just observed the two ways oil gets out of a well. Either the oil spews out on its own from pressure, or it's pumped out by some other means. Sometimes oil companies pour water into the well to force the oil to the surface. Remember, water is denser than oil. Sometimes gases are pumped into the oil to encourage it to come out. There are also other ways that pressure is increased.

Explain what you've learned so far about fossil fuels.

Countless Coal

Coal is an important and valuable resource and is very useful for creating energy in the world. Although coal used to create a dirty environment, modern equipment helps burn it cleanly—without adding a lot of pollution to the environment. Today, companies are developing even cleaner ways to burn coal. Coal is also much less expensive than oil and other forms of energy. This helps keep down the cost of turning on the lights and running the air conditioner. Although we can't find lakes with oil on every continent in the world, we can find coal on every continent—even Antarctica! In fact, this fossil fuel is still the main source of energy and electricity for most of the world. As you can imagine, coal provides many jobs for people all around the world.

This coal will be transported to power plants, where it can be used for energy.

We get most coal from coal mines. Coal mines are caves and caverns made deep in the earth. In the United States, coal is most commonly found in Montana, Illinois, Wyoming, West Virginia, Kentucky, Pennsylvania, Ohio, Colorado, Texas, and Indiana. People who go down into the earth to get the coal are called coal miners.

Coal is made up of dead plants that turned into carbon. In fact, coal is made up of carbon. As you know, carbon turns into something else when exposed to huge amounts of pressure. What is it? Diamonds!

This miner is deep within the earth, using special equipment to burrow through the earth and mine the coal.

Nature's Natural Gas

Besides a solid (coal) and a liquid (oil), fossils can also make a gas called methane. We just call it **natural gas** because it's made naturally under the earth. Many people use natural gas to heat the water that comes into their home. Some people even use natural gas to cook on their stove. If your stove has an actual fire that heats your food, it's using natural gas. Some people have natural gas coming into their fireplace as well.

Natural gas is found deep within the earth—inside layers of rock with tiny holes. The rock looks like a sponge, with lots of holes. Natural gas is stored inside these holes. People drill thousands of feet into the earth—using big wells and pumps—to bring this gas to the surface. The gas is then sent all over the country in huge gas pipes

Some fireplaces use natural gas and artificial logs to create heat and give the appearance of a real fire.

buried underground. The gas arrives at a utility company and is sent to your house in smaller pipes. In fact, the gas you use in your house probably came from a long way away!

Natural gas is extremely flammable and can even be explosive in large amounts. That's why it's important that natural gas is flowing into your house only when there's a flame burning it. This way it doesn't have a chance to build up to dangerous amounts. Natural gas is colorless and odorless. Therefore, utility companies add a sulfur-containing substance with an extremely strong smell to help make gas leaks easier to notice. If you ever smell a strange scent in your home like rotten eggs, you should tell someone immediately. The gas company will come to your home to see if you have a leak.

As you can see, fossil fuels are a hugely important form of chemical energy. Fossil fuels like oil, coal, and natural gas give power and heat to homes, automobiles, machines, and manufacturing plants. Those dead plants and animals are important natural resources in the earth, aren't they? If there had not been a worldwide Flood to bury them so rapidly—creating fossils so quickly—our world would be quite different wouldn't it? I bet the whales are glad we discovered the use of fossils for fuel!

Creation Confirmation

It was once believed that the huge oil reservoirs took millions of years to form. Today, some scientists are working to show that this may not be correct. In fact, scientists can create oil in a laboratory from dead plant and animal matter rather quickly. Further, the fact that there are so many oil reservoirs under the earth gives us evidence of the worldwide Flood which the Bible speaks of. It also explains why there are so many fossils of perfectly preserved bones under the earth.

In order for a fossil to form, the animal that died must not be exposed to the elements—the sun, wind, and rain—or of course to scavengers. How can a dead animal avoid being exposed to these elements? The only way is to be instantly covered or buried in the right material. In fact, for so many fossils to form at one time, there would need to be a massive burial of animals all at once. The oil and gas reservoirs and also the coal mines are evidence that the worldwide Flood indeed occurred. The Flood

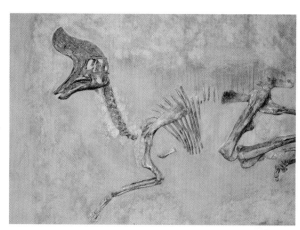

This fossilized dinosaur was buried in mud when it died. If it were not so, the bones would have decayed and disintegrated from exposure to the sun, wind, rain, and wild animals. This is evidence for a worldwide Flood.

poured enormous amounts of muddy water over the entire earth. This caused the death of every vertebrate land animal and many plants that were alive at the time. Although the plants could regenerate from seeds, the animals were lost forever—except those that were on the ark.

Explain to someone what you've learned so far today before moving on to learn about nuclear energy.

Nuclear Energy

We use energy every day for many important things like heating and cooling our homes, turning on the lights, driving our automobiles, cleaning our drinking water, and operating the factories that make our toys, games, devices, and cars. Energy is really important to people, so finding the best and easiest way to make energy is an important field of science. As it turns out, scientists have discovered that the most plentiful source of energy is found in something that surrounds us everywhere all the time—the atom! Even though it's so small, there's an enormous amount of energy inside the nucleus of a single atom. We call this energy atomic energy, or more accurately, **nuclear energy**.

In the 1930s, scientists learned that they could split the nucleus of some atoms if they hit the nucleus with a neutron. When an atom splits, it releases energy—huge amounts of it! We call splitting atoms **nuclear fission**. Nuclear fission produces nuclear energy.

Soon it was discovered that certain elements also produce nuclear energy naturally. We call these elements radioactive. The nucleus of these special atoms falls apart; it decays. When the nucleus decays, it's similar to an atom splitting—it gives off a great deal of energy.

In the 1940s, scientists realized they could create devastating bombs using nuclear fission. A famous scientist, Albert Einstein, wrote to President Franklin Roosevelt urging America to build such bombs before Germany could. Two of these bombs were dropped on Japan, the country that had started the war against the U.S. About a week after the bombs hit, Japan surrendered because of the widespread and terrible destruction these bombs caused.

After the war, scientists went about using nuclear power in a less destructive manner; they used it to create energy for homes and factories. By causing a nuclear reaction, they could generate a great amount of heat and energy. This nuclear reaction happens inside special containers and specially designed buildings that contain all the radiation.

These buildings, called nuclear power plants, were an amazing discovery that promised to give the world inexpensive, abundant energy. Nuclear power plants

This is a picture of a mushroom cloud from the atomic bombing of Nagasaki, Japan, on August 9, 1945.

can produce a lot of energy with little effort. In fact, a jelly-bean-sized pellet of uranium gives off as much energy as 1,500 tons of coal or 150 gallons of oil. However, nuclear power has its downside as well.

Nuclear fission might seem like the solution to our need for energy, but it does have some dangers. You see, radioactive elements can be harmful to cell life. Cells are what people, plants, and animals are made of. The radiation produced by the nuclear reactors can cause cell damage, leading to cancer and death. If people are exposed to a huge amount of nuclear radiation, they're at risk for developing cancer. Thankfully, the nuclear power plants take an enormous number of precautions to keep the radiation from leaking out of the plants.

These leftover uranium fuel rods still have a small amount of radioactivity left in them. The rods are sealed in drums for long-term storage in facilities or underground. It will take thousands, millions, or even billions of years before there's absolutely no radioactivity inside the rods.

There *have* been a few cases of nuclear power plants leaking, but they're extremely rare. One of the worst leaks of radioactive material was at a nuclear power plant in the Ukraine. In the town of Chernobyl, a damaged power plant exploded and leaked a lot of radiation. We say there was nuclear fallout. This means radiation was carried into the atmosphere and fell back to the earth in raindrops or as dust. The radiation went up into the air and was carried across Europe by the wind and clouds. However, very few people were harmed by this event. The amount of radiation people receive from fallout is smaller than someone might receive at the dentist's office.

Even more recently, in 2011, a huge tsunami and earthquake caused nuclear power plants in Japan to leak radiation. As a result, many people came

Before the discovery of radioactivity, uranium was primarily used in small amounts for yellow glass and pottery glazes, such as uranium glass and Fiesta dinnerware.

in contact with radiation. The amount of radiation they came in contact with was extremely small—less than someone might get through a CT scan at the doctor's office. It was rather harmless, yet people were alarmed. Although there are dangers of leaks, they're not usually as harmful as people have been led to believe.

This special container is holding radioactive waste. The waste will be safely transported to a place where it will be properly disposed of.

Another issue with nuclear power is that even though it doesn't create air pollution, it does produce radioactive waste. The power plants have to find a way to throw away the used-up radioactive elements. Even though the elements have been used, they still contain some radiation. Discarding them in a way that doesn't expose people to radiation is important. Thankfully, the amount of waste from a nuclear power plant is extremely small. In addition, in a typical fuel rod 80% of the radioactivity is gone within five years. Nonetheless, because of the risks to cell life, this radioactive waste has to be disposed of properly. Today, the waste is sealed in drums that radiation cannot penetrate.

As you can see, nuclear energy is not the perfect answer to our energy needs. However, engineers are making power plants safer, and others are working on solutions for handling the waste they produce. It's likely that, with the help of scientists and engineers, nuclear power will soon become one of the main sources of energy for the world.

Take a minute to explain what you've learned about nuclear energy.

Renewable Energy

I want to take a brief look at renewable energy since the news reporters and politicians are always talking about it. It's important for you to understand what the issues are. Eventually, our supply of oil, gas, coal, and nuclear energy may run low. It would likely be hundreds if not thousands of years before that would happen. However, people have become concerned that someday we'll use up all our natural resources. They would like to find ways to create energy from sources that don't run out.

We call energy made from sources that don't run out **renewable energy**. That's because the energy continues to renew itself over and over again. Coal, oil, gas, and even radioactive elements are not considered renewable. They can run out, and it takes a long time for them to be replenished. Energy from burning wood is considered renewable, but wood takes a long time to regrow. So when people think of renewable energy, they usually think of energy from sources that don't take a long time to renew—like the sun, wind, and water. Currently, less than 3% of the world's energy comes from these renewable sources. Scientists are working hard to create more renewable energy. Hopefully, this will help ensure our energy sources never run out.

There's another energy issue you'll hear about in the news—the negative impact of some energy sources on the environment. You see, many in people in America are concerned about our environment and work hard to take good care of it. These people want to protect the world from getting dirty and polluted. However, people can take this desire to protect the world too far, and it can have a negative impact on others. In fact, companies have been shut down and many people have lost their jobs because of unwise pollution concerns. It's not wrong to protect our environment. However, we have to be careful that our desire for a clean world doesn't negatively affect other areas of society.

Burning coal, oil, and gas does not pollute the environment the way it once did. Scientists and engineers have worked very hard to discover how to burn these fuels in ways that are not harmful to our environment. As a result, our air is 90% cleaner today than it was in 1970, even though we're burning more coal, oil, and gas. Sadly, many people don't know this. If you took a poll, you might find that most people think our air is *less* clean than it was in 1970 because of what they hear on the news. But that's not true. Our air quality has improved because we've worked hard to make it clean. The amount of pollution we're creating now is very small.

As you can see, we've come a long way in producing energy. However, some people still want to find a way to produce energy that has no chemicals or waste at all. We call energy that doesn't produce chemicals and waste

clean energy. A lot of money has gone into trying to find sources of clean energy in hopes we will no longer be dependent on coal, oil, gas, and nuclear energy. However, finding even cleaner ways to burn coal, oil, and gas may be a wiser use of our money. If we were to completely stop using these sources of energy, millions of people would lose their jobs. Many, many people work for companies that help mine, transport, and burn coal for energy. If millions of people lost their jobs, it would affect everyone in a very negative way.

Let's explore a few sources of renewable and clean energy that mankind is using. We'll also learn about the problems these energy sources produce. Then you can decide what you think should be done about all of this.

Hydropower

For many years people used the power produced by water mills to do work. Some people in other countries still use water mills to grind grain.

You may already know that "hydro" means water. So **hydropower** is the power of water. We can make energy with water! In fact, we've been doing this for a long, long time. For thousands of years, water mills have been used to grind grain and do other kinds of work for people. These devices use the force of falling water to strike paddles, which in turn generate power for machines that do work. Because electricity doesn't cost very much and is easy to use, water mills are no longer in use in most countries. However, less developed countries, like India, still use water mills to grind grain. Since they were such an important part of our history, you can still see water mills next to old buildings or bridges when driving through the country.

Can you guess what hydroelectricity is? **Hydroelectricity** is electricity from water—falling water to be exact! Have you ever seen a dam? Dams are large structures built on lakes and rivers. They're designed to make electricity. The dam creates a kind of waterfall from the backed-up water. As the water comes through, it turns turbine blades inside the dam. The turbine spins and produces electricity through a generator. You'll learn more about how this creates electricity in lesson 12. Just know that when you see a dam, people in the area are probably getting their electricity from it.

All over the United States, you can find hydroelectric dams that are producing electricity for thousands of people. These dams generate quite a bit of electricity, but not as much as coal or nuclear energy. Water coming down the river is renewable energy because it just keeps flowing. It's also clean energy because it doesn't release chemicals into the air.

However, sometimes it's not clean for the river. Hydropower plants typically cause the water quality in the river to be poor because they sometimes reduce the natural flow of the river. This can harm the fish and wildlife in the area. In addition, many communities don't want huge dams built on their rivers. However, sometimes the new lakes become very popular recreational spots. If a dam breaks, homes constructed along the river below get flooded. Although hydropower has some problems, it's probably the cleanest source of energy in the world with the fewest drawbacks.

Located on the border between Nevada and Arizona, Hoover Dam is one of our country's largest hydroelectric power facilities. It produces four billion kilowatts of electricity a year.

Wind Energy

As you already know, wind is moving air. Scientists have found a way to turn this moving air into electricity. Here's how it works: The wind turns huge blades called turbines. These gigantic turbines act like motors that create a little bit of electricity. If you add a lot of turbines, you can get more electricity. Although one regular-sized turbine won't power a home, three or more could. To power a community with thousands of homes, you would need several thousand wind turbines. Wind farms are places where thousands of wind turbines are built to power a community. As you can imagine, it takes a lot of land to build a wind farm. Texas and California have the highest number of wind farms in the United States.

These wind turbines are acting like motors, creating electricity people can use.

Wind is definitely renewable, and it doesn't produce any waste products or chemicals. However, there are many serious problems with this source of electricity. These enormous turbines don't generate much electricity compared to other sources of renewable energy; they can't compete with coal, gas, and nuclear energy.

Offshore turbines like the ones above are located in the middle of the ocean.

In addition, wind turbines require a constant flow of wind, which isn't available in most places. If the wind stops, so does the power. That's not very reliable. Although wind energy is considered clean energy, like hydropower, it's not great for the environment. Let's find out why.

First, these huge wind turbines change the natural beauty of the environment. Because a large amount of land has to be cleared to create a wind farm, many animals suffer the loss of their habitats. People have reported the disappearance of deer, bears, turkeys and other wildlife that once populated an area after a wind turbine was constructed. Perhaps these animals relocated to other areas to escape the noise. You see, the turbines are extremely loud, causing a great deal of noise pollution. People are also affected by the noise, preferring to stay away from areas where wind turbines are running. A study done in Australia showed that people living near wind turbines were harmed by the low-frequency noises the turbines produce. This constant noise may have caused problems such as difficulty sleeping, headaches, nausea, stress, irritability, and a poor ability to concentrate. These issues can lead to a reduced immunity to illness, resulting in more serious health concerns. This condition is called Wind Turbine Syndrome.

Birds and bats are often affected most by wind turbines. It was reported that within one month, thousands of bats were killed after the construction of wind turbines in one area. These kinds of animal deaths have occurred at many wind farms. Preserving the bat population is important because it keeps our insect population under control. If we disrupt one species of animal, we can potentially affect hundreds of other species. Birds commonly get injured when they fly through wind turbines. Many birds are killed every year because of these turbines. In fact, it's been suggested turbines should never be built near coastlines where birds fly on their migration routes. Sadly, this is exactly where many wind farms are constructed. Birds of prey—such as falcons, hawks, and eagles—are greatly threatened by the construction of wind farms. Clearing land to create wind farms draws small animals and rodents into the area—as well as birds of prey. The birds use the wind turbines as places to perch and are often killed flying toward them or away from them.

In addition to these problems, it's extremely expensive to build these turbines. Because they produce such a small amount of electricity and have such a negative impact on land and wildlife, it doesn't make sense to spend so much money to construct wind turbines. As you've learned, wind power is not necessarily a great solution to our energy problems.

Explain what you've learned so far about renewable energy, hydropower, and wind power. See if you can remember the problems associated with these energy sources.

The sun's heat provides much of the energy we use here on earth.

Solar Energy

"Solar" means sun. So it's easy to understand that **solar energy** is energy from the sun. Did you know that most of the energy we use is solar energy? The plants and animals that were buried long ago stored energy that originally came from the sun. When we burn those fossil fuels, we're actually releasing that stored energy. When we burn wood, we release the energy of the sun stored in the wood. Can you think of other examples of energy we use that originally came from the sun?

The sun has always been our main source of energy. Scientists have discovered a way to create energy by collecting the sun's energy! They do this by using solar collectors or solar panels.

There are two kinds of solar panels: solar thermal collectors and solar cells. Let's take a look at them.

Solar thermal collectors are designed to collect the sun's heat, piping it into homes and buildings. They're usually large, flat plates. You've probably seen them before. They're typically rectangular-shaped, blue plates placed on the roofs of buildings and homes. Each plate is designed with a black, metal plate on the bottom. This black plate absorbs heat from the sun, warming the water or air inside the pipes that run through the blue plates. The warmed water or air is then sent into a building or home, providing heat for the people inside. Since water heating is a big part of a home's power bill, this is an inexpensive solution for people's heating needs. However, these panels are very expensive.

Solar cells are another kind of solar panel. **Solar cells** are thin plates that turn solar energy directly into electricity. These thin plates are made of earth elements that conduct electricity, like silicon. We call these elements semiconductors because they can move electricity really well. What happens is this: When the photons from the sun hit the silicon, they excite the electrons in the silicon. These excited electrons create electricity. The electricity then begins flowing. You don't need a huge solar cell to get the electricity flowing. Even some calculators are powered by tiny solar cells. Several larger solar cells put together can give electricity to an entire home.

The positive side of solar energy is that it's free once you've paid for the equipment. It's also clean because it doesn't pollute the environment. Solar energy can be stored, so you don't lose it if it's not used right away. And, of course, it's renewable; it's not a resource that will run out.

The negative side of solar energy is that the equipment is extremely expensive. It usually takes a family several years to pay for the cost of solar panels. The panels are also large and take up a lot of room. Most people find them unattractive on homes. In fact, many cities and neighborhoods don't allow panels to be installed on the roofs of homes in the area because

The solar panels being installed on the roof of this house will turn the sun's energy into electricity.

The Hubble Space Telescope uses solar panels for energy.

141

they aren't nice to look at. But the most important problem with solar energy is that it requires sunshine, which isn't always reliable. If there are several days of overcast skies, you'll need a backup source of energy.

Here's an example. My uncle uses solar energy to heat his swimming pool. He built the entire system himself. The system works beautifully and gives him a nice, warm pool—even in the winter. The sun shines on the solar panels on his roof, heating the water pipes in the panels. These pipes run down under the ground into a tank and are sent into the pool. He enjoys a wonderfully heated pool free! However, trees growing over the panels have recently blocked the sunlight. His system isn't working as well as it did before. Once he cuts the trees back, he can enjoy his heated pool again.

These solar panels will create a lot of electricity to power many different things.

Solar energy can be used to power a wide range of things, from cars to homes to satellites. To create solar energy for a community, companies clear large areas of land to install hundreds or thousands of solar panels. Although solar panels take up a lot of land, they produce a great deal more electricity than wind turbines, and they don't hurt the wildlife in the area.

Solar thermal panels are often coated with black paint. Let's do an experiment to see how helpful that is when building a solar water heating system.

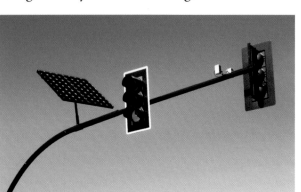
Solar energy is powering these traffic lights!

Try This!

You will need: An adult's supervision, 2 shoe boxes (one box should have a white interior and light-colored exterior), 2 water bottles, a thermometer, and black paint.

To begin, paint the inside and outside of the nonwhite box black. Let the paint dry. Next, put a water bottle in both the painted and unpainted box. Place the boxes side by side in a sunny location outside. After about an hour, test the temperature of each water bottle. Was there a significant difference in the temperatures?

The color black absorbs all the light from the sun. Because of this, the water bottle in the black box was able to absorb more of the sun's energy than the water bottle in the white box. That's why you discovered a difference in the temperatures of the water. The color white reflects the sun, while the color black absorbs it.

Explain what you've learned about solar energy.

There are three additional kinds of renewable energy sources that scientists are hoping to use more in the future: biofuels, geothermal energy, and hydrogen power. Let's take a look at them.

Biofuels

"Bio" means life. **Biofuels** are energy types that come from living things. Corn and sugarcane are often grown to create these special fuels. They produce a fuel called ethanol, which is a kind of alcohol that can be burned and made into energy.

Ethanol is a type of fuel produced by corn. It can be burned and made into energy.

Although the crops are renewable because they grow back quickly after being harvested (and they burn much more cleanly than other fuels), massive areas of land must be cleared to produce this fuel.

Geothermal Energy

Do you know how hot the center of the earth is? It's over 10,000°F! If we could find a way to get that heat from way down there to way up here, we'd have a great source of renewable energy. People are actually doing this! There are some places on the earth where the heat from inside the earth travels close to the surface. These places produce hot water that boils on the surface, called geysers and hot springs. People build structures over the hot springs because they create steam that can turn turbines and make electricity. This type of energy is called geothermal energy. In Iceland, geothermal energy provides heating and hot water for about 90% of homes. Geothermal energy can also be used to heat buildings directly by channeling the hot water through pipes into the buildings.

This geothermal power station in Iceland delivers around 1,800 liters (480 gallons) of water per second, servicing the hot water needs of people in the area.

Even though hot springs are great sources of clean, renewable energy, geothermal energy does have some problems. There aren't many of these hot springs and geysers around. So this kind of energy is only available to a few people in a few areas. Some companies have drilled deep into the earth and have found hot spots. They try to pump the water up to the surface to create steam. But the hot spots are often too deep, and the companies aren't able to bring up enough steam to turn a turbine. So although geothermal energy is beneficial for some, it's not a great solution for our energy needs.

Hydrogen

The last renewable source of energy we'll discuss is hydrogen. Hydrogen is pretty abundant. In fact, 90% of all atoms in the universe are hydrogen. But on earth, hydrogen is usually found combined with other compounds. The trick is to separate the hydrogen from the other elements and capture it. Separating atoms within molecules takes a lot of energy. So energy has to be used to get the hydrogen separated. Right now, we don't have an easy, inexpensive way of separating hydrogen and storing it. However, when hydrogen is separated and used for energy, it creates a lot of energy that doesn't produce any waste products—so it's very clean.

This image shows one of the main engines of a space shuttle. The engine is powered by liquid hydrogen and oxygen.

If we were to separate the hydrogen from the oxygen molecule in water and burn it to create energy, would it still be considered renewable energy? That's a question to think about. Whether it's renewable or not, scientists are working on ways to make hydrogen easier to get and store. It could be the energy of the future!

Final Matters

God thought about a lot of things when He made the world. He knew that one day, we would need the fossil fuels from the great Flood. He planned for that in advance. God knows everything that will happen and how it will all work out. We can trust God to take care of our needs, whether those needs are food, shelter, clothing, or even energy. We don't have to worry because He has a plan to bless us and take care of us!

What Do You Remember?

What is energy? What is kinetic energy? What is potential energy? What is the law of conservation of energy? What are some forms of energy that come from animals and plants buried long ago? What kind of energy is found in the nucleus of an atom? What is renewable energy? Name some forms of renewable energy and the problems associated with each.

Notebooking Activities

After you've recorded all the fascinating facts you've learned about energy, do the following activity.

Have you ever read the newspaper? If so, you may have seen letters people have written to the editor of the newspaper. These letters cover a range of topics that are important to people. They express opinions, give feedback on other articles, and inform the public of important issues. To begin this notebooking activity, read some letters written to the editor of your local newspaper. Then compose your own letter to the editor! This letter should address a topic you've learned about in this lesson. You can choose to write a letter about coal, nuclear energy, renewable energy, wind power, or any other energy topic. Your letter should be about two or three paragraphs long. Be sure to mention your age in the letter. Even if you choose not to send your letter, taking the time to write out your opinion is a good exercise.

If you do choose to send your letter, be sure to find out if there are any guidelines you should follow. Include your name, address, e-mail address, and phone number at the top of your letter. If you'd like to remain anonymous, you may want to add at the end of your letter: "Please note: I do not want my full name to be published with this letter." You never know. Your letter may even be published in the newspaper!

Experiment
Strike it Rich!

In this experiment, you're going to create a model of the earth with oil reservoirs in it. You'll be given $800 million to begin your exploration. If you strike oil, you'll earn another $800 million. If you hit a dry hole, you'll be out $100 million. This should be fun, so let's get started!

You will need:

- 6–10 eggs
- a shoe box
- enough sand to fill the shoe box about half way
- aluminum foil
- a bamboo skewer
- baking soda
- vinegar
- black powder paint
- a small funnel
- a plastic cup

1. Have an adult crack the tips of the eggs. Now peel back the shell to form a small hole. Empty out the contents of the eggs and wash out the shells. To sterilize the shells, heat them in the microwave for 2 minutes.
2. Fill each eggshell with 2 tablespoons of baking soda and 1 teaspoon of black powder paint. These are your oil reservoirs. They'll be buried in your earth model shoebox.
3. Pour a small bit of sand in the shoebox and position the eggs in different locations in the box. Now pour the rest of the sand around the eggs—enough to cover them to the top of the opening of each egg. The eggs should be almost completely buried, with the openings visible from the surface.
4. Make a map of where each oil reservoir is located by drawing a rectangle and putting an X in the location of each reservoir. If you wish, you can have a sibling or parent create the model and map so you don't know where the oil reservoirs are. However, it's often difficult to remember where the reservoirs are even with the map.

5. Cut a piece of aluminum foil the exact size of your box. Place it over your eggs and add sand. Pour a bit more sand on top of the foil, just enough to cover the foil.
6. It's time to begin drilling! First, make a chart for each person who will be drilling. Everyone begins with eight points, which equals $800 million.
7. Pour vinegar into the cup. This will serve as the water you'll use to force the oil up to the surface.
8. Study the map. Before you begin drilling, subtract one point from your chart for the $100 million you'll spend drilling the well.
9. Using your bamboo skewer, choose a location to begin drilling.
10. Insert your skewer into the sand. Make a hole just big enough for the funnel to fit inside. Pour about ¼ cup of vinegar into the funnel. If black oil bubbles up, you've struck oil and are now $800 million richer! Add eight points to your chart. If you don't have a gusher of black oil, you have a dry hole. The next person should now take his or her turn to drill. If you're the only person doing the experiment, have an adult drill the wells with you. Do this until you've located all the wells or have run out of money.

Sound of Energy

When you read the first chapter of Genesis, you find one form of energy mentioned right away. Let's read it and see if you can identify the first energy form mentioned: "Now the earth was formless and empty, darkness was over the surface of the deep, and the Spirit of God was hovering over the waters. And God said, 'Let there be light,' and there was light" (Genesis 1:2–3).

What form of energy do we read about after God was hovering over the waters? You may have said light. Yet before God created light, He did something else. He spoke! Speaking makes sounds, and sound is energy. What do you think it sounded like when God spoke? Well, the Bible talks about God's voice:

The voice of the LORD is upon the waters;
The God of glory thunders,
The LORD is over many waters.
The voice of the LORD is powerful,
The voice of the LORD is majestic.
The voice of the LORD breaks the cedars;
Yes, the LORD breaks in pieces the cedars of Lebanon. (Psalm 29:3–5, NASB)

The Bible also tells us many times that the voice of the Lord thunders. You've probably heard thunder before. Its sound shakes the earth and rattles our houses.

Have you ever wondered why thunder rattles your windows and shakes your house? How can sound rattle and shake things? If you know what *causes* sound, then you'll know the answer. Let's explore this form of energy together.

Sound Essentials

First, we need to understand what sound is. To put it simply, **sound** is a vibration. Put your hand to your throat and hum a little tune.

Do you feel the vibration? Well, that's what sound is: It's a vibration. The vibration flows out from your vocal cords and hits against the nearby air molecules, vibrating the air around you. In the same way, the sound of thunder vibrates the molecules in the air. These vibrating molecules may eventually rattle your windows. Sound flows out from its source in waves. It's a lot like when you drop a pebble into a pond. Have you ever done that? It's pretty amazing to see the waves span out in all directions, growing wider and farther apart as the waves move on until they finally die out.

Try This!

You will need: An adult's supervision, a large casserole dish, water, and several pieces of Cheerios cereal.

First, fill your dish a little over halfway with water. Now drop a piece of cereal into the center of the dish and watch to see what happens. Try another piece of cereal and watch again. Did you see the waves in the water travel out from the center of the dish where you dropped your cereal? This is very similar to how sound travels!

Did you notice how the waves you created spread out from the place where they began? They got farther apart and less pronounced as they spread out. It's easy to see this in the picture below. This is very similar to how sound waves travel. You may remember that air and water are very similar—both are filled with matter. By looking at the waves in the water, you can understand how sound waves travel in vibrations through the air.

Any sound you hear is just an invisible vibration traveling through the air hitting against air molecules. As you know, when you speak, your vocal cords vibrate. They are the source of the sound of your voice. The vibration created by your vocal cords vibrates air molecules. These molecules pass the vibration from one air molecule to another. This moving vibration is the **sound wave**. If the sound wave happens to hit someone's ear, it will vibrate his eardrum, and he'll hear the sound produced by the sound wave. If the person is really close, the sound will be very clear and loud. If he's really far away, the sound will be faint. Just remember this: The vibration of your vocal cords makes the air molecules around you move. This creates a very special sound wave known as your voice.

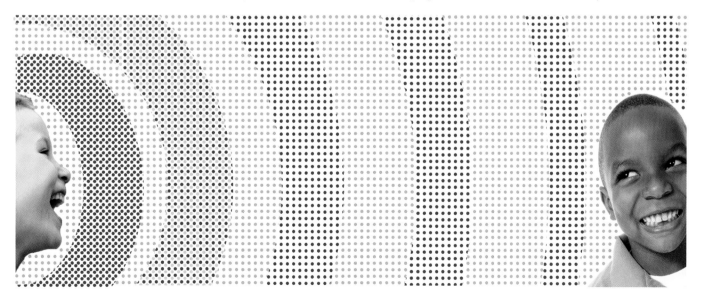

Each person's voice and every other sound moves the air differently. This is what makes all the different sounds we hear. Look at the recording of sound waves on the right. Each wave represents the sound of a different instrument. You can see they all vibrate in different patterns to make different sounds.

Let's get back to the air and water example we talked about. Do you remember learning about solids, gases, and liquids in lesson 2? Let's do a quick review to help you understand more about sound. Both gas and liquid matter can be pushed and moved. We can see water moving, but we don't really see air moving. However, air molecules *do* move. They get jostled as we walk by. When something causes a vibration, the air molecules start moving.

Because air is invisible, sometimes it's hard to remember that it is actually matter. Remember the experiment you did in lesson 2 when you put paper in a cup and turned the cup upside down in water? The water didn't go all the way up into the cup because air is matter and matter takes up space. So the air inside the cup stopped the water from going all the way up into the cup and touching the paper. As a result, the paper stayed dry!

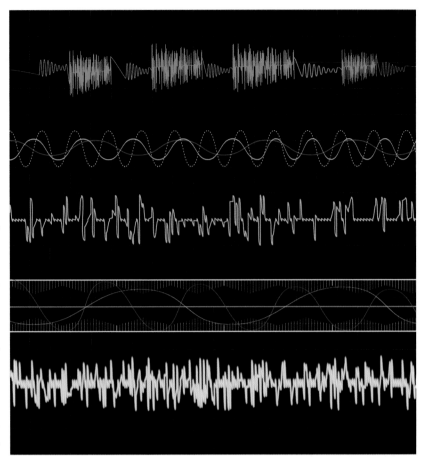

When musicians capture or create music, the vibrations look like this in the computer file. Each vibration wave is a different sound.

It's this same matter that moves when we make a sound. When something makes a sound—like a book dropping on the floor—the energy from that sound pushes against the air, jiggling it. The bigger the book and the harder the floor it hits, the bigger the jiggle. This jiggling creates the vibration as the matter in the air gets pushed. This push then makes a push on the matter next to it, which pushes the matter next to it. It goes on and on, creating a wave of matter. Of course, the matter closest to the object gets pushed the most, and the wave is strongest next to the source of the sound. A stronger wave makes a louder sound.

Try This!

You will need: An adult's supervision, a set of dominoes, and a flat surface.

Stand up the dominoes in a line, one behind the other. Make sure the dominoes are close enough to each other to touch when they fall forward but far enough apart that you can see the dominoes fall into each other. Now tip over the first domino in the line. Watch to see what happens!

The falling dominoes created a chain reaction—a series of changes. When one thing changes, it causes another thing to change, which causes another thing to change, and so on. This is what happens when a sound is made. The vibrating sound moves the air molecules next to it. Then those molecules move the air molecules next to them, and so on.

Let's create a sound cannon that will enable you to actually see the vibrations of sound on water.

Try This!

You will need: An adult's supervision, a long cardboard tube (such as a gift wrapping paper tube), a balloon, a rubber band, paper, tape, scissors, a baking dish, a candle, a lighter, and some water.

First, cut off the long, skinny end of the balloon. Stretch it over one end of the cardboard tube, making sure it's tight. Now secure it with the rubber band. Next, make a cone out of the piece of paper. Be sure there's a small opening at the narrow end of the cone. Tape the wide end of the cone over the other end of the tube. Now fill the baking dish with water. Point the end of the cone toward the water and snap your finger very, very close to the other end of the cannon (the end with the balloon attached). What happens to the water? Talk into the end with the balloon; talk softly and loudly. What happens to the water then? Experiment with different noises. Finally, have an adult help you light the candle. Point your sound cannon toward the flame. Now tap the balloon with your finger. What happens?

The sound cannon created enough energy to make ripples in the water and blow out the candle. Now let's see if you can direct sound energy through a tube that's even longer.

Try This!

You will need: An adult's supervision, a long garden hose, and a partner.

To begin, shake any water out of the garden hose. Next, have your partner hold one end of the hose while you hold the other end. Now you and your partner stand far away from each other, stretching out the hose completely. Hold your ear to the end of the hose while your partner speaks to you through the other end. Then you speak while your partner listens. How does it sound?

What happened? Why were you able to hear your partner? The reason is that the sound waves traveled through the garden hose until they reached your ear. Unless something like water was in the hose to stop the sound, you could hear your partner from a long distance. The hose prevents the sound energy from being spread out.

Explain to someone all that you've learned today about sound. If you're taking a break, record in your notebooking journal what you did and learned.

3-D Dynamics

It's important to understand that sound waves don't just flow along a flat plane the way the water waves and dominoes did in the experiments. When a sound is made, the sound waves fill the entire space in three dimensions. They go up; they go down; they go forward and backward. They make a round wave, spreading out from the source.

Imagine sound waves as you snap your fingers. First, snap your fingers right next to your ear. Now snap your fingers far away from your body. Finally, snap your fingers with your hand under a table and your face far above the table.

Were you able to imagine the waves coming from your fingers as you snapped them? Why did the snapping sound different when you changed the location of your fingers?

As you noticed, the air molecules closest to the source of the sound moved the most and made the loudest sound. The air molecules farther from the source weren't moving with as much power and sounded a lot quieter. The sound energy was spread over a wider area, so there was less sound to detect.

You probably realize that sound waves keep moving outward unless something blocks them. For example, when you put your fingers under the table, the table blocked some of the waves, and the sound was quieter. However, you'll find out in a minute that sound does travel through objects like tables, walls, doors, and windows.

Cheerleaders use megaphones to increase the sound of their voices. This helps the players and fans far away hear their encouragement.

Directing Waves

Have you ever seen someone use a megaphone? A megaphone is a funnel-shaped device designed to direct sound from its source to a certain area. It makes the sound louder for those who are receiving it. You can control the direction of sound using devices like these.

If you cup your hands over your mouth, you can make a miniature megaphone, enabling the sound waves to be sent in a specific direction. People often do this so that the hearer can easily make out their words.

Let's make a megaphone to direct sound!

Try This!

You will need: An adult's supervision, a piece of thick paper (like card stock), tape, and a partner.

Roll the paper into a megaphone shape and tape it together. You and your partner are going to take turns speaking to each other across the room through the megaphone. First, say something without the megaphone. Now, using the megaphone, say the same thing. Was the sound louder? Try directing the sound in different areas. How does the megaphone affect the sound of your voices?

Echoes

Have you ever heard your echo? If you've ever had a bad phone connection, you probably heard your voice shortly after you spoke. That's an echo. An **echo** is a sound you hear a second time—very soon after you hear it the first time. It's basically a sound bouncing back and returning to its source. It's kind of like throwing a rubber ball at the wall; it bounces right back at you. An echo is a reflected sound. You can actually use an echo to measure the speed of sound.

Conductor of Sound

The sounds we hear usually travel right through the air around us, hitting our ears. The air conducts the sound to our ears. To **conduct** means to lead something from one place to another, like a conductor on a train. But did you know that a gas, like air, is not the only phase of matter that conducts sound? Sound can travel through liquids and solids as well!

I remember when I first discovered that sound could travel through water. I was a young child, swimming with my brother in the pool. We both went under the water and looked at each other, and then he spoke. I was astonished that I could hear him! We spent the rest of the summer trying to find out how far away we could be from each other and still hear one another's voice. We also played guessing games to see if we could figure out what the other person was saying. We didn't even know we were doing a physics experiment!

Which of the three phases of matter is the best conductor of sound: a gas, a liquid, or a solid?

Consider this interesting tidbit from history: Many years ago, Native Americans would put their ear to the ground to listen for herds of buffalo in the distance. Amazingly, the buffalo could be heard from

Because liquid is a conductor of sound, these children will be able to hear one another speak underwater.

hundreds of miles away! Also, in early American history, people could put their ear to a train track and know if a train was near. The train could have been miles and miles away, but it could be detected with an ear pressed to the solid track. At certain depths of the ocean, whales can hear other whales communicating with them from thousands of miles away—practically on the other side of the world! Through the air, you could never hear buffalo or trains hundreds of miles away, nor could you hear an animal on the other side of the world. I hope you've figured out that gas is not the best conductor of sound.

Whales are able to hear one another from thousands of miles away because the ocean is a good conductor of sound.

Although it would be easy for me to tell you which materials sound travels through best, I think it would be more fun if you could figure it out for yourself. But before you do, I want you to make your best guess. Look at the images below to remember how molecules are organized in each phase of matter. Then try to determine which organization of molecules will help sound travel most easily from one molecule to the next.

Solid

Liquid

Gas

Did you figure it out after looking at the images of the three states of matter? Let's do an experiment to help you further understand how well sound travels through a gas, a liquid, and a solid.

Try This!

You will need: An adult's supervision, a partner, 2 metal spoons, a Sheetrock wall, a car hood, a large container filled with water (such as a plastic bucket or aquarium), and a wooden table.

First, let's see how well sound travels through air. Hold a spoon in each hand and make a sound by hitting one spoon against the other. Listen to the sound by hitting the spoons in the air in front of you. What do you hear? Now let's see how well sound travels through a solid Sheetrock wall. Place your ear on the wall and, with your hands stretched out in front of you, put one spoon on the wall and hit it with the other spoon. Did you hear a sound? Was it loud? Now do the same test on the hood of a car. Be careful not to scratch the car with your spoon! Hold your hands the same distance away as you did on the wall and tap the spoon against the spoon resting against the car. Finally, let's see how well sound travels through water. You'll need a partner for this. Put your ear on the large container filled with water. Now have your partner hit the spoons together under the water. Was the sound louder than when you hit the spoons in the air? Finally, try this activity on a wooden table.

Which material conducted sound the best? If you were able to do the water experiment, you realized that sound travels well through water. Hopefully, though, you discovered that sound travels *best* through solids. The sound was much louder traveling through the metal car hood than the Sheetrock wall, wasn't it?

This car's metal hood conducts sound better than most other things.

Why does sound travel best through solids? Most solid objects have molecules that are close together. This makes it easier to move the sound vibration along. Think about how much more difficult it is to vibrate molecules that are farther away. Gas molecules are much farther away from one another than are solid molecules. Liquid molecules are in between. So you can see why sound vibrations travel better through solids. Depending on how the solid molecules are organized, some solids conduct sound better than others. The atoms in metal make a much louder sound than the atoms in wood because they're stiffer and more tightly packed. Metals are better conductors of sound than most other things. That's why telephone wires are made of metal!

Stiffer materials pass on vibrations better from molecule to molecule. Solids are stiffer than liquids, which are denser than gases. Metals are stiffer than wood, so they conduct better. If something conducts sound better, it also speeds the delivery of the sound. That means sound is not only traveling better from molecule to molecule, but it's also traveling faster! Let's talk a little more about the speed of sound.

Explain to someone what you've learned so far about sound.

Speedy Sound

As you probably know, the speed at which sound travels changes depending on what the sound is traveling through. You learned that metal conducts sound better than Sheetrock. Look at the chart on the next page to see how fast some things conduct sound compared to other things.

The Speed of Sound in Meters per Second (m/s)*

Gases at 32°F or 0°C	Liquids at 68°F or 20°C	Solids
Air 331	Chloroform 1,904	Aluminum 5,100
Air (68°F or 20°C) 343	Ethyl alcohol 1,162	Copper 3,560
Carbon dioxide 259	Fresh water 1,482	Diamond 12,000
Helium 972	Mercury 1,450	Gold 3,240
Hydrogen 1,268	Seawater 1,522	Iron 5,130

*To work out miles per hour, multiply these figures by 2.237.

What did you learn by studying the chart? Did you notice that copper conducts sound better than gold? Aluminum is an even better conductor because it's less dense. This allows the molecules to jiggle a little more freely. Iron is even better because it's stiffer. Stiffer materials make sound travel faster. The more spongy or soft a material is, the less it's able to transfer sound waves.

Which solid transmits sound the best? Diamonds! Why do you think that is? Diamonds increase the speed of sound because they have a low density but a high **stiffness**. Of course they have a high **stiffness**—they're the hardest natural substance in the entire world!

Consider helium. Sound travels a lot faster through helium than through air (which is mostly nitrogen and oxygen). Perhaps you've breathed in the helium from a helium balloon. What happens to your voice? It becomes extremely high and very silly sounding, doesn't it? That's because even though the wavelength of your voice is the same, it's traveling at a higher speed. That makes the frequency higher. So you hear your voice at a higher pitch. On a side note, when you breathe in helium, you're not breathing in oxygen. This isn't good for you; your body needs a constant supply of oxygen to survive. Breathing in pure helium is like holding your breath; you would probably pass out from a lack of oxygen if you did this too much.

Do you think sound travels faster in warm temperatures or cold temperatures? Think about the molecules again. Which are most active? Now look at the chart again and look at air. It's mentioned twice—once at a very cold temperature and once at a warmer temperature. Which one conducts sound faster? Can you guess why sound travels faster in warm air? The reason is that the molecules in warm temperatures are full of energy, while the molecules in cool temperatures are sluggish and slow.

These telephone wires conduct electrical impulses that are converted into sound waves.

Look at the difference between sound travel in air and in seawater. Sound travels almost five times faster through seawater than it does through air. If someone dropped an anchor in the water from a boat, who would hear the sound first—the person who dropped the anchor from 10 meters above the water or a diver who was 10 meters below the water? Of course the diver would!

This U.S. Marine Corps F/A-18 Hornet has a top speed above Mach 1.

153

The speed of sound in seawater gives us a good clue why whales can hear other whales so far away at certain ocean depths. Seawater carries sound well.

Measuring Mach

The ThrustSSC (Supersonic Car) was the first land vehicle to break the sound barrier, carrying passengers at 763 mph.

People often ask, "What is the *exact* speed of sound?" There isn't an easy answer. Usually what people are really asking is, "What is the speed of sound through air?" If we were measuring the speed of sound in miles and hours, we would say sound travels at 760 miles per hour. This speed is called **Mach 1**. If anything travels faster than 760 miles per hour, we say it travels at a **supersonic speed**. We also might say it broke the sound barrier. That means the object traveled faster than the speed of the sound. If something travels twice as fast as the speed of sound, we would call it Mach 2. Three times the speed of sound would be Mach 3, and so on.

In 1947, an American fighter pilot named Chuck Yeager wanted to be the first person to fly a plane faster than the speed of sound and break the sound barrier. He realized that sound travels more slowly in colder temperatures. And he knew that the higher you go in the sky, the colder it gets. So he flew his plane 13,700 meters (45,000 feet) above the ground and managed to reach the speed of Mach 1.06 (361 m/s or 807.2 mph). Since then, many people have created machines that can travel faster than the speed of sound.

When anything travels at or faster than the speed of sound, it won't sound like a regular moving object to the person it passes. That's because it's going faster than the speed of sound; the sounds coming from it don't travel in a normal pattern to our ears. When it passes by, all we hear is a big boom—like an explosion. We call it a **sonic boom**. Sonic booms come from all objects traveling faster than the speed of sound. If you've ever heard a gunshot from a very powerful gun, you may have heard a sonic boom. Some bullets travel faster than the speed of sound and make a sonic boom sound when they're shot out of the barrel. A warplane can also travel faster than the speed of sound. A warplane's sonic boom is much louder than the sonic boom from a speeding bullet; the warplane is bigger and is moving more air particles with more intensity and force.

You may be wondering why some bullets and warplanes produce a boom rather than their normal sounds. Here's why. When the object passes through the air, it creates sound waves in front of it and behind it. These waves all travel at the speed of sound. However, because the object is traveling *faster* than sound, the sound waves are forced together or compressed. That's because they can't get out of the way of each other. This causes them to combine into one single sound wave that's more like a shock wave. This shock wave starts at the front of the plane or bullet and ends at the back.

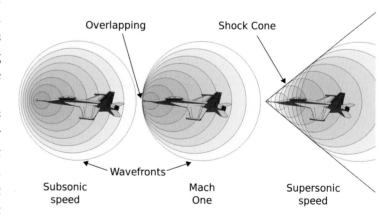

The first image shows a warplane flying slower than the speed of sound. You can see the normal sound waves coming from the plane. When the plane flies at Mach 1, you can see an overlapping group of sound waves, creating a boom-like sound at the point where the sound waves overlap. The third image shows the plane flying above the speed of sound, at a supersonic speed. This causes many overlapping sound waves, creating several boom sounds as the plane passes by and as several sound waves crash into one another.

Bullwhip Boom

Planes, cars, and bullets aren't the first man-made items that travel faster than Mach 1. In fact, an item made thousands of years ago, called a bullwhip (yes, for whipping bulls), can produce a sonic boom. When someone swings the whip in just the right way, it makes a loud cracking sound at the tip. It creates a small sonic boom because the whip is traveling faster than the speed of sound!

Explain what you've learned so far about the speed of sound.

Loud Waves

Have you ever been to the beach? When our family arrives at the beach, the first thing we do is check to see how big the waves are. If the waves are big, we grab our surfboards and head out to ride them. Have you noticed that when the ocean waves are big, they're very loud? The bigger they are, the louder they are.

It's the same with sound waves. When something makes a loud sound, the sound waves it makes are really high and tall. The height of a wave is called the amplitude. This is easy to remember because an amplifier is something we plug a musical instrument into to make the sound fill the room. The amplifier makes the instrument louder.

Study the waves in this picture to understand high and low amplitude.

This amplifier amplifies the sound of the guitar, allowing others to hear it from a greater distance.

Higher amplitude
Louder sound

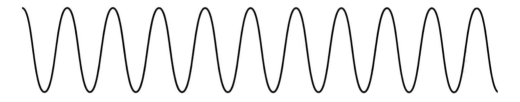

Lower amplitude
Softer sound

As you can see from the image, a large wave has a high amplitude, and a small wave has a low amplitude. It's pretty easy to see which one is louder. Would you rather listen to music at a high amplitude or a low amplitude? If you listen to something with an amplitude that's too high, the big and intense sound wave can damage your eardrum.

When we measure how loud or soft a sound is, we use a measurement called decibels. If the sound is loud, it has a lot of energy and also a high decibel count. Study the chart on the next page to see the decibel counts of common sounds you may hear each day. What sound do you hear around you right now? About how many decibels do you think that sound is? For every 10 decibels a sound increases, the sound is 10 times louder.

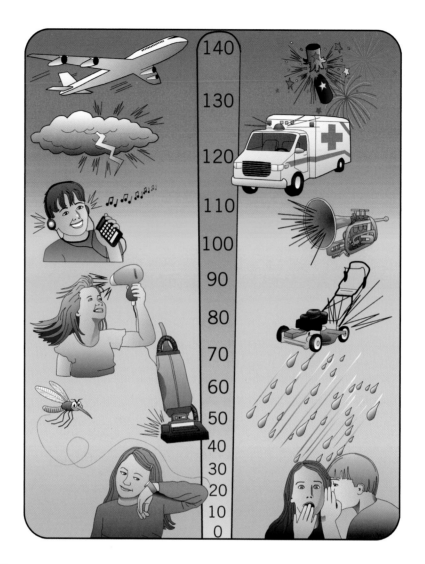

Frequent Frequency

There's something else you need to know about sound waves to really understand how they work and how they're measured. Have you ever heard of sound frequency? The distance between each wave, or the frequency of the waves, also affects the sound that hits your ear. Let's explore frequency.

Do you know what the word "frequency" means? Here's an illustration to help you understand: How often do you eat? How often do you brush your teeth? If you eat a lot but rarely brush your teeth, then you eat with high frequency and you brush your teeth with low frequency. Being a high-frequency tooth-brusher will probably make your parents happy. Being a high-frequency eater may not.

Let's put a high-frequency eater/low-frequency brusher child on a chart.

Eating frequency

Tooth-brushing
frequency

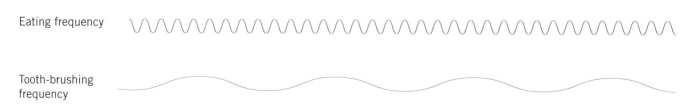

One week

If you examine the chart, every time a wave goes up, the child has completed the eating or tooth-brushing behavior. This chart spans one week. As you can see, the child is eating with a lot more frequency than he is brushing his teeth. In fact, in one week, the child has only brushed his teeth four times—but he's eaten 33 times! He'll likely need to visit a dentist soon to fill the holes in his teeth. I hope you brush your teeth two or three times a day as dentists recommend. That way, you'll be sure to keep the bacteria in your mouth from making holes in your teeth.

Let's get back to this concept of frequency. There's high frequency and low frequency in sound. We're going to explore both.

Measuring Frequency

We measure frequency using hertz. This measurement is named after Heinrich Hertz, a German physicist who first detected radio waves. To understand hertz, just remember that a sound that produces 20,000 waves per second is actually 20,000 hertz. We'd say it's 20,000Hz, or 20 kHz (kilohertz).

Low Frequency

As you know, a sound wave with a low frequency goes up and down less frequently. This sound is very low to our ears. A sound that's 20 hertz or lower (making 20 waves or fewer in a second) is too low for our ears to hear. If a sound is too low for our ears to hear, we call it an **infrasound.** We call the vibration it makes infrasonic.

Many animals use infrasound to communicate over long distances. We mentioned earlier that whales can communicate with other whales more than a thousand miles away. The frequency of their sounds is too low for our ears to hear. Scientists have to use special equipment to hear their sounds. Elephants communicate over long distances using infrasound as well. Instead of traveling through water, their sound waves travel through solid ground. These waves are sensed by other herds of elephants far away—right through their feet! Other animals that use infrasonic vibrations to communicate are hippos, rhinos, giraffes, and alligators.

Elephants communicate using low-frequency sounds. These infrasounds are too low for human ears to hear. (Photo: Muhammad Mahdi Karim.)

Almost every animal can sense infrasonic waves moving through the earth during natural disasters. You may remember the tsunami that hit Sri Lanka in 2004. Many of the animals in the area had already moved to higher ground before the wave hit. Most scientists believe it was the ability to sense these low frequencies that kept these animals safe.

Dogs and cats can hear high-frequency sounds that are too high pitched for human ears.

High Frequency

If a sound wave has a high frequency, that means the wave goes up and down a lot of times in a short period of time. This makes a high-pitched sound. The more waves, the higher the sound. If a sound has a wave that goes up and down more than 20,000 times in a second, it's too high for our ears to hear. We call that an **ultrasound**—making an ultrasonic vibration.

Have you ever been in the same room with your cat or dog when suddenly he becomes startled for no reason? You don't hear a thing, yet all of a sudden your cat shoots up with eyes wide open and ears stretched back. Your dog becomes agitated and starts barking. It could be that your pet hears something you don't. Cats and dogs can hear sounds that are too high for humans to hear. These high-frequency noises come from machines or devices that create extremely high-pitched sound waves. To your pet, these high-pitched waves might sound like a fingernail scratching the surface of a chalkboard, a fork scraping a plate, or a whistle blowing on a playground. After all, we'd be startled if we were sitting on the couch enjoying a book when suddenly someone blew a whistle in our ear. These sounds startle animals and are probably unpleasant for them to hear.

Because of dogs' unique hearing ability, special whistles are made just for them. The owner blows the whistle, and the dog comes running. However, to all the humans around, the whistle never makes a sound! It does make a sound to the dog, however. It's just too high for us to hear.

Rhinos are able to hear extremely low-pitched sounds.

Sumatran rhinos can detect frequencies as low as 3 Hz, while beluga whales and porpoises can detect frequencies up to 123,000 and 110,000 Hz. Bats, mice, and owls can also hear extremely high-pitched sounds.

What do you think is the highest frequency *your* ears can hear? I was surprised to learn I can hear sounds only up to 14,000 Hz. What about the lowest frequency that you can hear? I can only hear sounds that are at least 200 Hz. You can go to www.apologia.com/bookextras to find a site that will test your hearing.

Normally, people lose some of their hearing as they age. Depending on whether or not they experienced ear damage from an illness or loud noise, some people can hear better than others.

Would you like to experiment with frequency? Let's do that now.

Listening to loud music with earphones or earbuds will damage your hearing. Keep the volume down to protect your hearing.

Try This!

You will need: An adult's supervision, a glass of water, and a drinking straw.

To begin, place the straw far down into the water and blow across the top of the straw so that it makes a whistling sound. Now lift the straw slightly and blow again. Lift it a bit more and blow again. Continue to lift the straw higher and higher out of the glass as you continue blowing. Make sure to keep the straw under the water each time you blow.

What did you discover in the straw experiment? Did you notice anything interesting about the sounds? You may have noticed the sound was higher when the straw was farther down in the water. As you lifted the straw out of the water, the sound got lower, didn't it?

Can you guess why this happens? When you blow on the straw, you're rattling the air molecules inside the straw. This causes them to bump against other air molecules in the straw. Then those molecules bump into other air molecules, creating a wave—a sound wave! The longer straw makes a lower sound because a longer wavelength is able to resonate or produce a deeper sound within the straw. The smaller straws can support only small wavelengths.

Let's test this in another way.

Try This!

You will need: An adult's supervision, a rubber band, a large metal can, a small metal can, a table, and a chair.

First, put the cans on the table in front of you. Sit in a chair about 3 feet back from the table and shoot the rubber band at the large can. Now shoot the rubber band at the small can, using the same amount of force you used before. What do you notice about the sounds?

Which can made the higher-pitched sound when the rubber band hit it? The small can. Why? Because the large can is able to support longer wavelengths than the small can. The small can isn't big enough for a long wavelength that's needed to make a lower-frequency sound.

Do you know what happens when a person blows air into a musical instrument? The air makes a sound as the molecules being pushed vibrate inside the instrument. What is the lowest-sounding instrument you can think of? How about a tuba? Now compare that to a small instrument like a flute. Can you explain why the flute makes a higher-pitched sound than the tuba?

A flute is an instrument that makes a high-pitched sound. A tuba is an instrument that makes a low-pitched sound.

Pitch

Did you notice I used the word "pitch"? **Pitch** is how we describe the sound we're hearing. High-frequency sounds are high-pitched sounds, and low-frequency sounds are low-pitched sounds.

The tones of the instruments in this orchestra blend together, creating a very pleasant timbre.

Sound Quality

What makes a sound pleasant or unpleasant? Why does a guitar sound so different than a piano? It all boils down to sound quality. We call the quality of a sound its **timbre**.

As you know, sounds are made by vibrations that come from a certain source. Often the source of the sound sends out vibrations in several different frequencies, not just one. This blending of different frequencies is what gives the sound its timbre. The sound coming from one particular thing is called its tone. When you speak, the sounds coming from your voice are several different frequencies blending together, giving your voice tones. Instruments have their own tones as well. Some people have voices that are uniquely designed with a lovely mix of tones. These people usually have good radio voices.

What do you consider noise? I don't like the sound of the radio between stations; it's too noisy for me. I also find it noisy when a lot of people are talking at the same time. Noise does not have a pleasing quality, and it has no particular pitch; the sounds do not blend well together. Noise is missing a clear pattern and clear pitch.

You've learned a lot about sound. You now know about amplitude, frequency, and sound quality.

Before we discover the use of sound for science, tell someone what you've learned so far.

Technology and Sound

Sound can be amazingly useful. Let's explore some of the ways scientists have used sound to help us.

Bats send out ultrasonic frequencies to navigate in the dark and find prey.

Sonar

Did you know bats send out high-frequency noises from their mouths when they fly around? It's true! They use echoes to locate food. This is how it works: The ultrasonic waves bounce off objects (such as walls, insects, or animals) and reflect back to the bats. We call this echolocation. The bats are able to find their food without ever seeing it. They can fly around in total darkness without bumping into anything. This enables them to locate prey and predators very easily. Bats aren't really blind, but they certainly could be with this God-given talent!

Scientists often study the amazing designs of God's creation so they can figure out how to create those designs themselves and use them in the world. Not surprisingly, scientists now use ultrasonic sound much like bats. Ships and submarines use high-frequency sound waves to navigate through the dark depths of the ocean. High-frequency ultrasonic waves are used in a system called **sonar**, which stands for Sound Navigation and Ranging. The ship or submarine sends a sound wave into the water. This wave then travels in a straight line until it reaches an object, which stops the wave. The wave then reflects back to the ship. The time it takes for the sound to travel to the object and back is measured by a sonar device. This helps to determine the exact depth of the object.

Sonar devices are also used by fishermen to locate schools of fish under the ocean and by geologists to find oil and minerals under the earth. Your car may even have a sonar device that tells you when you're getting too close to something when backing up.

This boat is sending down sound waves to locate fish under the water. Dolphins also use sonar.

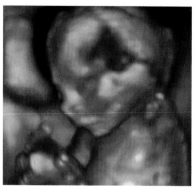

This is a 3-D ultrasound image of a four-month-old baby inside the womb.

Ultrasound

Doctors also use high-frequency sound waves for medical reasons. When you were a baby inside your mother, she probably went to the doctor. If she did, she was most likely able to see you as you developed inside her. But how? Scientists have discovered they can turn sound waves into pictures. A device called an ultrasound machine is able to do this. If your mom has a picture of you when you were inside her, ask her to show it to you. Doctors use this ultrasound machine to watch developing babies move around to see if everything is normal.

Ultrasound is also used to look at organs in the body to determine if they are healthy. Medical technicians called radiologists are trained to use these machines.

Bioacoustics

Bioacoustics is the study of sound made by wildlife. Some animals create certain calls that are like an alarm sounding, warning other animals of danger. Scientists sometimes reproduce these sounds and play them over loudspeakers at airports so that birds and other wildlife will stay clear of the area. This prevents birds from flying into airplanes that are taking off and landing at the airport.

If a Tree Falls

The question that must be answered is this: If a tree falls in the woods and no one is around to hear it fall, does it still make a sound? What do you think? We now know that sound is really a vibration that travels in waves. Let's look at how the dictionary defines sound. It gives two different definitions:

If no one were around to hear this tree fall, did it make a sound?

1. a sensation produced by stimulation of the organs of hearing by vibrations transmitted through the air or other medium
2. vibrations transmitted through a medium, traveling in air at a speed of approximately 1,087 feet (331 meters) per second at sea level

The second definition of sound says that no one needs to hear the sound for the sound to exist. From that definition, a tree falling in the woods makes a sound even if the sound waves didn't hit the eardrum of a person or animal. The first definition of sound requires the sound to be heard. So the answer depends on the definition you choose!

Sounds in Space

If a tree fell in space, do you think it would make a sound? It wouldn't. Do you know why? Think back to what you learned about sound vibrations. What is vibrating? The air molecules vibrate. There is no air in space, so there are no molecules to move.

It was recently discovered that the sun makes sounds. Deep within the sun are bubbles that create sounds. However, we can't hear them because sound can't travel through empty space. In fact, outer space is utterly, completely silent. If a giant asteroid crashes into another giant asteroid and breaks into a million pieces, it's a silent explosion. The vibration of the collision can't move any air molecules because there is no air. When an astronaut drives a big moon rover vehicle on the moon, does he hear the moon rover making a sound? No. However, he probably *feels* the vibrations made by the moon rover. Did the vibrating moon rover make a sound? You decide.

Final Matters

Sound is one of the Lord's amazing inventions. Can you imagine the world without sound? Although some people cannot hear sound here on earth, everyone who loves Jesus will enjoy the sound of the Lord speaking to them in heaven. That's going to be the most marvelous and beautiful sound we'll ever hear!

See how many of the questions on the next page you can answer correctly, then let's finish our lesson with some fun projects and activities.

What Do You Remember?

What is sound? What phase of matter does sound generally travel through best? What measurement do we use to measure loudness? What is frequency? Which has more waves per second—a high-pitched sound or a low-pitched sound? What do we call a sound too high pitched for human ears to hear? What do we call a sound too low pitched for human ears to hear? Name one way we use what we know about sound to help us.

Notebooking Activities

After writing down the fascinating facts you've learned about sound, create a story about an instrument that makes a sound. Be sure to include information you've learned from this lesson in your story (amplitude, frequency, and tone). Your instrument could have a problem with being too loud, or maybe it isn't playing at the right pitch. Perhaps your instrument is perfect but has no one to hear it. I'm sure you'll come up with a creative way to explain all that you've learned!

Project
Soundproof Box

There are many reasons why people may need to soundproof a room. When someone is making an audio recording for a CD, he needs to record it in a soundproof room so that no other sound ends up on the recording. If someone plays loud music in a band, a soundproof room enables him to play without disturbing others in the same building. People use many things to soundproof a room. They usually put special soundproofing foam on all the walls.

You're going to create a soundproof box using materials you think will absorb sound. You can use old pieces of carpet, foam, cardboard, plastic, fabric, carpet padding, or anything else you think will work for your soundproof box. Be creative and consider what items will not transfer sound well.

You will need:

- a shoe box (or similar-sized box)
- materials that will absorb sound
- tape or glue
- an object that produces sound, like an iPod, cell phone, alarm clock, or small radio

1. You're going to build a soundproof barrier around the outside and on the inside of your box. Use tape or glue to attach your materials to your box. If you're doing this with others, you can have a competition to see which box is the most soundproof.
2. To test whether or not your box is soundproof, place your sound-producing object inside the box. Now put the top on the box.
3. Listen for sounds coming from the box. You could also put a small recording device inside the box and record to see if a sound that's made outside the box can be heard inside the box.
4. If your materials aren't absorbing sound very well, experiment with other materials or maybe add more soundproof material to your box.

Light of the World

"And God said, 'Let there be light,' and there was light" (Genesis 1:3).

What comes to your mind when you think of the word "light?" Light is such a big part of our lives. Even the Bible talks about light a great deal.

"When Jesus spoke to the people, He said, 'I am the light of the world. Whoever follows me will never walk in darkness but will have the light of life'" (John 8:12).

The Bible says God's light shines in us: "For God, who said, 'Let light shine out of darkness,' made his light shine in our hearts to give us the light of the knowledge of God's glory in the face of Christ" (2 Corinthians 4:6).

The Bible also says we should shine God's light to others: "In the same way, let your light shine before others, that they may see your good deeds and glorify your Father in heaven" (Matthew 5:16).

What do you think these verses mean? What does it mean to walk in the light? What does it mean that God is light? What does it mean to "let your light shine"?

In this lesson, we aren't going to study the spiritual significance of light. However, as you study the principles of light, think about God's light and how it pertains to what you're learning. Maybe you'll discover spiritual truths as you learn scientific truths!

Let There Be Light!

You may think that when God said, "Let there be light," the sun started shining. But that's not what happened. Actually, the sun wasn't created for a few more days after God spoke light into action.

What was shining the light? The Bible tells us that one day we won't need the sun's light. Instead, God *Himself* will be the One who gives us light (Isaiah 60:19, Revelation 21:23). Since the Scripture tells us one day God's light will replace the sun, we can safely assume it was *His own* light that shone on the world during that first day of creation.

Perhaps God's light has the same qualities as the sun's light. After all, He created the plants on day three. In the natural world, green plants are fully dependent on the sun in every way. Without the light from the sun, they can't survive unless light is supplied from another source.

Fire in the Sky

On the fourth day of creation, God created the sun. The sun seems pretty important up there in the sky, doesn't it? Like plants, we are completely dependent on this very sun God created. It's the main source of light that enables us to see. But all other sources of light, such as light bulbs and fire, are also dependent on the sun. That's because they use energy that would not exist were it not for the sun. Almost everything is dependent on the sun. Let's explore this incredibly important source of energy.

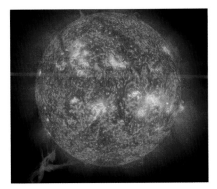

Nuclear fusion joins hydrogen atoms together and causes large explosions within the sun. These explosions give us light and heat.

Hydrogen and Helium Explosion

You probably know the sun is a huge ball of burning gas. Do you remember from our chemistry studies what the two main gases on the sun are? Right—they're hydrogen and helium. The sun uses the hydrogen and helium to become ablaze with fire. Those hydrogen atoms produce nuclear energy. Let me explain how it happens on a very basic level.

Every single second of the day, explosions are happening in the very center of the sun. The explosions happen when hydrogen atoms fuse (or join) together to become helium atoms. Remember that hydrogen has only one proton and helium has two protons and neutrons. On the sun, the hydrogen atoms are becoming helium atoms. They make a loud bang when they do this.

This joining of hydrogen atoms happens over and over again. We call it **nuclear fusion** because particles are fusing or joining together. This makes a whole different particle. What happen is this: Hydrogen nuclei join together to form into helium atoms, releasing a lot of energy in the process. It's the opposite of nuclear fission. Fission involves dividing the nucleus. You learned about that in the last lesson. One divides the nucleus; the other joins the nucleus. Both fusion and fission release enormous amounts of energy. They both create nuclear explosions! The fusing of hydrogen atoms on the sun creates light and heat for us on the earth.

Creation Confirmation

When nuclear fusion happens, the sun gets hotter and releases more energy. If you could fast forward several billion years, the sun might be too hot to support life on earth. The opposite might be true if you could go backward in time. The sun would have less energy, so the earth might be too cold to support any living organisms. Some scientists call this the faint young sun problem. It is evidence for the biblical view of creation.

Tell someone what you've learned so far about light.

Radiating Race

When light leaves the sun, it radiates in all directions. What happens when light leaves a light bulb? It radiates in all directions as well. When you shine a flashlight, the light radiates from that small bulb to make light for a larger area. When you light a candle in a dark room, the light radiates from the candle flame to give light to the area around the candle. It's the same with fire. It's also radiating light. To radiate means to spread out from the center. Because of this, we call all light **radiant energy**. Let's explore how radiant energy travels.

Light travels extremely fast. In fact, it travels faster than anything else in the entire universe. That's why you can see a lightning bolt a few seconds before you hear that bolt of lightning make a thundering sound. In space, light travels 186,000 miles per second (300,000 km/s). That's really, really fast! That's about 11 million miles a minute. Scientists call that the speed limit for the universe since nothing can travel faster than light. It's as fast as anything can go: 186,000 miles per second. That may be fast, but it still takes the sun's light a bit of time to get from the sun to earth. After all, we're a long way from the sun—about 93 million miles away! It takes the light that leaves the sun eight minutes to reach the earth. The light coming from your light bulb or a fire travels a little more slowly because it's traveling through a thicker substance than space—air, which as you know is full of matter.

Since the sun's light travels in all directions, only a very, very small part of it reaches us here on earth. When the light hits the earth, it warms and illuminates it. This light is stored as energy inside the cells of plants and is even used to make electricity!

We call the energy we get from the sun solar energy because the word "solar" comes from the Latin word for sun, *sol*. Without solar energy, life on earth wouldn't be possible. As we saw a minute ago, we wouldn't have plants. Without plants, there would be no animals at all. In fact all animals—whether they eat plants or animals—need plants to survive. Plants produce oxygen for animals to breathe and food for plant-eating animals. Even the carnivorous animals depend on plant-eating animals and the oxygen plants produce for survival. Humans need plants in their diet to be healthy as well. Every single living thing on earth is dependent on the sun for survival.

The sun is the primary source of light. But there are also other sources of light on earth. Let's take a look at the these sources of light.

SPEED LIMIT

186,000
miles per second

The speed limit of the universe is the speed of light.

Sources of Light

When my dad was a child and wanted to see his way through the house after the sun went down, he had to carry a candle. On a moonless night, he would need several candles. Candles and other sources of fire were very valuable to my father, especially in the winter when the sun went down early. Although electric light was in existence back then, only the wealthy had electric lights in their homes.

For many thousands of years, fire was the only way to light the night. As you know, fire is a chemical reaction that releases light and heat. Fire releases as much light as it does heat, much like the fire on the sun. Sometimes we want light without all that heat. This is one reason why electrical lights have been helpful.

Electrifying Light

In 1879, Thomas Edison made a great discovery. He created a light bulb that produces what we call **incandescent light**. "Incandescent" means hot enough to glow. Edison learned that if he ran an electric current through a filament (an electrically conductive thread), the filament would heat to up to 5,500°F (3,000° C). This would cause the filament to glow brightly. The glow would continue until the filament partly evaporated and eventually broke.

Edison and his friends tried many different threads in the bulb. They used carbon filaments and other fabrics, but those burned out pretty quickly. They tried thread after thread. Eventually William D. Coolidge discovered the perfect material: the element tungsten. Tungsten

The invention of the light bulb changed lives in many ways. Instead of everyone going to sleep when it gets dark, people are able to stay up much later. Big cities have so much light late into the night that it drowns out the light from the stars for many miles. We call this light pollution.

is a metal, and metals conduct electricity. Tungsten has the highest melting point of all the pure metals. It won't melt until it reaches 6,192 °F (3,422 °C). It also evaporates the least. Tungsten happens to be the strongest metal too. Tungsten lasts far longer than cotton and other filaments and is also very inexpensive. It was discovered that the tungsten thread would evaporate more slowly if the bulb were filled with an inert gas—argon. With this new invention, people could have electric lights right in their own homes! Years later, every home was built to include electric lights.

This amazing new invention provided the world with another source of light besides fire and the sun. Today, incandescent lights aren't the only type of electric light bulb. There are many other kinds of light bulbs, such as halogen, fluorescent, and LED lights.

Tungsten filament

The discovery of the tungsten filament provided the world with a source of light that changed people's lives.

Fluorescent lights are filled with mercury vapor. When electricity is pumped into these mercury-filled tubes, the mercury electrons get so excited that they release heat and light. But this is invisible ultraviolet light so the bulbs have a special coating that emits visible light when the ultraviolet light hits it. Only a little energy is required to produce fluorescent lights. That's because only a small amount of heat is released with the light. With incandescent bulbs, 90% of the energy released is heat. Because mercury is a poisonous metal, care has to be taken when handling fluorescent lights. They could break, releasing the mercury into the environment.

Halogen lights are used in stage lighting. Their brightness and low heat allow performers to be seen without getting too hot under the lights.

LED, which stands for **light emitting diode**, is also becoming an extremely popular type of light. A diode is made of something we call a semiconductor. A semiconductor is a material that can conduct electricity. It doesn't conduct electricity as well as metal, but it does *semi*conduct electricity. When electricity flows through the electrons in some diodes, they release energy as light.

These special little lights can be found in digital clocks, remote controls, watches, and every appliance in your kitchen that has a little red light telling you whether it's on or off.

Because they don't release much heat at all, lots of LED lights can be combined to create a very bright light. Today they're used to light up large televisions and make traffic lights red, green, or yellow. LED lights don't have a filament. They don't get very hot. They also take a long, long time to burn out. They are especially practical because they're placed in a small plastic bulb, not a glass one. Therefore, they don't break as easily.

This LED light can be grouped with many more LED lights to create a very bright light.

Just for fun, you can see how many LED lights you have! Go through each room in your house and count the LED lights. Be sure to look for any electronic devices. How many LED lights did you find in your entire house?

Tell someone what you've learned so far about light.

Just Passing Through

Light travels in a straight line. It doesn't bend around corners. Light can pass through some objects but can't pass through others.

If you shine a flashlight on your hand, does the light pass through your hand? If light can't pass through an object, we say that object is **opaque**. However, if light *can* pass through an object, we say that object is either **transparent** or **translucent**. Transparent materials allow nearly all of the light to pass right through, so we can see clearly through the materials. Clear glass and clear plastic are transparent. Do you see anything around you that's transparent? The windows in my house are transparent.

Have you ever seen stained glass windows? They aren't transparent; they're translucent. Translucent materials let light pass through; however, the materials scatter the light, sending it in all different directions. Because the light doesn't go straight through the translucent material, it's hard to see clearly through it.

Everything around you is opaque, transparent, or translucent. In your kitchen, you probably have plastic wrap, waxed paper, and aluminum foil. These three materials represent transparent, translucent, and opaque materials. Examine them right now and see if you can guess which is which.

You probably noticed the plastic wrap is transparent, the waxed paper is translucent, and the foil is opaque.

Stained glass windows are translucent. Although light passes through, the light is scattered to give us these beautiful window pictures.

Shadows

When light rays encounter an opaque object that's smaller than the beams of light, some of the light will pass by the object and some will be blocked. The blocked light will make a **shadow**. Shadows fall across the back of the opaque

This sundial uses the sun's shadow to tell time.

object. I remember being extremely frightened of my shadow—that dark person following me everywhere I went. I wondered why sometimes the dark person was there and sometimes she wasn't. Sometimes my shadow was very small, but other times she was terrifyingly enormous! Later on I learned it was the direction and angle of the sun that caused my shadow to change shapes. Our shadows change throughout the day, depending on where the sun is in the sky. Many years ago, intelligent scientists created a clock that uses the sun's shadow to tell time! This device is called a sundial.

Beams and Waves

We talked about how light travels in straight lines. Those straight lines are sometimes called beams of light. These beams of light are actually particles called photons. We don't understand a lot about photons, but we do know photons aren't made up of elements. So they're not matter. What are they then? We don't really know. We *do* know that photons are strange particles of light that travel in a straight line from the sun (or other source of light). Scientists are still learning about photons, but one interesting thing they've discovered is that when these photons travel, they travel as a wave.

Let's explore these light waves a bit. Do you remember why sound waves can't travel through space? It's because there's no matter in space to carry the waves along. Light and heat travel through space. How can light travel through space if it's a wave, like sound? As you've learned, sound waves involve vibrations of molecules. Light waves vibrate electrical fields. Vibrating electrical fields make a magnetic field. A vibrating magnetic field makes an electrical field, and so on. You'll learn more about this in lesson 12.

Because light creates electrical and magnetic fields, it's considered **electromagnetic energy**. This energy reaches all the way from the sun to the earth. Light also travels out from fire and light bulbs as electromagnetic energy. It doesn't need matter in order to travel from the fire to you. It radiates from the source of light electromagnetically

These beams of light coming through the trees are made up of photons.

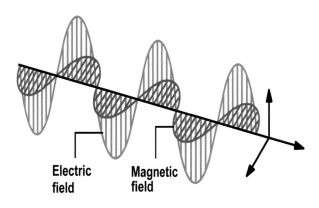

Electric field Magnetic field

In lessons 12 and 13, you'll learn about how electricity and magnetism work together. Light is made up of electrical and magnetic waves going back and forth. These waves can travel through empty space. That's why the heat and light from the sun can reach us here on earth.

through space. This electromagnetic energy reaches us as, light, and radiation.

Light, radio waves, microwaves, X-rays, and other radioactive energy waves travel electromagnetically. This is unlike sound, which travels mechanically as vibrating matter. When you get to high school, you'll study all the waves that travel electromagnetically. Today we're only going to focus on light waves.

The electromagnetic waves of light give us all the colors of our world. The light of the sun is made up of every single color we can see—and many colors we can't see. These electromagnetic waves bring color to our world!

Spectrum of Colors

All the colors in the world make up what we call the **color spectrum** or **visible spectrum**. Look around you. Every color you see is part of the visible spectrum. Yet there are many, many more colors coming from the light. There are many more colors we *can't* see than ones we can see. The colors we can't see are part of the **invisible spectrum**. We'll talk more about those colors in a moment.

Look at the image below to examine all the colors in the spectrum. Do they look familiar? Those are the colors of the rainbow! The colors on either end of the color spectrum aren't visible to our eyes.

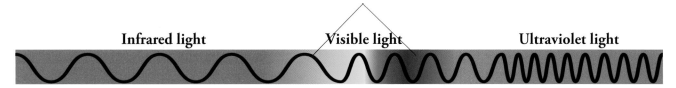

Infrared light Visible light Ultraviolet light

The rainbow reminds us of God's promises. It also shows us the order of colors in the color spectrum we see as visible light. These colors make up everything we see around us.

Look at the wave that's passing through the colors. Do you notice that part of the wave has a longer wavelength, while other parts have shorter wavelengths? The low-frequency colors are on the red side. The high-frequency colors are on the violet side.

If you've ever seen a rainbow, perhaps you've noticed that the colors are always in the same order, usually described as red, orange, yellow, green, blue, indigo, and violet. Sometimes the blue and violet colors blend a bit, but this is the actual order of the colors in the visible spectrum.

You might even use the acronym "Roy G. Biv" to remember the order of the rainbow colors. The apparent colored stripes are the result of the way our eyes and brain see color. The colors indigo and violet are actually extremely similar. Isaac Newton, who discovered and explored the visible spectrum, included both violet and indigo so that the spectrum would have seven colors, instead of six. He was a strong Christian and believed that seven was a more spiritual number than six. It's also the number of notes on a musical scale. So the spectrum includes indigo and violet, but if you look at it, you'll notice that these two shades really blend into one.

When the sun is bright and there's a dark cloud behind the rainbow for contrast, we can often see a fainter secondary rainbow—with the color order reversed.

Would you like to create a rainbow to see the visible color spectrum? Let's do that now.

Try This!

You will need: An adult's supervision; a straight-sided, thin drinking glass; water; white paper; duct tape; a bright flashlight; and a very dark bathroom.

First, fill your glass of water almost to the top and place it at the very edge of the bathroom counter, slightly hanging off. Place the sheet of white paper on the floor, angled away from the counter. Now put at least two pieces of duct tape over the front of the flashlight so the light comes out of a slit about ⅛ inch wide. Make sure to seal the tape directly on the lens up to the edge of the rim and over, not just straight across. Now place the flashlight slit just at the top back edge of the glass, almost touching. Darken the room and shine the light at a diagonal into the water. Keep repositioning the light until you see a spectrum on the sheet of paper. Wherever sunlight falls on water, glass, or plastic that has a tapered shape, you'll see a rainbow!

Colorful White

The most interesting thing Newton discovered about the rainbow of colors is that all these colors are contained in a beam of sunlight—the white light that comes from the sun. He realized that when you blend all these colors together, you get white light. But you can also split that white light and separate all the colors. That's what you did when you created the spectrum by shining the white beam of light from your flashlight through the glass. Newton passed a beam of white light through a prism—a triangle made of glass. What do you think happened when he passed that beam through the prism? The light split up into all its different colors and came

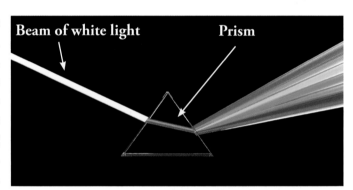

Beam of white light   **Prism**

When the beam of white light passes through the prism, it separates all the colors of the white light, showing light's true colors—which we see as the visible spectrum.

out the other side as a rainbow of colors! But Newton didn't stop there. He then sent the rainbow light through another prism. Guess what happened? It became white again! You could say he took the light apart, then put it back together again! If you have access to two prisms, you can repeat the exact experiment Newton did.

Try This!

You will need: An adult's supervision, a copy paper box, a knife, 2 prisms, and a sunny day.

To begin, cut out a rectangular notch in the center of the top edge on the narrow side of the box. Make sure the notch is slightly smaller than the prism so the prism can be wedged tightly into the notch. Now place

the prism in the notch and go outdoors on a sunny day. Position the box so the sunlight is able to project the rainbow image onto the bottom of the box. You may need to prop the box up. When you see where the image falls, set up your second prism to catch the light. It must be positioned upside down. You can do this by putting the prism on a small block in the correct position.

Wavelength

Making rainbows is a delightful activity because color is a gift from God that makes the world a brighter place. Color gives our world so much beauty. Imagine if everything were in black and white. God could have created the world this way, but instead, He chose to give the world color! How did He cause all those colors to come out of a beam of white light? Let's find out.

As I mentioned earlier, God created the colors of light by creating different wavelengths in those electromagnetic waves. Just as sound waves create different frequencies based on their wavelengths, every color has a different wavelength or frequency. You remember that high-frequency waves of sound make high-pitched noises. High-frequency waves of light make blue light, and low-frequency waves make red light. Look at the color spectrum again.

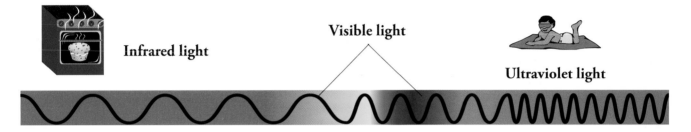

Infrared light

Visible light

Ultraviolet light

Very Violet

If the wavelength is even faster than blue, it becomes indigo. Indigo wavelengths have a high frequency. If you could relate the indigo wavelength to sound, you might say it's a high-pitched squeal. After indigo comes violet, which is an even higher-frequency wave. Guess what happens if it's an even higher frequency than violet? It becomes **ultraviolet**, meaning beyond violet. Ultraviolet is light we can't see with our naked eye—somewhat like the high-frequency sounds we can't hear. We can't see ultraviolet light because it's not in the visible spectrum for humans. We can, however, *feel* ultraviolet light because this kind of light gives us a suntan—and a sunburn, if we aren't careful. The higher the frequency, the higher energy the photons have. Indeed, the highest frequency of ultraviolet light, with energetic photons, turns our skin pink and can even cause cancer if we get too much of it.

An aquarium shines ultraviolet lights on these jellyfish to make them glow with a purple-blueish color.

A frequency of ultraviolet light that isn't harmful gives us the purple lights used in amusement parks. These lights make fluorescent materials glow in the dark.

The discovery of ultraviolet light has been helpful in many ways. It has been shown to kill bacteria and is used in many places to purify medical equipment, water, and many other things. Also, some important documents contain special information that can be seen only under ultraviolet lights. For example, passports and visas (which allow you to go in and out of the different countries of the world) have secret seals that can't be seen. When the official puts your passport or visa under an ultraviolet light, he looks for the symbol and knows whether your passport is real or fake.

You're Getting Warmer

Scientists have measured the heat coming from each color of the rainbow. Interestingly, the color red is always warmer than the other colors. This is because the light on the red side of the color spectrum, called **infrared**, has longer wavelengths and generates heat. Although we can't see infrared light, it causes molecules to vibrate. Remember, vibrating molecules make heat.

Infrared light is what gives us the warmth from the sun. If you're out in the sun and feel really hot, blame infrared radiation. Without infrared light, we couldn't feel the warmth from the sun or the warmth from a fire on a cold night. We also couldn't feel the warmth from a light bulb. So when you go outside to get warm in the sun, the sunlight you're seeking is not visible light; it's invisible, infrared light.

Although we can only see colors in the visible spectrum, some animals can see ultraviolet light and some can see infrared light. Let's learn a little more about this.

This hunter is wearing a color that deer are unable to detect.

Animal Vision

Many insects can see ultraviolet light. Some flowers have special ultraviolet patterns designed to lead the insects to the food inside the flowers. This also helps the flowers because the insects pollinate the flowers while they get food. These insects are able to find the food they need because God gave them the ability to see ultraviolet colors. What's really interesting is that with the ability to see ultraviolet light, many actually don't have the ability to see the colors at the other end of the spectrum. Bees, for example, can't see red.

Deer are similar. They see some ultraviolet colors but can't see red or orange. That's one reason hunters wear orange jackets when they're hunting deer. It's dangerous to be out in the woods shooting at anything that moves. But if a hunter is wearing a bright orange jacket, he's less likely to get shot. He also won't scare off any deer because they won't see that bright orange color; it's not visible to them. However, laundry detergent has ultraviolet brighteners in it. It's possible the deer might see the ultraviolet brighteners in the clothes whether they're orange or not.

Although deer can't see red, snakes and other reptiles have been given the ability to detect infrared light. Many snakes wouldn't be able to survive without this ability, as their prey is good at hiding under leaves and in holes.

Scientists use infrared technology to help mankind. Heat-seeking missiles are able to search out the infrared heat coming from another missile and destroy it before it can hurt anyone. When searching for people lost in the forest, rescuers use infrared scopes to detect infrared heat that comes from humans. This also helps police find escaped prisoners who are hiding out. In addition, infrared light can be used to see at night. Night vision devices allow soldiers and hunters to see in the dark. Weather satellites also use infrared technology to see the height, shape, and speed of clouds. Astronomers use infrared technology to detect heat coming from galaxies and planets. Infrared technology can also be used to see through paintings to detect if anything was painted or drawn beneath the visible artwork. This can help art collectors and museums determine whether a painting is real or a copy made by someone else.

Tell someone all that you've learned about colors.

Snakes use their ability to see infrared light to detect where the hidden creatures around them are.

172

Eye See

Have you ever wondered how you actually see these beautiful colors that are all around you? Some children imagine they're able to see because beams of light shine out of their eyes and capture images of everything around them. However, if you go into a dark room, you won't see light coming from people's eyes. We don't see because light comes *out* of our eyes; rather we see because light comes *into* our eyes.

What happens is this: The sun explodes with light, and all the colors in the world are contained in that light. The sun is white to our eyes because white light contains all the colors of the color spectrum. That light radiates in every direction. When this light enters our atmosphere, it shines onto everything it encounters. Newton's experiments with colored light prove that the colors we see are the result of reflection. So the color we see is actually the light waves that are reflected off the object we see.

If light waves hit a pair of jeans, all the colors of the light are absorbed except the blue light waves (assuming they are blue jeans). These blue light waves bounce off the jeans and into your eyes, making you see the jeans as blue. Blue is the color of the jeans because blue light bounces off the jeans. Whatever color an object is to your eyes is the color that bounces off that object.

When light hits a red object, all the colors except red are absorbed into that object. The red light is reflected off that object, bouncing up into our eyes. As a result, we see red.

This is the reflective nature of light. When it bounces, it's actually *reflecting* off something. Most things in the world are a mixture of different colors. An object that's white is actually reflecting all the colors of the rainbow off of it. All the colors bounce off the white object and hit our eyes, so the object appears white. That's why white objects can seem bright and hurt our eyes when the sun is shining. Black objects absorb all the colors of the rainbow; therefore, no colors bounce off the black object and into our eyes. This is why black is not really considered a color. It's actually the *absence* of color. Not a single light wave is bouncing off a black object; they're all being absorbed.

The sky and this girl's eyes are blue because of the way light scatters.

Blue Skies

Have you ever wondered why the sky is blue? The gas molecules in the atmosphere scatter the light that comes through the atmosphere. Higher-frequency light, like blue light, scatters much more easily than lower-frequency light. As light comes through the atmosphere, the blue light is scattered the most, causing it to bounce off the gas molecules and other particles and into our eyes. That's why the sky is blue!

Maybe you've wondered why some people's eyes are blue. Blue eyes are blue for the same reason the sky is blue. In every eye there's a dark substance called melanin. There's less melanin in blue eyes, so the light scatters the melanin in the iris, making the eye appear blue. In dark brown eyes, there's much more melanin, so it simply reflects the brown color coming from the eye. Melanin also causes dark hair and skin.

The sun usually looks white. However, it's orange at sunrise and sunset. At these times of the day, the sun's rays are coming at a shallow angle, so they pass through much more air. The blue light waves are scattered away, so the colors at the other end of the spectrum—the orange colors—are what we see when we look beyond the atmosphere. The blue light is taken up by the scattering, and the orange light is what's left. So the sun looks orange.

This is also what happens to the moon during a lunar eclipse. The moon usually looks white or silver because it reflects all the colors of the sun and stands out against the blackness of the night sky. During a lunar eclipse (and when the moon is low on the horizon), the moon appears a rich, orange color because of its position in the sky. Light waves from the sun must pass through an enormous amount of the earth's atmosphere as they hit the moon. When the waves pass through our atmosphere, the blue light waves are taken up, and the moon appears orange.

To understand this, let's do an experiment.

The moon looks orange at times when it appears near the horizon. That's because the blue light is scattered by particles in our atmosphere, leaving only the orange light for us to see.

Try This!

You will need: An adult's supervision, a glass of water, milk, a white wall, a darkened room, and a flashlight.

First, pour a small amount of milk into the glass of water. Now place the glass of water near a white wall in a darkened room. Next, shine the flashlight on the glass of milky water. Look at the color of the light that shines behind the glass onto the wall. You should see an orange hue.

Primary Colors

As I've said before, all the colors you see come from the sun's pure white light. It's kind of hard to believe that all the colors mixed together make white, isn't it? You've probably mixed paint colors together and have gotten brown or black, not white. Let's do a couple of experiments to see if we can make white by mixing colors.

Try This!

You will need: An adult's supervision; red, blue, and green plastic wrap or cellophane; scissors; 3 cardboard tubes; tape; 3 flashlights; 2 friends; and a white wall.

First, cut out squares of red, blue, and green plastic wrap or cellophane big enough to fit over the ends of the cardboard tubes. Fit the colored squares onto the ends of the tubes using tape. Now place the flashlights on the other end of each colored cardboard tube. Have each friend shine her flashlight on the wall, allowing a spot of color to mix with the other two colors. The colors should mix together. In the center, the lights should touch on the edges. Are you surprised by what you see?

In this experiment you could see that three colors can actually be mixed together to form white light. Believe it or not, those three colors are the primary colors of light: red, green, and blue.

Let's do another activity to form white light from colors.

Try This!

You will need: An adult's supervision; a piece of white cardboard; scissors; a sharp pencil; and either markers, crayons, or tempera paint (in the colors purple, blue, green, yellow, orange, and red).

To begin, cut a circle out of the cardboard. Now divide the circle into six different segments and color each segment with a different color of the spectrum in order of the rainbow. Next, push a sharp pencil through the middle of the cardboard circle. Spin the circle by turning the pencil with your fingers. Do this as fast as you can. What do you notice about the colors?

Do you know what a primary color is? Three primary colors make up all the other colors when mixed together. You may have been taught that the primary colors are red, blue, and yellow, but that's not exactly true. There are actually *two* sets of primary colors. There are the primary colors of light—red, green, and blue—which you experimented with a moment ago. You can mix these colors in any combination to make many other colors.

There are also the primary colors of paint. But these primary colors are not red, blue, and yellow as you may have been told. They're actually cyan, magenta, and yellow. When you mixed the red, blue, and green lights in our first experiment with color, you may have been able to see cyan, magenta, and yellow when red, blue, and green crossed over one another. That's because blue light and red light, when mixed together, make a pinkish light called magenta. Look at the image on the right to see this. You will also notice from that image that green light and red light mixed together make yellow light. Blue light and green light make a greenish-blue light called cyan.

Red, green, and blue are the primary colors of light. You're able to see cyan, magenta, and yellow when you mix these colors together.

Why are there two sets of primary colors? The primary colors of light are called additive primary colors because you add the colors together to get new colors. Your television and computer screens use the additive primaries red, green, and blue, called RGB. If you look closely at your television screen, you may be able to see that the picture is made up of thousands of tiny blue, red, and green dots. If you ask an adult to put a drop of water on your computer or television screen, you'll be able to look at the colors that make up everything you see on the screen.

The primary colors of paint are cyan, magenta, and yellow. You can see red, green, and blue— the primary colors of light—when you mix these together. Printers use a color process called CMYK. The K stands for key, which is black. Black must be added as these colors don't make black.

The primary colors of paint are called subtractive primary colors because when you mix them, they subtract or lose some of their original color. If you have a color printer and have bought printer cartridges, you've probably noticed the colors of the cartridges you need are cyan, magenta, and yellow, along with black.

Beams of Monochromatic Light

Before we leave the study of color in light, I want to tell you about one more really amazing kind of light. As you know, light coming from a light source contains many different wavelengths of light and travels in many directions. Even an ultraviolet light gives off many different ultraviolet wavelengths. What if you could isolate a single wavelength of light—just one color—out of the millions of colors that come from a single beam of light? Believe it or not, scientists have done this. They've created light that produces a single wavelength, which produces a parallel beam that is sometimes extremely powerful. We call them lasers (Light Amplification by Stimulated Emission of Radiation).

This U.S. military scientist is experimenting with laser beams.

Lasers come in many different wavelengths—from ultraviolet to blue to green and all the way to infrared. Every laser is used for a different purpose. Today, the most frequent use of lasers is to scan barcodes on store bought items. Lasers are also used to read CDs and DVDs so people can listen to music and watch movies. The newer Blu-ray uses blue (actually violet) lasers. These are considered better because the

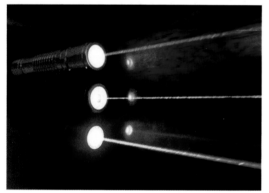

wavelength is shorter, so the disk can store five times as much data. Lasers are also used for surgery, especially surgeries that involve the eyes. They're used for cutting objects with precise, quick cuts. Police officers use them to read the speed your car is traveling. Lasers even make nifty toys for kids. Just never, ever look directly at the light of a laser. It's too powerful and could harm your vision.

As I mentioned, some lasers are made up of light in the invisible spectrum. If you own a digital camera and a newer television with a remote control, you can do an experiment to see light that's in the invisible spectrum.

Try This!

First, press the "on" button on your remote control while looking (not directly) at the end you're supposed to point toward the television. If nothing lights up, you have a remote that uses the invisible spectrum. Now darken the room. As you press the remote, have someone snap a digital picture of the remote. Cell phone cameras work best. You're able to see the beam with the camera because the newer digital cameras can detect light in the invisible spectrum.

Tell someone what you've learned about color before moving on.

Bouncing Light

Do you remember that light photons bounce off of things? We say they reflect. Being **reflective** is a special property of light that causes it to bounce off of things. To understand how light reflects off objects, let's do a simple experiment.

Try This!

You will need: An adult's supervision and a bouncy ball.

First, throw your ball on the ground from the side, at an angle. Do you see how it bounces off the ground at the same angle at which you threw it?

This is how light photons bounce off objects. They bounce at the angle at which they hit the object. If the object is smooth, all the light that hits it bounces off at the same angle. If the object is rough, the light bounces off in many different directions. This makes the object less reflective.

As you know, some objects reflect more light than others. What are some of the most reflective things you can think of? What objects seem to shine the most? What objects give off the most reflection of light when light hits them?

Try This!

You will need: An adult's supervision, 2 pieces of white paper, a piece of aluminum foil, and a sunny day.

First, crinkle one of the pieces of paper into a ball and flatten it back out. Now take the foil and papers outside and hold them in the sun. Which item is most reflective? Which item is least reflective?

Most mirrors have three layers. The bottom layer is the protective layer, made of a dark material. The middle layer is the reflecting layer, made of aluminum or another shiny metal. The top layer is the transparent layer, made of glass to protect the reflecting layer.

You probably found the foil to be the most reflective. The smooth white paper was reflective as well but not quite as reflective as the foil. It definitely was bright to your eyes, though. However, the crinkled paper bounced the light in many different directions, making it the least reflective.

If something is extremely smooth, it can often reflect an image of what's in front of it. Mirrors are so reflective that we can actually see ourselves in them! Some mirrors are more reflective and produce a better reflection than others.

We see objects in a mirror because of how the image is reflected. Everything absorbs or reflects different amounts of light. When photons of light hit a mirror, all the photons bounce off the mirror at the same angle and back into our eyes. Photons that hit a rough surface bounce off the surface in a disorganized, jumbled way and at many different angles—some going this way, some going that way. It's the *angle* of the light reflection that allows you to see your reflection. If the surface is smooth and flat, you should be able to see your reflection in it.

When you're looking in the mirror, the photons stream out of the light bulb and bounce off all the different parts of you. These bouncing photons bounce into the mirror. The mirror reflects back all the photons at the exact same angle at which they hit the mirror, and they go into your eyes so you can see yourself! Every smooth, shiny surface should give you a reflection.

Because the water is calm, it can clearly reflect the image of the land, just like a mirror.

Some surfaces *appear* smooth but actually are not. If you can't see your reflection in a smooth surface, it's probably because the surface isn't as smooth as you think. For example, a piece of paper seems smooth and even shiny sometimes. However, if you look at paper under a magnifying glass, you'll see it's actually quite rough. Light particles are tiny and can pick up on the roughness, even though we can't. Because paper is not really smooth, it reflects light in a random, chaotic way—unlike a flat piece of metal that reflects light at a definite angle. This is why you can't see your image in a piece of paper.

However, even if a surface is genuinely smooth, it might not be able to give you a reflection. This is because some smooth surfaces absorb most of the light. As a result, not much light is reflected off the object. Smooth surfaces—such as smooth metal, mirrors, and calm water—are all light-colored objects. They reflect all the light at the same angle the light struck, which allows you to see an image in the reflection.

You can experiment with how light reflects off the surface of a mirror by doing the following experiments.

The angle at which you shone the flashlight on the mirror affected the direction of the light that landed on the wall. That's because light bounces at the same angle at which it shines on a surface. Scientists call the incoming direction the **angle of incidence**. The law of reflection tells us that the angle of incidence equals the angle of reflection. Let's do another experiment with reflections.

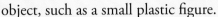

Try This!

You will need: An adult's supervision, 2 small square mirrors, tape, and a small object, such as a small plastic figure.

Place the mirrors at an angle next to each other and secure them together with tape. Put a small object between them. Can you count how many reflections you see? As light is reflected from one mirror to the other, an infinite number of images can be seen. Experiment with holding the mirrors at different angles. Do you see how the angle affects the number of images reflected?

Explain your understanding of reflection to someone before moving on.

Bending Light

You learned that light is made up of photons. These photons travel in a straight line and bounce off objects. You also learned that light passes *through* some objects. But did you know that when light passes through things, it behaves rather strangely? This leads us to another property of light: Light changes speed and bends as it passes from one substance to another. This bending of light is called **refraction**. Let's see this in action!

Try This!

You will need: An adult's supervision, a glass of water, and a long pencil.

Put the pencil in the glass of water. Now look at the pencil from the side. What do you notice? The pencil looks different, doesn't it? That's because the light slowed down and bent as it entered the water, causing the pencil to appear broken.

When you're in a bathtub or swimming pool, you'll notice light bending as well. But why does this happen? Light slows down as it enters different substances. This makes the light bend. Think of it like this: Imagine you're walking in water, pushing a train of wagons in front of you. You keep walking at a particular speed, when suddenly, you enter a huge area of mud. You slow down quite a bit as you continue to move forward. You were able to walk much faster before you hit the thicker substance. The moment you entered the mud, your speed changed. This is what happens to light when it enters thicker substances like air and water.

Let's try another light-bending experiment.

This little girl is able to put on her mother's lip gloss with the help of a mirror. Without a mirror, many tasks adults do—such as shaving and putting on makeup—would be difficult.

Try This!

You will need: An adult's supervision, a penny, a teacup, a partner, and some water.

To begin, place the penny in the bottom of the teacup. Now lower your head until the coin just disappears from view. Hold your head still in that exact place. Next, have your partner very slowly pour some water into the cup. What happened to the penny? Why do you think that happened?

It's much easier to spear fish under the water where all the light is traveling at the same speed.

The penny became visible because the light bent, and the visual location of the penny changed, enabling you to see it. The *physical* location didn't change. But from your perspective—above the water—the penny seemed to change locations. Things aren't always where they appear to be when you're looking into a different medium—from water to air, from air to water, or from space to earth.

How do you think this affects how hunters spear fish in the water? Do they throw the spear at the fish where it *appears* to be from above? With practice, hunters can determine where the fish actually is. Would it be easier to spear the fish from under the water or above the water? When you're under the water, everything seems to be properly placed because all the light is hitting the object at the same speed from your perspective. It's only for those seeing the light at two different speeds that things appear out of place.

Now you see that light bends. But you may wonder *why* light bends. We can understand why it would change speed, but why does it bend? It's actually the slowing down that causes the light to bend.

It's difficult to explain why light bends, but imagine if you and your entire family—your parents, siblings, cousins, uncles, aunts, and grandparents—were lined up shoulder to shoulder walking to the park. You're in the front and slightly ahead of everyone so that every single person is at a slight diagonal. Suddenly, you encounter a four-inch-thick slab of mud in front of the entrance to the park. You all must trudge through the mud, shoulder to shoulder, to get inside the park. Now imagine everyone is walking at the same pace. You hit the mud first and slow down a bit—but the others continue to walk at the same pace as before, causing your line of family members to bend.

This is similar to how light behaves when it enters a substance. It's traveling at the same speed, but the photons that enter the substance first move more slowly once they enter the substance. The light appears to bend because the photons in the substance are moving at a slower pace than the photons that have not yet entered the substance.

Final Matters

I hope you've enjoyed your study of light. What was the most interesting thing you learned in this lesson? Remember, you're called to be a light to the world. I hope you'll reflect God's light to all the people around you. It's now time to finish this lesson with some questions and interesting activities!

What Do You Remember?

What are the two most common elements found on the sun? What is nuclear fusion? What is the order of colors in the electromagnetic spectrum? Name two kinds of invisible light. What kinds of surfaces reflect light the best? What happens to light when it enters a different medium?

Notebooking Activities

Record the fascinating facts you've learned in this lesson as well as the projects and experiments you did. Then create a color spectrum, recording information you've learned about each of the colors in the spectrum. The *Chemistry and Physics Notebooking Journal* has templates for these activities.

Did you know God talks about light a great deal in the Bible? Sometimes Jesus is referred to as the Light. Sometimes we are told to let our light shine and to walk in the light. I'd like you to research the word "light" in the Bible using a concordance or Bible search tool, such as www.Bible.cc. Read all the verses that talk about light. Pick your favorite verse and copy it into your notebooking journal. Below that, write down what the verse means to you.

Experiment
Build a Periscope

Although light can travel only in a straight line, by using reflection, we can make light go around corners. When a submarine is underwater, it can see what's on the surface of the water without having to come all the way up out of the water. The submarine does this with a periscope, a device that reflects light, enabling the submarine to see around corners. Johannes Gutenberg (1398–1468), who is best known for inventing the printing press, also invented the periscope.

Let's build our own periscope!

You will need:

- reusable adhesive putty
- one 18-inch length of 2-inch outer diameter PVC pipe
- two 2-inch inner diameter PVC pipe elbow joints
- two small, round mirrors measuring 2 inches or less in diameter

Note: You can use pieces of different-sized PVC pipes as long as the diameters of the pipe and the elbows are the same.

1. Begin by putting the adhesive putty on the back side of both mirrors.
2. Position the mirrors inside the PVC elbow pipes so that each mirror sticks to the bend of the elbow at a 45-degree angle.
3. Connect the elbows with mirrors to the long PVC pipe on either end.
4. Turn the bottom elbow facing toward you and the top elbow facing away from you.
5. You can now look through the bottom elbow to view what someone would see outside the top elbow. You can also hide behind a couch and see what's happening on the other side. Or you can look around a corner.

The image should reflect off the mirrors so that you can see out the other end of the periscope. You may want to use a drill, an X-ACTO knife, or razor blade to make a one-inch slit in the long pipe, near the top mirror, to allow more light into your periscope.

Thermal Energy

Imagine walking in the cold wilderness of the Yukon in far western Canada. What would you need to survive this climate, where the temperature can reach 100 degrees below zero? Would the warm clothes you normally wear be enough for you in a climate where water freezes in midair as it falls to the ground? Would wool socks be enough in temperatures where your blood doesn't want to flow into your arms and legs because it freezes in your veins? Jack London wrote a short story called "To Build a Fire." It's about a man who was in this freezing place and didn't have what he needed to survive the climate. Though the story ends tragically, it gives us a powerful picture of how dependent we are upon heat to live.

As you know, God created the sun to provide us with light. In addition to light energy, the **thermal energy** (heat energy) we receive from the sun is absolutely essential for our survival on this great big planet called earth.

People living in cold climates like the one pictured above are dependent on reliable sources of heat for survival.

Thermodynamics

You've probably heard the word "thermal" before. You may have heard of thermal underwear. Perhaps you've heard of a thermos. A thermos is a bottle that keeps liquids warm or cold by keeping heat in or out. I bet you've heard of a thermostat and a thermometer. A thermostat controls the temperature of your house. A thermometer measures the temperature of objects, places, and even people. By now you've probably figured out that "thermal" is a word used in science that refers to heat.

Thermal energy leaves the sun and is transferred to the earth. Do you remember the law of conservation of energy? This law states that new energy is never created; it's only transformed into different *kinds* of energy. There are four special laws that deal with energy and all of matter. These are called the **laws of thermodynamics**. **Thermodynamics** is the study of thermal energy. The laws of thermodynamics are like the laws of motion, but they apply to all of matter. I think you'll find them extremely interesting and important. Before we explore heat, let's learn about these laws.

A thermometer is an important device we use to determine whether or not we have a fever.

Once this lady's hands warm to the same temperature as the hot coffee, there will be no more transfer of heat. This is because of the zeroth law of thermodynamics.

The Zeroth Law of Thermodynamics

Can you believe it? Scientists named the very first law the *zeroth* law. That's because they discovered this law *after* they had named the other three. They realized it's the most important law to put first, so it's called law number zero! Instead of calling it the first law of thermodynamics, we'll call it the primary law, since primary means first.

To understand the **zeroth law**, we need to know the term "thermal equilibrium." If two objects are in thermal equilibrium, it means they don't transfer net heat (thermal) energy to each other. Objects in thermal equilibrium are at the same temperature. If the two objects are *not* in thermal equilibrium, heat flows from the hot thing to the cold thing.

Can you explain the primary law of thermodynamics in your own words?

The First Law of Thermodynamics

The next law of thermodynamics is called the first law of thermodynamics. It was once thought to be the primary law, but now it's the second law after the zeroth law. I hope that's not confusing to you! The **first law of thermodynamics** tells us that energy and matter can never be created or destroyed. They can only change from one kind of energy or matter to another. The total amount of energy and matter in the universe is already set. We can't add to it, and we can't take away from it. Do you remember that we call this the law of conservation of energy?

Let's explore what this means a little more since it's such an important law for you to know. Think of it like this: Let's say you decide to create a miniature world, so you go to the store and buy four cans of Play-Doh. You use *only* the Play-Doh in those four cans to create your world. After your creation is complete, you decide to change things around a bit. You take a tree you made and form it into a house. You take a person you created and make it into grass. No Play-Doh is created or destroyed; it's only made into different things.

Does that help you understand the first law of thermodynamics? I hope so! It's a scientific law all scientists know, understand, and believe.

Creation Confirmation

Before we move into the next law, let's talk about how the first law of thermodynamics gives evidence for the

The amount of matter and energy in the universe was set when God created the world. Once it was created, no amount of matter or energy could be added to or taken from the universe. It can only be changed into different forms.

Bible's account of how the world was created. For everything to exist, it had to be created at some point. But the law says that nothing can be created or destroyed. There must have been something *outside* the laws that govern nature that created everything.

Some people believe the whole world and everything in it came from nothing but a few random molecules. They think the molecules collided and created a big explosion, which they say created everything we see. People call this idea the big bang theory. This theory says that all matter and energy came from nothing. But this breaks the law; it violates the first law of thermodynamics. Never, ever in the history of the world has something come from nothing on its own—not even through a scientific experiment.

So where did everything come from if the natural laws that

govern everything in the universe prohibit anything coming from nothing? We only have three possible ways to explain how everything came about: Everything came from nothing, everything originated from something, or everything came from something supernaturally. Of these three choices, the only one that can explain the existence of the world is the third choice: Everything came into existence by a supernatural God who instantly created all things from nothing—supernaturally! The natural law proves to us that choices one and two—everything came from nothing and everything came from something— are impossible. If things can't come about naturally, then they must have come about supernaturally. To say that something can come from nothing is a serious violation of science and the scientific laws that rule the universe.

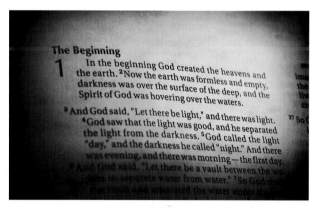

The first law of thermodynamics confirms the Bible's teaching that the world was supernaturally created by God.

Before we explore the second law of thermodynamics, take some time to explain what you've learned so far about thermodynamics.

Does your room go from organized to disorganized very often? This should remind you of the second law of thermodynamics.

The Second Law of Thermodynamics

Now it's time to explore the **second law of thermodynamics.** It explains why things are always wearing out, falling apart, and decaying. This law can be described in various ways. If you study this law, you'll see it expressed in many different ways by many different people. Here's the basic idea: The universe as a whole is always becoming less and less ordered or organized. Think about it: There are many more ways to be disorganized than organized. Let's take your bedroom as an example. There's pretty much one way for your room to be clean and organized—with everything in its place. But there are *many* ways your room can be disordered and messy—

with everything *out* of place.

If you've ever visited a landfill (the place where everyone's trash goes), you've seen this in action. In a landfill, you'll find new trash and old trash. If you look at the really old trash, you'll notice that everything begins to break down with time (except those pesky plastics and glasses we talked about earlier).

It goes like this: A shiny, new tricycle is exposed to the sunlight in the backyard. First, the shine begins to wear off the bike. Then the red paint begins to peel. Next, the metal begins to rust. Eventually, if it's not taken care of, holes will wear into the metal of the bike. If the bike is thrown into the trash, it will sit in the landfill and begin to completely wear away until it becomes part of the soil! Did you know that most everything can turn back into soil? It's true! Some things take longer than others, but almost everything can become dirt. Eventually, everything breaks down, wears out, falls apart, and decays.

Some people call this the law of entropy. In simple terms, **entropy** is a measure of disorder. If the red tricycle reaches a state of total entropy, we won't be able to tell it was once a tricycle. It has become a pile of elements at the landfill and will eventually become dirt. Really, entropy is the fabulous recycler! So next time something breaks, you can tell your parents, "It's the law."

As I said, everything is experiencing the second law of thermodynamics. *Everything* wears out and breaks down eventually. Even when we're trying to take really good care of something, that item is constantly attempting to go from a state of order to a state of disorder. This includes our clothes, our cars, our yards—even our own bodies! Can you think of some things you really enjoyed having that eventually wore out? It's that second law at work. Entropy, entropy, entropy. It gets us all! It's the law at work in the universe—a law that just can't be broken but causes everything to break.

The law of entropy is what causes a tricycle to deteriorate if not cared for properly.

Some creation scientists believe that the second law of thermodynamics is great evidence for creation. You see, evolutionists believe that the world started out as chaos and became more and more structured and orderly over time, eventually evolving into the beautiful world we have today. Can you find something wrong with this theory based on your knowledge of the second law of thermodynamics?

Take a few minutes to explain the second law of thermodynamics and how it supports creation.

The Third Law of Thermodynamics

We have one more law. Are you ready to learn it? This law will lead us into our study of thermal energy (or heat) because it has to do with heat. Actually, it has to do with the lack of or *absence* of heat. Let me explain.

You'll learn in a bit that temperature is a measure of how quickly or slowly molecules are moving. As you already know, when something gets colder, molecules slow down. But there's a limit to how cold something can be. That limit is called absolute zero, or zero kelvins (0 K, -273.15°C, -459.67°F). Try to remember that. The third law is dealing with this temperature—absolute zero. Look at how cold that really is!

If something *could* reach this cold temperature of absolute zero, it would reach zero point energy. When something reaches zero point energy, that doesn't mean there's no motion at all in the object. Many people believe that. But the great physicist Albert Einstein discovered that things always have *some* energy.

So the **third law of thermodynamics** is about this temperature of absolute zero—and it's also about entropy. It says the entropy of something approaches its minimum as it's cooled toward absolute zero. When something keeps getting cooler and cooler—closer to absolute zero—it's getting closer to the smallest amount of entropy it can have. That means it's becoming less and less disordered or disorganized.

Some scientists explain this using a crystal as an example. They say the entropy of a perfect crystal is zero when the temperature of the crystal is absolute zero (0 K). If the crystal is not perfect, there will be some disorder in it. If the temperature of the crystal is above absolute zero, there will be too much energy and motion in the crystal, also causing it to be disorderly.

As the crystal gets warmer and its temperature rises above absolute zero, the particles in the crystal start to move. That creates some disorder. Entropy (disorder) increases as the temperature increases. Imagine what happens when the crystal reaches its melting point. It becomes a liquid! Compared to a solid, a liquid is not very well ordered. That means it has more entropy. By adding even more heat, the entropy of the liquid increases even more. When it reaches the boiling point, there's a huge increase in the entropy of what was once a perfect crystal, making it a random, chaotic gas.

And that's what this law is all about—what happens as things are cooled toward absolute zero!

These are the four laws of thermodynamics God designed for our world. There may be more laws we haven't yet learned about or discovered. But God knows all the laws of the universe because He was the one who designed this world for us. He was the one who determined the laws of the entire universe!

Spend some time explaining to someone all that you've
learned about the four laws of thermodynamics.

In some places, the summers are hot enough to fry an egg on the sidewalk!

The Heat of the Moment

What exactly is heat? Do you think you can come up with an answer? I bet you can come up with a pretty good answer because you've learned so much this year! Essentially, **heat** is atoms in motion. When we increase the temperature of something, we're increasing the energy and excitement of the atoms. This energy is transferred from one atom to another atom. Everything is atomic, isn't it? Atoms are always moving. Not only that, but they also *love* to get other atoms in on the action. In fact, when the heat from the pavement burns our feet, it's actually the atoms in the pavement that are transferring their energy to the atoms in our feet!

Heat is always—and I mean *always*—on the move. In fact, it's so much on the move that we're often trying to figure out how to stop it from moving. We want to keep the heat in our house in the winter, so we close the curtains and seal the cracks under our doors and around our windows. When we go outdoors in the cold, we try to keep the heat from leaving our bodies by dressing warmly. On the other hand, in the summer, we try to keep the heat from moving into our house. Sometimes we love the heat; sometimes we don't. However, heat is always, always moving. It moves from the sun to the earth, from the hot pavement to our feet, from our warm cup of cocoa to our hands, from the stove to the pan to the water in the pan to the macaroni in the water in the pan—and so on!

What do you think would happen if you left a cup of hot cocoa on the table next to an ice cube? The heat from the cocoa would transfer into the air. At the same time, the heat in the air would transfer to the ice cube. Within a short time, everything in the room would be the same temperature: the cocoa, the water that was once an ice cube, the table it sits on, the spoon next to the cup—everything. If there's a temperature difference between two things, there will be a transfer of heat.

Here's an important point to remember: Heat always moves from the hotter item to the cooler item. Cold things never transfer their coldness. Do you remember there's no such thing as coldness? When things are getting cooler, they're actually losing heat, not receiving cold. It's all about heat transferring to cooler things.

Have you ever held M&M'S in your hand? Within a short time, the M&M'S melted into a mushy mess, didn't they? This is because the heat from your hand moved into the cooler M&M'S. You might say the energetic and warm molecules in your hands transferred their heat and energy to the molecules in the M&M'S. Also, the moisture from your hands dissolved the colored outer coating. Of course, M&M'S should always melt in your mouth, not in your hands—just as the slogan says!

The heat from this child's hand transferred to the candy and melted it. Heat is always transferring its energy from the warmer thing to the cooler thing.

Source or Sink

In every transfer of heat, there's a heat source and a heat sink. The item that's hotter is called the **heat source**, and the item receiving the heat is the **heat sink**. The sun is the heat source, and the pavement is the heat sink. Once the sun heats the pavement, the pavement is now the heat source, while your feet are the heat sink. In the picture above, the hand is the heat source, while the candy is the heat sink.

In the images below, which is the heat source, and which is the heat sink? You'll find the answers in the answer key in the back of this book.

Explain what you've learned so far in your own words.

Traveling Heat

What's your favorite way to travel? Do you love road trips in the car? Do you enjoy biking in the mountains? Have you ever traveled by airplane or boat? There are many ways we can get from place to place. However, heat travels in only three ways: radiation, convection, or conduction. Let's explore each of these ways that heat journeys from place to place.

Radiation

When you build a fire, you don't need to touch the fire to feel its heat. The heat travels through the air and reaches you through a process called radiation. You've heard the word "radiation" a lot in this book. As you know, **radiation** is energy that moves through space. Radiant heat doesn't need materials to transfer energy. This radiating heat can warm the environment around you. This is how the sun heats the earth.

Heat traveling through the air from a campfire is radiated toward you through electromagnetic radiation. The other two ways heat travels—convection and conduction—require a material for the heat to travel through. As you may remember from the last lesson, electromagnetic waves can transfer heat through empty space. In fact, that's what the sun's heat does. It travels through empty space in every direction, heating the entire solar system. Of course, some parts get warmer than others. We call heat that moves through empty space **radiant heat.**

This fire can warm these hands and cook the marshmallow through electromagnetic radiation.

Try This!

You will need: An adult's supervision, a thermometer, and a desk lamp that's turned on.

First, write down the temperature on the thermometer. Now place the end of the thermometer near the bulb of the lamp. Keep the thermometer near the lamp for 10 minutes. Check the temperature again. Did the temperature change? Why did the temperature on the thermometer go up? Because of radiant heat! The heat from the light bulb radiated out, warming the thermometer and causing the temperature to increase.

Now let's take a look at the second way heat travels.

Convection

What do you do when your bath water is too hot? You probably add cold water. The cold water pours into the tub, but it stays near the faucet, doesn't it? So what do you do? You swish the water around to transfer the cooler water around the tub. The warmer water then transfers its heat to the cooler water, causing the warmer water to lose some of its heat. This makes your bath water just the right temperature. It's convection in action!

My college apartment was heated by a wall unit. When I felt cold, I would turn the setting on the wall unit to warm. It would blow warm air into my apartment. The warm air coming from this one small device would eventually heat my entire apartment as the warm air molecules transferred energy to the air molecules around the room. This, too, is convection. **Convection** is heat that transfers in fluids—liquids and gases. I've just described forced convection. Forced convection occurs when an outside force causes the mixing of hot and cold fluids. A convection oven uses forced convection.

There's also natural convection. Natural convection is important for understanding weather. As you know, heat radiates toward the earth from the sun. But the earth is also heated and warmed through natural convection as air moves all around the earth, changing the temperature everywhere. Let's explore how natural convection works.

Did you know that warm gases always rise, as do most liquids? This happens because the molecules in warm air and warm liquids are more active. They need more room to move around, filling up more space. So there are fewer molecules in the same amount of space. Warm air and warm water (above 4°C or 39°F) are less dense than cool air and cool water. Do you remember learning about that in the first lesson of this book? Air and liquids rising because they become less dense leads us to the next thing you should know about convection.

If you've ever been to the beach in the summer, you've probably noticed it's rather windy near the shore. This happens because of convection. Here's what happens: The land heats up the air that hovers over its surface. When the air gets hot, it rises. But the air that hovers over the ocean isn't as hot because the water is rather cool. So as the air that's heated over the land rises, the air over the ocean rushes in to fill the empty space that the rising air left. This is called a **sea breeze.**

But things that heat up quickly also cool quickly. At night, the land cools faster than the sea. So air rises over the sea, and air from the land flows in to replace it. This is called a **land breeze**. This happens over and over again, every day-night cycle.

Let's do an experiment to see if hot water rises.

During the day, the sun heats up the land, and the hot air near the land rises. The cool air over the ocean then rushes in to fill the empty space, creating a breeze. At night, the land is cooler than the water, so air from the land flows in to replace the rising air over the water, creating a breeze in the other direction.

Try This!

You will need: An adult's supervision, an aquarium or large transparent container filled with room-temperature water, a large bowl (or two small bowls) that will fit in the aquarium, 2 plastic film canisters with lids (or 2 four-ounce plastic GladWare containers), a hammer, a nail, scissors, boiling water, ice water, and red and blue food coloring.

First, place the bowl (or bowls) upside down in the aquarium to make a flat surface upon which you'll place the film canisters. Make a hole in the lids of both film canisters using a hammer and a nail. Now cut the hole bigger, making a half-inch slit. With an adult's help, fill one canister with boiling water. Drop red food coloring into the canister. Now fill the other canister with ice water. Drop blue food coloring into that canister. Finally, place both canisters in the aquarium on their sides. Right away they should begin leaking the water that was inside them. Watch to see what happens next!

What happened in this experiment? If it was done correctly, you noticed that the red water from the hot film canister rose to the top of the aquarium, while the blue water from the cold canister sank to the bottom of the aquarium.

Now let's look at the convection action of air that's heated.

Try This!

You will need: An adult's supervision, a balloon, a pot of boiling water, and an empty glass bottle.

First, stretch the balloon over the mouth of the bottle. Now place the bottle in the pot of boiling water. Can you predict what will happen? Watch what happens to the balloon when the air molecules begin to heat up!

As you saw, the hot water heated the air inside the bottle. As the air warmed, the pressure rose, causing the balloon to expand.

Before you put all your experiment supplies away, ask an adult to take the bottle out of the water. When it's a bit cooler, feel the sides. The bottle was also warmed by the water because it came in direct contact with the hot-water molecules. That's conduction—warming through direct contact with the heat source. Let's explore conduction.

Conduction

Conduction occurs when the heat source and the heat sink are connected through matter. The heat flows from the warmer thing to the cooler thing by direct contact. This usually involves a solid. You may remember we said that a conductor moves things from one place to another. If heat travels through something, that thing is conducting heat—moving it from one place to another. Some materials are better conductors of heat than others. What materials do you think conduct heat the best?

Let's find out with this experiment!

Try This!

You will need: An adult's supervision, peanut butter, a metal spoon, a wooden spoon, a plastic spoon, and a container of hot water.

To begin, place a dab of peanut butter in the middle of each spoon. Now place all the spoons at the same time in the container of hot water. Watch to see what happens!

As you saw, metals are the best conductors of heat. Aluminum, iron, and other metals conduct heat very well, but silver and copper conduct heat the best. That's why many people have copper pots and pans.

A metal spoon feels colder than a wooden spoon because of conduction.

Good conductors of heat are also usually good conductors of electricity. One exception is the diamond. It's a better heat conductor than any metal, but it doesn't carry electricity. We'll learn about that in the next lesson. You may also remember that these conductors of heat conduct something else really well that we already studied. Sound!

Have you ever noticed that metal feels cold when you touch it? If you touch a wooden spoon and a metal spoon that are the same temperature, the metal spoon will feel colder than the wooden spoon. Why? Because metal is such a great conductor of heat that when you touch it, the heat from your hand is quickly transferred to the metal spoon! The metal is pulling heat from your hand, which makes the metal feel cool. It's actually your hand that's losing heat, not the spoon.

Many things are heated through conduction. One of these is the stove. It heats pans that are placed directly on it. The food inside the pan is also heated by conduction. When we drink a warm beverage on a cold day, we feel conduction in action.

In this picture, we see the three forms of heat travel: radiation, convection, and conduction. The air traveling up is warm air rising through convection. The heat traveling to the hot dog and the people sitting by the campfire is electromagnetic radiation. The pot on the fire is heating the contents inside the pot through conduction.

Heating Our World

Many things are heated through a combination of radiation, convection, and conduction. You can cook popcorn through conduction, convection, or radiation. If you place popcorn in a pan with oil and put the pan on a stove, you're using conduction. The heat is transferred directly to the popcorn from the pan, which received direct heat from the heating element on the stove. You might also use a popcorn popper, which moves hot air around a machine, heating the popcorn through the circulating air—convection. But the most common method is through radiation. When you place a bag of popcorn in the microwave, the radiant energy from the microwave heats the corn kernels until they pop.

A house using solar energy to heat water uses all three forms of heat transfer. The radiant energy warms the water-filled pipes inside the wall panels. The panels are usually black, to absorb as much radiant energy as possible. They pass this heat to the water by conduction. The hot water moves through the pipes, which warms cooler water through convection. The hot water then comes through the faucet and is used for showering, cleaning the dishes, washing the clothes, and helping with many other tasks that require hot water.

This popcorn was popped by an air-based popping device that uses convection.

Most people, however, don't use solar panels to heat their water. They use a hot water heater—a tank filled with water that has a small fire or electrical element underneath. The fire transfers the heat through radiant energy and conduction at the bottom of the tank. What happens when the water at the bottom of the tank gets hot? It rises to the top of the tank. This is convection.

This happens on and off all day long. As you use hot water in your house, the hot water from the water heater is pumped out of the tank. Cooler water then comes into the tank to be heated, replacing the water that was used. The little fire under the hot water heater is quite important, isn't it?

As you can see, although fire is an ancient source of heat, it is still used a lot today. In fact, fire is probably the most important source of thermal energy in the world. It's so important that we should probably take some time to study it.

Chefs prefer to cook with wooden spoons. After learning about heat transfer, can you think of some reasons why?

This popcorn was popped using conduction.

You've learned about the three different ways heat travels: radiation, convection, and conduction. Spend a few minutes explaining what you've just learned to someone before moving on.

Insulators

You noticed in the experiment that wood is not a great conductor of heat. If something doesn't transfer heat well, it's called an insulator. Glass, wood, plastic, and rubber are good insulators. Look at the pots in your kitchen. What are the handles made of?

Air is also a pretty good insulator. That's why you should dress in layers of clothing on cold days. Air gets trapped between each layer as well as between the fibers, reducing heat loss. This is also true when you're in bed on a cold night. Several light blankets can be warmer than one heavy blanket.

Typically, homes built in the United States are equipped with insulation in the attic. This insulation is often made up of glass fibers with lots of air trapped inside. This material is designed to stop the transfer of heat. If you heat your house, the insulation keeps the heat from escaping through the roof. If you cool your house, the insulation keeps outside heat from invading your house.

Let's experiment with insulation.

Try This!

You will need: An adult's supervision, water, a pan, a thermometer, 5 empty baby food jars with lids, masking tape, and insulation materials. You can use fiberglass (use gloves and take care when handling this material), down-filled fabric, cotton cloth, a wool sweater, or wool socks.

To begin, have an adult help you boil some water. Now measure the temperature of the water and write it down. With an adult's help, fill each jar with the boiling water. Secure the lids on the jars. Then cover four of the jars with your insulation materials. Use tape to attach the insulation to the jars. Be sure to wear gloves when handling the fiberglass. Try to make sure each jar has the same amount of insulation. Now make a guess about which material will be the best insulator (which will best keep the water warm). Keep the jars in the same location for 30 minutes, then test their temperatures. Which jar had the best insulator?

Set on Fire

Since we're talking about heat energy, we should spend some time learning about fire. Did you know that fire is extremely helpful for humankind? Fire gives us light and warmth. It makes our cars run and heats our water. Fire makes steam for power plants that provide electricity. It's used to cook food and melt metals.

Yet fire can also be a horribly destructive force. It can be used in war. A house fire can, in one day, turn a lifetime of work and memories into ash. Sadly, it can eliminate a beautiful forest in only a few days.

Thousands of years ago, ancient scientists believed fire was not just energy on the move but was an actual element. It seemed logical. After all, you can touch gold, you can touch water, and you can touch fire. You can see gold, you can see water, and you can see fire. However, you know that fire is really just a chemical reaction,

Forest fires can start in many ways.

It's important to know what to do when a house catches on fire so that you don't get burned or worse.

causing one substance to change form and become a different substance. Fire is the heat and light given off during that chemical reaction.

How do fires start? A fire can start through radiation, convection, or conduction. If you place a piece of tissue an inch above your stove, it will catch on fire through convection: The heated air causes the molecules in the tissue to become so excited that they eventually burst into flames, releasing that energy as fire. If you place the tissue directly on the stove, it will burst into flames much more quickly—almost immediately—through conduction. If you take a tissue outside and focus the sun's light on it with a magnifying lens, the tissue will burst into flames through radiant energy.

Fires can also start in forests when the ground is very dry. The sun can shine its heat with such intensity that the dry ground bursts into flames. Although most forest fires begin with lightning or human carelessness, radiant energy can cause dry grass to ignite unexpectedly.

With the supervision of an adult, you can burn a tissue with the sun's radiant energy. Let's try that now!

Try This!

You will need: An adult's supervision, a tissue, a magnifying glass, a pitcher of water, a sunny day, and a paved surface outside.

Go outside and put the tissue on a paved driveway or sidewalk. Be sure to bring your pitcher of water with you. Now position the magnifying glass in such a way that there's a tiny point of light on the surface of the tissue. Leave the magnifying glass in that position for a bit. Watch the tissue closely to see what happens. You'll notice the radiant energy heating the molecules in the tissue. They'll begin to smoke and will eventually catch on fire! Allow the fire to burn until it burns out. If the tissue begins to blow away, pour water on it immediately.

The radiant energy from the sun was focused through the lens into a small point of light, which contained a great deal of energy. That energy caused the molecules in the tissue to become so excited that they burst into flames.

Combustion

Fires burn through a process called combustion. **Combustion** is simply a chemical process in which some material reacts quickly with oxygen to give off heat. The material that reacts is called the fuel. Do you remember when we talked about fuel in lesson 8? A fire must have fuel to burn. In fact, the fuel is actually what's on fire.

In addition to fuel, a fire must have oxygen to burn. Let's do a common experiment to test this idea.

Try This!

You will need: An adult's supervision, a jar with a lid, a candle (that fits inside the jar), and a match.

Have an adult light the candle and help you put it in the jar. Now screw the lid tightly on the jar. What happens to the candle's flame?

The candle's flame eventually ran out of oxygen and went out, didn't it? That's because the fire was using oxygen to burn. Once it used up all the oxygen in the jar, the fire could not continue to burn.

Let's do a less common experiment to see what happens when the air is filled with another gas besides oxygen.

Try This!

You will need: An adult's supervision, a jar with a lid, a candle (that fits inside the jar), vinegar, baking soda, and a match.

First, pour some vinegar into the jar. Now have an adult light the candle and help you put it in the jar. Be sure the vinegar doesn't reach the top of the candle and put out the flame. Next, sprinkle baking soda all around the candle, into the vinegar. Watch to see what happens.

What happened? The vinegar and baking soda caused a chemical reaction that produced carbon dioxide. The carbon dioxide filled the jar and cut off the oxygen. As a result, the candle could no longer burn.

Triangle Truths

Having oxygen and fuel isn't enough to have a fire. We also need something to *start* the fire. We need thermal energy—heat! With heat, fuel, and oxygen, we can have a fire. Some people call this the **fire triangle**. If one of these three things is missing, a fire will not start—or it will go out. Once the fuel burns out, the fire goes out. You saw that when your tissue burned. Eventually, the tissue burned up, and there wasn't any more fuel for your fire. Campers know how important it is to keep adding fuel to a fire. Once a log burns up, the fire goes out. So campers have lots of sticks and logs nearby to fuel the fire. Campers also know they need something to ignite the fire. They need heat.

Heat comes from many different sources. The heat used to start a fire must be hot enough to heat the fuel, which in turn must be hot enough to ignite and catch on fire. We call this the **ignition temperature**. It's the temperature a substance must reach in order to ignite. You already know that not everything has the same freezing or boiling temperature. So it shouldn't surprise you that not everything has the same ignition temperature. It takes a lot more heat to ignite most metals than it does to ignite wood. It takes a lot more heat to ignite wood than paper.

At the end of this lesson, we'll do some activities to learn about fire safety. In the meantime, let's learn about measuring temperature.

Explain what you've learned about fire to someone so you won't forget.

Measuring Heat

You already know that heat is energy, and energy is the ability to do work. Do you think heat is potential or kinetic energy? It's actually energy in motion, so heat is at work. That means it's kinetic energy. However, energy can be stored in chemicals, such as oil and coal, as chemical energy. The heat is not being used, so it's potential energy. The heat we're discussing here, though, is in motion.

Heat moves molecules. The more the molecules move, the more kinetic energy the molecules have, and the hotter the substance is. We measure how much energy something has by measuring its temperature. **Temperature** measures how active the molecules are in the substance.

Let's say you have one atom of hydrogen. Imagine you add energy to it. It begins to move up and down and all around. All that moving around of an atom is temperature!

Have you ever had your temperature taken? If so, your parents probably used a thermometer. If you had a mouth temperature of greater than 99.9°F (37.7°C), you had a fever. Most people have a temperature range of 97.7–99.5°F (36.5–37.5°C). A healthy person's temperature is often 98.6°F (37.0°C). Anything above that means your body is working harder than usual and heating up while it does. What's it doing to make your body heat up? It's fighting germs! Whenever a germ enters your body, your cells get busy. If it's a bad germ, more cells are called into action. With more cells in action, more energy is being used. The cells are busy fighting the germs in your body. They're moving around so much that it makes your temperature rise higher and higher!

There are three ways we measure temperature: by using the Fahrenheit scale, the Celsius scale, or the Kelvin scale.

Fahrenheit

The most common way in the United States to measure temperature is to use the **Fahrenheit** scale, the classic English form of measuring things. It's named after David Gabriel Fahrenheit, the man who invented the first modern thermometer in 1714. He based the scale on the temperature of the human body. It was thought the human body's temperature was 100°F (37.7°C), but it's actually 98.6°F. Fahrenheit was rather close, wasn't he? On the Fahrenheit scale, water freezes at 32°and boils at 212°.

Celsius

Today, most of the world outside the United States uses the **Celsius** system, which fits in with the metric system. Using this scale, the freezing point of water is 0°, and the boiling point of water is 100°, which makes everything nice and orderly—100 equal degree points between boiling and freezing. Look at your thermometer. Does it have Fahrenheit or Celsius temperatures? Maybe it has both.

Kelvin

Kelvin is another form of measuring temperature that's used only by scientists. A British scientist named Lord Kelvin developed this scale using the very coldest temperature an object can reach and the very hottest temperature an object can reach. We mentioned this temperature earlier when we talked about absolute zero, which is zero kelvins. That's when a substance can't get any colder because it has reached minimum entropy; it can't release any more heat. That's 0! I mentioned that mankind isn't able to make something reach this cold temperature. That shouldn't be surprising. Remember, heat moves from hot things to cold things. To remove enough heat from something to cool it to 0 K would require something *colder* than 0 K, which is impossible. There's always *some* heat that's being transferred to the thing being frozen. Therefore, nothing has ever reached zero entropy and the temperature of 0 K.

You can find the temperature of anything in kelvins by adding 273.15 degrees to it when you measure it with the Celsius scale. On the Kelvin scale, water freezes at 273.15 K and boils at 373.15 K.

Thermometer

Have you ever wondered how thermometers work? Thermometers are able to measure temperature because they're filled with matter—usually a liquid—such as mercury or alcohol. This liquid expands when heated. As it expands, it rises in a narrow glass cylinder, which allows us to measure what the difference in temperature is.

So what's happening? When the liquids in the thermometer are excited because they're in contact with energy (a hot room or a boiling liquid in a pot), the molecules inside the liquid get agitated and move around more and more. As they move, they begin to push away from each other. This causes the liquid in the thermometer to expand, needing more room for the molecules' activity. As the liquid expands in the glass cylinder, it begins to rise in the thermometer—which causes the thermometer to measure a higher temperature.

You can make your own homemade thermometer using these principles. Let's do that now.

The liquid in this thermometer will rise as it's heated by the rising temperature surrounding it.

Try This! **You will need:** An adult's supervision, a narrow-necked glass bottle, room-temperature water, food coloring, a plastic straw, a piece of clay, and a thermometer.

To begin, fill the bottle almost full with water. Now add food coloring. Place the straw in the water with half of the straw out of the bottle. Mold clay around the top of the bottle, holding the straw in place. Make sure there's a tight seal of clay around the straw so air cannot get in or out of the bottle. Place the bottle near a warm location like a fireplace or stove. You can also place it outside in the sun. As the water temperature rises, the water in the bottle will expand and move up the straw. Keep your eye on your thermometer for a few days and watch what happens! You can test out your thermometer further by placing it in the refrigerator.

You probably noticed as the water in your bottle warmed up, it expanded and moved higher up the straw. As the temperature decreases, it will go down the straw.

You've learned a lot today. Explain to someone in your own words all that you now know.

Thermal Expansion

Whether you realize it or not, you've run into the concept of thermal expansion quite a bit in this lesson already. When things begin to heat up, they begin to expand. That's **thermal expansion**. Let's close this lesson by looking a little more closely at thermal expansion and doing some fun activities to understand it better.

Thermal expansion is an important scientific concept to know, especially if you're an engineer or builder.

Have you ever been walking along a sidewalk and suddenly noticed it has spaces every few feet? This is necessary because of thermal expansion. Without these spaces, the sidewalk would expand and crack. The spaces allow room for expansion.

When engineers are building bridges, they have to take this into consideration. Builders place metal links throughout the bridge so it can expand and shrink

Sidewalks have joints or spaces to keep them from buckling or cracking when they expand.

This bridge is built with expansion joints that move in and out as the air heats up or loses heat.

without affecting the safety of the bridge.

As you already know, when a solid heats up, the molecules in the solid begin to vibrate. Even though they're in a fixed position, the energy causes them to move farther away from the other molecules. This increases the distance between all the molecules in the solid, causing it to expand. This also happens with liquids and gases, as you saw in our convection experiment. When the hot water was released from the canister, it rose to the top because it was less dense. When a molecule needs more space to move, it expands, causing the material to be less dense. Almost every object is less dense when it's warm and more dense when it's cold. However, there is *one* substance God created to behave quite differently. And it's a good thing too!

Let's take a look at the strange phenomenon of nature called frozen water.

Ways of Wonderful Water

As we mentioned earlier in this book, the ways of water are quite different from solids, gases, and other liquids on the earth. Water expands when it freezes!

God designed this special feature of water, and it's a good thing He did. Think of midwinter ponds. If water was like other liquids, as the air above the pond cooled it, the cold water would sink, pushing up the warmer water to be cooled in turn—convection style. Any ice would sink. This would eventually freeze the whole pond from the bottom up. But because very cold water and ice don't sink, they protect the warmer water underneath so fish can still live in it.

As I said before, water behaves differently from other substances by expanding when it freezes. This is why ice cubes float. Would frozen cubes of other liquids float? Let's find out!

If water froze the way other liquids do, this entire lake would freeze, killing all the fish. This boy is able to ice fish on a frozen lake in Michigan by cutting a hole in the ice and catching the fish that swim below the surface.

Try This!

You will need: An adult's supervision, 4 paper cups, rubbing alcohol, nail polish remover, oil, water, a freezer, and a large glass of water.

Pour some rubbing alcohol into the first cup. Next, pour nail polish remover into the second cup. Pour oil into the third cup. Finally, pour water into the fourth cup. Now place the cups in the freezer. (Three of the substances will not fully freeze but will become cloudy instead.) After the one liquid has frozen, pour the contents of each cup, one by one, into a large glass of water. Watch to see what happens! Can you explain why the different substances behaved as they did?

Let's do another experiment to learn more about what happens when water freezes.

Try This!

You will need: An adult's supervision, a thin plastic bottle with a cap, water, and a freezer.
To begin, fill the plastic bottle all the way to the top with water. Now secure the cap on the bottle. Place the bottle in the freezer and leave it there overnight. Remove the water bottle from the freezer the next day and examine it. What happened? You probably noticed the bottle was misshapen. This happened because the water expanded as it froze, distorting the bottle.

Let's see if you can figure out how thermal expansion affects everyday things. Can you think of the answer to the questions below?

Why do you think power lines might be droopy on hot days but straight and tight on cold days? What might happen if water is left in the pipes outside your house and the temperature outside drops below freezing? Why do you think your car's windshield washer container is made out of plastic? Why does a car require a substance called antifreeze in its radiator? When a jar won't open, why do you run hot water on the metal lid? If one glass is stuck inside another, how could you use thermal expansion to separate it? To find the answers to these questions, look in the answer key in the back. All of these things are designed by engineers who had to understand thermal expansion and the expansion of water.

Tell someone what you've learned about thermal expansion and the expansion of water.

Final Matters

When God created heat, He knew it would be an important part of our lives. Without heat, we couldn't live. And without heat, we couldn't enjoy many of the amazing things God created. Let's thank God for the wonderful gift of the sun.

What Do You Remember?

Which law tells us there is no transfer of heat between two objects in thermal equilibrium? What is the first law of thermodynamics? What is the second law of thermodynamics? What is the third law of thermodynamics? How is radiant heat transferred? Describe how heat is transferred through convection. Describe how heat is transferred through conduction. What are the three things a fire needs to ignite? What is temperature? Which temperature scale has water freezing at 32 degrees? Which temperature scale has water freezing at 0 degrees? Which temperature scale has water freezing at 273.15 degrees? Explain thermal expansion. What substance expands when it freezes?

Notebooking Activities

After recording all the fascinating facts you've learned about thermal energy, do the following activity.

Fire safety is one of the most important topics you'll ever study. That's why I think it's important you research and record in your notebooking journal what you learn about fire safety. Go to www.apologia.com/bookextras to find websites that discuss fire safety. Then create a notebooking page that explains the most important things you can do to prevent fires. On another sheet of paper, create your home escape plan. Make a line drawing of your home with the window and door exits, including any items you have to help you escape quickly. Then make a list of what should and should not be done in the event of a fire. The *Chemistry and Physics Notebooking Journal* has pages for these assignments.

Experiment
Build a Solar Oven

You will need:

- 2 cardboard boxes, one smaller than the other. The smaller one needs to hold a cooking vessel. There should also be a few inches of space around the smaller box when you place it in the larger box.
- aluminum foil
- glue
- a pot or glass jar with a lid, painted black
- a newspaper
- a sheet of cardboard
- a pencil
- scissors
- plastic wrap or a clear sheet of plastic or glass that is roughly the same size as the top of the larger box
- some food to cook (grilled cheese sandwich, hot dog, etc.)

1. Line the inside of the smaller box with aluminum foil, shiny side up. Glue it in place, making sure it's flat.
2. Place the smaller box in the larger box.
3. Place your pot or jar in the smaller box.
4. Fill the space between the outside of the smaller box and the inside of the larger box with crumpled newspaper.
5. Crumple some more newspaper and put it around the pot or jar in the smaller box.
6. Lay the sheet of cardboard on the top of the larger box and trace the outline of the box. Add a few inches to the outline you traced and cut the piece to this size. This will be the reflector. Line one side of your reflector with aluminum foil, shiny side out. Attach this to the outside of the larger box, near the top, so there's maximum reflective area sticking up.
7. To cook something in your oven, place the food you want to cook in your black vessel.
8. Lay the clear plastic or glass over the top of the opening of the larger box.
9. Point your solar oven toward the sun. Move it as necessary to follow the sun's path while cooking.

Electrifying Our World

This is where the study of energy becomes truly electrifying! You might remember that when God created the universe, He made it very electrical. Everything is electrical: the earth, the planets, the stars, the oceans, the land, the flowers, the fish, the birds, and even the mammals. Can you explain why? I'll give you a hint: The word "electricity" comes from the word "electron." Yes—electricity is all about those little electrons. Now you see why understanding chemistry is so important.

Let's review electrons and charge. This will help you learn how electricity works.

All Charged Up

You already know that protons have a positive charge and electrons have a negative charge. Do you know what happens to the charge of an atom when it has the same number of electrons and protons? The positive and the negative cancel each other out. These atoms are considered uncharged or neutral. We might say they have a charge of 0. When an atom has too few electrons, it's positively charged. If it has extra electrons, it's negatively charged.

I explained earlier that electrons can jump from one atom to another. Those little electrons do this *all the time*. As you know, this jumping around of electrons changes the charge of atoms. Changing location and changing energy is part of an electron's job. In fact, there's a law I should mention: As with all things God created, new charge cannot be created or destroyed; it can only change locations. Does that sound like some other laws you've heard about in this book? Well, it's true of charge too. What happens when an atom gets positively or negatively charged? You may remember, but let's talk about it anyway.

The electricity that lights neon signs is made up of atoms in motion.

Attraction

You probably remember that opposites attract. So what happens if a positively charged atom comes near a negatively charged atom? Like a magnet, they'll be attracted to each other. A force between them will draw them together. We'll do some activities in a moment to illustrate this.

If opposites attract, what happens to atoms that have the same charge? You probably figured out that they repel or try to get away from each other. All of this is important to the study of electricity. In fact, it's the reason for electricity.

Can you explain what's happening with the atoms pictured above?

Amber flows as resin from wood, then hardens. This ant was trapped in the resin and became part of this amber rock.

Electron Electricity

We get the word "electricity" from the ancient Greek word *elektron*, which means amber. Amber is a glassy rock-like material that's formed from fossilized tree sap. We often find amber with ancient bugs inside. That's because as sap runs out of the trees, bugs get stuck in it. The sap hardens and becomes amber after many, many years.

You may wonder what amber has to do with electricity. The story goes like this: In ancient Greece, a man named Thales of Miletus was trying to polish a piece of amber by rubbing it with a piece of fur. After doing this, he noticed something strange. Small pieces of material jumped up onto the amber as the amber got near the material. Thales thought the amber had a special force inside it.

When you rub anything really hard against hair, it will get those little electrons moving. When those electrons starting moving around, the object gets charged. If just a *few* of the atoms in an object get charged, the whole object becomes charged!

Let's see if this is true by doing an experiment!

Try This!

You will need: An adult's supervision, a balloon, a mirror, a plate, and black pepper (coarsely ground).

First, shake some pepper onto the plate. Now blow up the balloon and rub it 30 times on your hair. (Your hair will need to be clean and free from oil for this to work.) Hold the balloon close to your hair while looking in the mirror. What happens? Finally, hold the balloon close to the pepper. What happens now?

Note: Be aware that if it's an extremely humid day, this experiment may not work properly. This is because the water in the air gets involved in electron transfer, enabling the electrons to leak off the balloon—thus neutralizing the charge.

When you rubbed the balloon on your hair, the electrons moved from your hair to the balloon. This left your hair with a positive charge and the balloon with a negative charge. When you held the balloon near your hair, your hair was attracted to the balloon. It moved toward the balloon when it encountered its invisible electrical field. Why were your hair and the balloon attracted? Because the hair atoms lost electrons when you rubbed the balloon against them. Your hair became positively charged, and the balloon gained electrons—making the balloon negatively charged. Remember, opposites attract. When your hair encountered the electrical field, the electrical force moved the atoms toward the balloon. Electricity really has some power, doesn't it?

What happened with the pepper? Although the pepper particles are neutrally charged, they're made of atoms. All atoms contain charged particles. When the balloon was close to the pepper, its negative charge pushed away anything negatively charged. This means the parts of the pepper grains closer to the balloon were positive, and the parts farther away were negative. So the pepper particles jumped onto the balloon. After a bit of time, some of those pepper particles gained an extra electron from the balloon. They then had the same charge as the balloon. So they were repelled and jumped back off!

As you can see, this girl's hair is electrically charged!

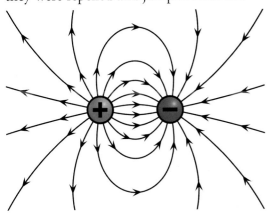

This illustration shows the electrical field around an atom. It also shows two atoms of opposite charges in an attractive relationship.

Is your hair still standing on end? That's because all the hairs that lost an electron are positively charged. This causes those particular strands of hair to be repelled by the other hairs that also lost an electron. In their effort to get away from each other, they stand up on end! If you rub your hair with your hand, you'll probably transfer some of the electrons from your hand back into your hair, causing it to calm down.

Every charged object—whether it's a piece of polished amber, an electric fence, or a balloon—has an invisible electrical field around it. Anything that gets close to that field will be either attracted to or repelled by that charge. An **electrical field** is the field around electrically charged objects. It's like an invisible force that extends beyond the object.

Static Electricity

You've just explored a special kind of electricity we call static electricity, or electrostatic energy to be more scientific. **Electrostatic energy (static electricity)** is stored energy. Do you remember what stored energy is? It's potential energy. Many things around you carry this static electricity. Have you ever touched someone or something and gotten a shock? That's because one of you was electrically charged.

Whenever an object gets charged with static electricity, the electrical energy eventually leaves that object and is transferred here and there. Sometimes it gets transferred onto another object. But normally those extra electrons escape into the air. They usually catch hold of the water

Although you don't typically see it, when electrostatic energy is transferred, it creates a tiny lightning strike between the two objects.

molecules floating around in the air. If there isn't much water in the air, static electricity is much more noticeable. On dry days, we're likely to get an electric shock or two. That's because there aren't as many water molecules in the air to discharge the static electricity that's built up in objects—or in us! What happens to the charged object when it lets go of its extra electrons? It becomes neutral again. That's why your pepper eventually fell off the balloon.

Let's try to create some static electricity!

What happened when you touched the doorknob? You should have felt a shock of electricity. The electrons transferred between your socks and the carpet, making you electrically charged! The charge transferred from your finger to the doorknob, causing a spark of electricity. If it was dark in the room, you may have seen a flash of lightning.

Do you realize the electricity that was generated is the same kind of electricity that illuminates the lights in your house? It's just a whole lot *less* electricity than the energy flow coming into your house. That energy flow is a continuous current rather than a buildup of energy that suddenly discharges.

This light bulb is powered by an electric current running through it.

However, a lot of electrical devices have small gadgets inside that store static electricity to be discharged when needed. These little gadgets are called **capacitors**. A capacitor is made with two plates separated by an insulator. One plate stores positive charges, and the other stores negative charges. The insulator prevents electrons from flowing from the negative plate to the positive plate. Capacitors come in all shapes and sizes, as you can see from the images below.

Let's take a minute to discharge electrostatic energy in the most unusual place—your mouth!

What happened in the last experiment? As you broke the mint apart with your teeth, you were breaking apart sugar crystals in the candy. These sugars released little electrical charges that attracted the nitrogen in the air. When the two met, they reacted and produced a tiny spark you could see.

Did you notice the electric discharge that came from the mint looked like a tiny bolt of lightning? That's because it *was* lightning—but on a much smaller scale than the lightning in the sky. Lightning is one of the most powerful electric discharges you'll ever see. It's basically static electricity with a bang!

You'll study lightning in great detail when you study weather. For now, you should know that lightning strikes to release the stored energy in clouds.

You may have heard that it's not safe to be near a tree or on a hill during a lightning storm. This is true! Can you guess why? When an electrically charged cloud is looking to release energy, it's going to release that energy on whatever is closest. The object it touches will direct the energy to the ground, becoming the pathway for the lightning to travel through. Trees and hills are closest to the clouds and are often struck by lightning. Tall buildings usually have metal lightning rods on them. The rods attract the lightning, sending it safely to the ground without harming anything or anyone.

If there's a lightning storm, the best thing to do is stay inside. But if you can't get inside, stay away from metal, water, and electrical objects. Another safe place is inside a car because the lightning will travel around the outside of the car before heading to the ground. The people inside the car will be safe.

Holding an umbrella during a lightning storm can be dangerous if you're the tallest object around with an umbrella in hand. However, if there are a lot of other things taller than you, an umbrella is safe to hold while you run for safety.

Explain all that you've learned so far about electrostatic energy

Current Events

The electricity that comes into our houses runs along as a current. What's that? Well, let me tell you a story. One day I wanted to fix the outlet into which my computer was plugged. So I took off the cover and, with my screwdriver, began to unscrew the entire thing. When I touched my screwdriver to the metal inside the outlet, a huge bolt of electricity flung me back across the room about five feet. Well, the electricity itself didn't fling me; rather, the electricity caused the muscles in my legs to contract violently, throwing me back. When I looked at my screwdriver, I discovered the electric current that came from the wall outlet had melted the metal of my screwdriver. Now that's power! You should know that the electricity flowing into your house is extremely powerful. That's why parents often put plastic protectors over all the outlets—so young children won't be tempted to stick objects in the plug and get a terrible shock. That much electricity entering a human body can be deadly. I'll explain why I didn't get injured in just a moment.

When electricity is flowing from one place to another, it usually flows in currents. A **current** is like a stream of electrical energy that flows without stopping. The electricity flowing into your house rides on electrical wires. It flows through the wires into whatever object is placed in the outlet.

All the outlets in your house are connected to an electric current flowing into your house. A huge amount of electrical energy flows through these outlets.

It's Great to Insulate

So why didn't the electric current enter my body and melt me? If it could melt my steel screwdriver, how was I protected from that powerful current of electricity flowing out of the outlet? I was protected because the handle of the metal screwdriver was made of plastic. Plastic doesn't conduct or carry electricity. That plastic handle insulated or shielded me from being electrocuted.

If electricity flows really well through something, we say it's a good conductor of electricity. You learned about this in the last lesson. Everything that conducts electricity is called a conductor. Metal conducts electricity really well.

If something doesn't conduct electricity, like the plastic handle of my screwdriver, we call it an insulator. To insulate means to protect or shield. An **insulator** is a protective shield against the flow of electrons. Plastics and wood don't conduct electricity; therefore, they are insulators. It's a good thing people who make screwdrivers understand the importance of insulators, or I might not be writing this book right now!

You may be wondering, "How does electricity actually flow through conductors?" That's a great question! Let's use copper as an example so I can explain how it works.

Copper is one of the best materials to use to conduct electricity. When power is applied to copper, electrons are able to jump off their atoms easily and pass quickly from one atom to the next. This movement of electrons, or flow of electrons, is an electric current. Scientists say an **electric current** is a flow of electricity through a conductor. Think of it as electrons streaming from one atom to another.

The ions in this acidic lemon are generating electricity through a circuit.

Electrical Ions

But metals aren't the only things that conduct electricity. Electricity can flow through liquids as well. That's why

Tools used on electrical equipment are protected with insulators.

lifeguards tell you to get out of the water when there's a lightning storm. Liquids that are great conductors of electricity usually contain ions. Do you remember that atoms are called ions when they gain an extra electron or lose an electron? When you rubbed the balloon on your hair, you created ions. Ions are electrically charged molecules, so ionic fluids are great conductors of electricity, too. Believe it or not, your body is full of ionic fluid. So you are a great conductor of electricity as well! The ions in your organs and tissues cause electric currents to flow through your brain, nerves, and all your other organs to keep them working properly. Yes—God made you an ionic bonding machine operating with electrical energy from the top of your head to the tips of your toes!

Now you understand that without the screwdriver's plastic handle, the electricity would have flowed from the wires of my house into the metal of the screwdriver and right through me—being passed along by all that ionic fluid inside my body. I would have been cooked!

Before I started working on the outlet, I should have turned off the flow of electricity into my house. Let's explore how this huge amount of power got into my house and how I could have turned it off.

Circling Power

In order to have a flow of electricity, we need something that produces electricity. We also need something to conduct the electricity to where we want it to go—in order to light our house or turn on the heater. All electricity that flows from one place to another has a source or beginning. Do you remember where all the powerful electricity that turns on your lights comes from? It comes from power plants. Once the electricity reaches your house, it turns around and goes back to the power plant. Flowing electricity must always move in a circle. Electricity can't continue to flow unless it's running through a **circuit**—a circular path that starts

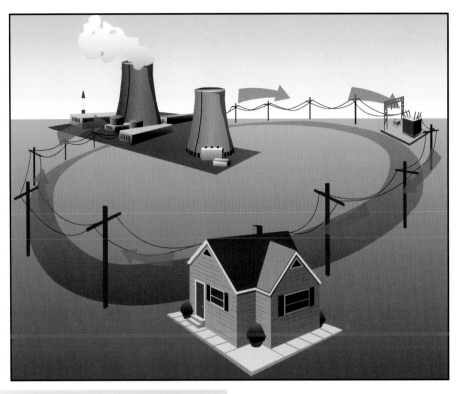

and finishes at the same place. Let's see how this works.

Lines of Power

To light a room, we flip a light switch. Electricity flows from the wires inside the walls of our houses into the light bulb. It goes through the light bulb and back out different wires. Those wires inside our houses are connected to wires outside our houses, which travel to the source of all that power—a nearby electrical power plant.

As you may have guessed, the power plant that brings electricity into your house is incredibly important. It provides all the electricity you need to run almost anything you desire to operate— whether it's a night light, vacuum

This dam is an electric power plant, providing electricity to residents of a nearby city. Nuclear and coal-run plants provide electricity for many cities through a power grid.

cleaner, computer, stove, oven, or television.

Take a minute to think of everything you depend on that uses electrical power. Consider things that plug into an outlet, whether it's to charge the object or turn it on. How many things can you count that you depend on every week? How about every day? How would your life be different if you had no electricity?

Electrical Grid

The power you use travels from the power plants into your house through a special system called the **electric grid**. An electric grid includes three things: power plants, power lines, and transformers. Power plants make the power. Power lines carry the power, sometimes from one state to another. Transformers change the level of power so it isn't too much when it's sent to our houses.

Power lines that go into people's homes are found along the streets and are sometimes buried underground. Are the power lines that go into your home visible above the ground on poles? If not, they're probably hidden under the ground. Before you dig deep holes in your yard, you're required to have a city worker come out and put a mark where all the power lines are located. You wouldn't want to accidentally cut into a power line with a metal shovel, would you? I sure wouldn't.

Planting Power

How does all this work? The power originates or begins at a power plant. Usually, coal, oil, or nuclear energy is used to heat water. This heated water creates steam. As you know, steam is produced when hot water changes phases from a liquid to a gas. This steam turns the blades of a large fan called a turbine. The turning turbine generates an electric current.

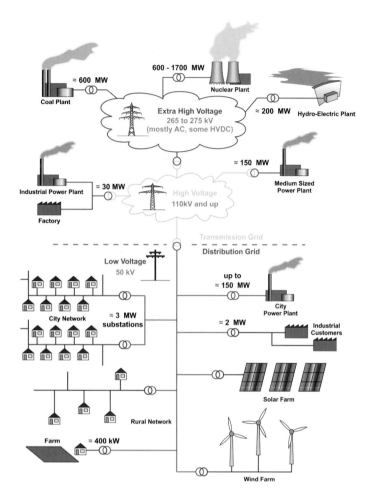

This electric grid shows the different producers of power and the network that sends the power to houses and buildings. Some power plants create more energy (measured in megawatts) than others.

The spinning turbine blades cause a large power generator to begin spinning as well. The word "generate" means to make or create. So a power generator is a power maker. The generator has coiled copper wire that spins quickly inside a magnetic field. It's like a big motor. We'll make a small version of this in the next lesson when we study magnets. This spinning copper produces an enormous flow of electrons—which is electricity! This electricity is then sent along a circuit.

Because of the way the coil spins, the electricity is sent out in one direction. It then switches and is sent in the other direction. It alternates back and forth between the two wires that come in and go out of the circuit. You probably think of electricity flowing in only one direction—going out one particular wire and coming back in through the other. This isn't how the power coming into our houses works, though. The way a generator or motor spins around automatically causes the current to keep changing directions.

You'll understand this better in the next lesson when you build a motor. We call this kind of current an **alternating current** or **AC**. Electricity produced by anything with a motor usually produces an AC. Batteries produce a different kind of current that flows in only one direction. We'll learn about that in a moment.

Once the generator produces electricity, it's sent through wires to an electric substation. You may have seen these around your town or

These enormous generators spin to create a flow of electricity, providing power to homes and businesses.

Substations like the one above can be smaller or larger, depending on the needs of the people who are getting the power.

city. A huge amount of power enters the substation. The substations have transformers to lower the power level. It's then separated into different lines to be sent to different places.

As the electricity heads out the power lines, it stops at different locations. These locations regulate the power to make sure it's not too much or too little.

When the electricity reaches your house, it runs through another transformer. The transformer is either a cylinder mounted high on a pole or a green tube buried in your lawn. This takes that huge voltage and reduces it to a smaller amount, suited for your particular house. Too much voltage would blow out the light bulbs when you turn them on. Too little voltage would be insufficient to power your appliances.

Some transformers are up on poles like this one. Others are buried underground.

When you turn on the light switch, you open the circuit that allows power to flow into your house. The electric current begins to flow from the transformer through a meter outside. The meter is there to keep track of all the power you're taking into your house. A meter reader from the power company comes by every month to check how much electricity you've used. They send your parents a bill each month charging them for the power. So if you're not using the lights in the room or watching the television, please turn them off!

Try This! If you have a nondigital meter, turn off all the lights and electrical equipment in your house, including your air conditioner (or heater) and even your refrigerator. Leave them off for just a few minutes. Now go outside to your meter box and watch the dials on the meter. They should not be moving at all. Go back inside and turn everything on, including every single light in your house and even your oven. Now go back outside and check the meter. Are the dials moving around? They should be.

Try This! Ask your parents to show you the circuit box for your house and have them tell you what they know about it. Do they know which circuits go to which areas of the house? If not, you can help them find out. Turn on the lights in the kitchen. Now go to the circuit box and turn off the different circuit breakers until the kitchen light goes off. You've just discovered which circuit goes to the kitchen! You can label that breaker with a "K" for kitchen. You can do this for every area of your house if it hasn't already been done.

After learning how your meter works, you're probably more motivated to turn off the lights when you're not using them. You saw how much the dials spun, which means the electric company will charge you for all that electricity you used unnecessarily!

Back to your house: After the electricity leaves the meter, it moves along wires into your home, where it enters a special device called a distribution board or panel board (circuit breaker box). The panel has a main on-and-off switch for the electricity flowing from the outside into your home, as well as many additional on-and-off switches for each area of your house. We call these switches circuit breakers. They can turn the circuit on or break the circuit, turning the electricity off. You can manually turn the electricity off and on if you need to work on the electricity in that part of the house. If there is a short circuit, the switch can turn off the circuit automatically to prevent a fire. Imagine if a wire in your house became loose and touched the ground. It would cause all those volts of electricity to electrify your house! Instead, when a powerful surge of electricity goes back into the panel box, it automatically flips a switch and opens the circuit so that the electricity does not flow. So a circuit box is an important protective device for your home.

The power flows through the circuit box into the wires of your house. Those wires are connected behind the walls and into the different outlets and switches. Remember, for anything to work, the electricity has to flow out as well as in. For the electricity to flow into anything, it must be connected to a circuit—the circle of connected wires. When the electric current flows into the lamp on your table, it goes through the light bulb. But it doesn't stop there with the light shining. It goes through the light bulb and back out again through a different wire. It flows out of that wire, following the same path it started with. It then travels all the way back to the transformer where it makes another loop, and another. This is how electricity flows in a circle—a circuit circle! Of course, it alternates back and forth between the wire it comes into and the wire it goes out from. But it's always flowing in a circle.

Before you work on the electrical wiring or outlets in your home, you should turn off the power coming into your home by flipping the switch on your circuit breaker box.

Most electric cords have obvious ridges where the incoming and outgoing power flows.

Look at a lamp in your room. Notice the cord that plugs into the wall. Most cords have an indention between the two wires. If you were to take the plastic off the wire, you'd see that it's actually two different wires. They're both needed to complete the circuit. Electricity flows into the lamp through the bulb from one wire and out of the bulb into the other wire—and round and round it goes. Why do you think the cords are covered with plastic? As you know, plastic is an insulator. It protects the metal wires inside so the current doesn't flow out of the cord and the two wires don't touch.

What happens if the wires touch? Electricity prefers to flow through the shortest path. So instead of going all the way through the light bulb, it will flow into the wire, then out the wire it's touching before it ever reaches the bulb. This creates a shorter path or a **short circuit**. The flow of electricity will not go all the way through the wires. Instead, it will take the shorter circuit with the touching wires.

All electrical devices reduce the current because they use some of the electricity. When the current flows out through the other side of the electrical device, it's a reduced current. We call it resistance when something reduces an electric current. But in a short circuit, this resistance is lacking. So a huge current now

If you ever see a damaged cord on an electrical appliance, make sure the appliance is not used until the cord is fixed.

flows through the circuit and back out. Fortunately, this large current will melt the fuse and break the circuit. The circuit is turned off when there's a short circuit (sometimes called a short). That way, there won't be a fire or some other hazard from the exposed, powerful current.

If you ever see a cord that has some of the plastic broken or missing and you can see the metal wires, replace the cord or cover it with electrical tape. Electrical tape is a plastic insulating tape that prevents electricity from flowing through it.

Generators

Some people live far from the city and aren't connected to the city power grid. Some of these people rely on solar energy. Others must produce their own power with a generator. A small generator is a lot like the giant ones found at the power plant, but it's only about as big as an ice chest. It's powered by gasoline that spins a wheel to generate electricity. Places that experience frequent storms or heavy snowstorms often lose power because the severe weather can bring down power lines. People living in these places usually have a backup generator. Because some patients in hospitals are placed on machines to stay alive, it's important for the hospitals to have generators as a backup source of energy in case they lose power.

Explain in your own words all that you've learned so far.

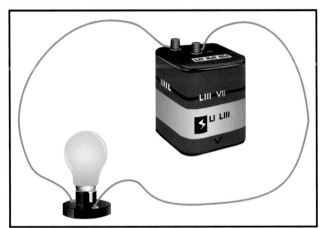

This image shows how electricity flows in a circle, called a circuit.

Loading the Circuit

Now you understand that electricity flows in circles called a circuit. Circuits are an important part of understanding electricity. We'll make some circuits in just a moment. Here are a few things we'll need: a power source, a load, and wires. The **load** is the object we're trying to turn on with an electric current. You could use a light, a motor, or a buzzer. Loads are sometimes called resistors. A **resistor** is any device that slows down the flow of electricity through a circuit. The source of power we'll use is batteries. Because they have less power, batteries are safer to use than the power that comes into your home. Let's first explore what a battery is and how it's made. Then we'll have some fun with circuits!

Battery Power

I know you probably understand what batteries do, but let me give you a little history of the battery. An Italian physicist named Alessandro Volta wondered if he might be able to create electricity with things that conduct electricity: metals and ionic fluids. So Mr. Volta soaked some cardboard in saltwater and cut it into little round discs. He created a stack, inserting the cardboard discs between pieces of silver and zinc. Then he attached wires to each end. Finally, Mr. Volta touched the wires together and—BAM! Sparks flew! Alessandro Volta made something we call a wet cell battery.

This is a painting of Volta explaining electricity to Napoleon in France.

A **battery** is a combination of different items that conduct electricity. Every item is touching the item next to it. The way these items are set up generates a current of electricity.

Do you think a battery has potential or kinetic energy? A battery actually stores potential energy—chemical energy. But when it's in use, that potential chemical energy turns into kinetic electrical energy.

Unlike the alternating current of a motor, batteries create a direct current that flows out one side of the battery, through the circuit, and back inside the other end of the battery. The current always flows in the same direction. We call this kind of current a **direct current** or **DC**.

You may have noticed that batteries have a plus side and a minus side. That's the positive end and negative end of the flow of electricity. Sometimes the positive side of the battery has a little bump on the end.

The electricity always flows out the negative side of the battery, through the circuit, and back in the positive side, repeating the cycle over and over again. Many drawings show the electricity flowing out the positive side. However, those drawings aren't correct.

Because Alessandro Volta discovered how to produce electricity, we measure it with a measurement called volts. **Volts** measure the energy of the electrical charge. Most batteries are 1.5 volts. The electrical sockets in houses provide 120 volts. That's a big difference in energy, isn't it?

Do you think you might be able to make a wet cell battery like Volta did? I think so. Let's give it a whirl!

Electricity flows out the negative end of the battery, through the circuit, and back into the positive end of the battery.

Try This!

You will need: An adult's supervision, 6 pennies dated after 1982, a piece of rough sandpaper, a piece of thick cardboard, electrical tape, a small LED, 1 cup of water, scissors, 1 teaspoon of salt, and vinegar.

Using the sandpaper, sand the copper off the "tails" side of 5 pennies. You should see a silver color under the copper. This metal is called zinc. Next, add salt to the water and stir until it's dissolved. Do you remember what this kind of solution is called? A saturated solution! Now add 1 tablespoon of vinegar to the solution. Cut your cardboard into 5 square pieces the same size as the pennies. Drop them into the water and let them soak. Next, stack the sanded pennies with the silver side up and place a wet piece of cardboard between each penny. Be sure

the pennies do not touch each other. Also, make sure the pieces of cardboard do not touch each other. In addition, be sure your stack is not dripping wet. Now place the unsanded penny on the very top of your stack. Wrap the entire stack with electrical tape, leaving the top and bottom pennies exposed. Connect the LED by touching the longer wire to the top unsanded penny and the shorter wire to the bottom sanded penny. Make sure the wires don't touch any other layers. Congratulations—you just made a real battery!

Let's explore how the battery actually works. When two different metals are connected by an ionic solution, a chemical reaction occurs at each metal surface, causing the metals to give or take electrons. When these metals are connected by a wire, electrons move from one surface to the other, creating an electric current.

So how did this happen with your battery? The zinc electrons transferred to the copper atoms. The salty cardboard was the electrolyte that moved electricity from one penny to the next and between the two wires.

Each zinc-cardboard-copper stack represented a single cell. By stacking additional cells, you made a battery. A battery is actually a series of cells. You created a battery that's almost exactly like Volta's battery.

Now you know what to do if the power goes out and you don't have any batteries!

Current Flowing

You may be wondering what makes the current flow through the circuit. Why is it leaving the battery and returning to the battery?

Think of it like this: Imagine water flowing down a hill. It's moving from a higher elevation to a lower elevation. That's similar to how and why electrons move through a wire. They move from a place of higher electrical energy to a place of lower electrical energy.

Inside a battery, one side has

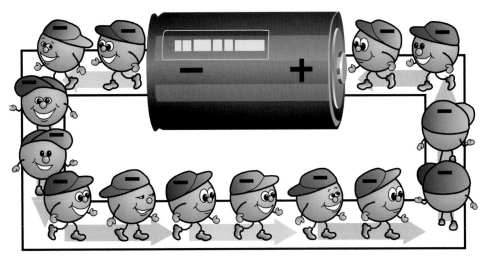

The electrons exit the negative side of the battery and flow around the circuit, entering the positive side.

a place of higher electrical energy than the other side. It's not balanced. Things like to be balanced. So when you attach a wire to both ends of the battery, electricity will flow from the place of higher electrical energy through the wire to the place of lower electrical energy. This balances out the energy.

The current flowing through the battery is seeking to get to the other end of the battery. Just like water flowing down a hill, the electrons naturally flow from the higher electrical energy to the lower electrical energy.

Circuit Central

Now it's time to explore more about circuits. You'll be building circuits and exploring them as you learn. Let's begin by building a simple circuit.

Try This!

You will need: An adult's supervision, a 6-volt lantern battery (preferably with screws on the positive and negative connectors), 2 coated copper wires, and a load (a small 6-volt light bulb works well).

Connect these items as shown in the picture. Now that you've built a simple circuit, let's experiment with it!

We talked about the fact that some things are great conductors and others are not. Let's do an experiment to find out which items are the best conductors and what materials don't conduct electricity well.

Try This!

You will need: An adult's supervision, the simple circuit you created in the last experiment, plus an extra wire.

First, remove one of the wires from your load and attach the new wire to the load. Now you have an open wire leading away from the load and an open wire leading into the battery. Try to see if you can close the circuit and keep the electricity flowing by connecting the two wires to different objects. If the object conducts electricity, the light will continue to glow. If the object does not conduct electricity, the electricity will not flow through the circuit. Attempt to complete the circuit with different items, such as those listed below. You can use different items from the ones listed, but you'll need to create your own chart with the items you're testing. The *Chemistry and Physics Notebooking Journal* provides a blank chart for you to use. Before you test each item, be sure to make a hypothesis (a good guess) about whether or not the item will conduct electricity. Will the item prove to be a conductor or an insulator? Here are some items to get you started:

- a piece of silver jewelry
- a steel nail
- a penny
- a pencil sharpened at both ends
- gold jewelry
- a dime
- a fork
- a piece of wood

Now we're going to test which solutions conduct electricity. If it conducts electricity, it's an ionic solution!

Try This!

You will need: An adult's supervision, your circuit, 4 drinking glasses, milk, water, salt, and vinegar.

Fill one glass with milk, one with water, one with salt water, and one with vinegar. To test the circuit, place each side of the open wire into each of the cups of solution, one at a time. What did you learn?

Wow! You've learned a lot about conductors of electricity. Take some time to explain to someone what you've learned.

Switching Things Around

I want to teach you a little about making a device that opens and closes circuits. When you turn on a light in your house, you close the circuit, enabling electricity to flow to the light bulb. However, when you turn off a light, you *open* the circuit, preventing electricity from flowing to your light bulb. It's much like the experiment you just performed. You closed the circuit when you put good conductors between the wires. However, when you placed items that didn't conduct electricity between the wires, the circuit stayed open. You didn't have anything to close the circuit and make the electricity flow.

Switches are devices we use to open and close circuits. Think about all the different things you turn on and off every day. How do you turn on the light in your room? How do you turn on a lamp? How do you turn on the oven? What about your computer? Do you have any toys you can turn on? What do all these switches look like? Can you think of any other switches that are different from the switches I just mentioned? As you can tell, there are many different kinds of switches. Let's take some time now to build a switch using common materials.

Try This!

You will need: An adult's supervision, the circuit you created, 1 paper clip, 2 paper fasteners, tape, and 1 piece of corrugated cardboard (about 2 inches).

Position the paper clip in the middle of the cardboard. Poke one paper fastener through one end of the paper clip and the cardboard. Push the fastener all the way down through the cardboard and open the prongs underneath. Position the second paper fastener so that the other end of the paper clip touches it. Now swing the paper clip away and push the paper fastener into the cardboard. Open the prongs underneath. Turn the cardboard upside down and wind the ends of the wire from your circuit around each prong. Make sure the prongs of the fasteners aren't touching each other on the back side. Tape down the prongs with the wires so the prongs never touch each other. Now use your switch to turn on and off your load!

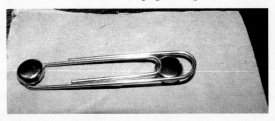

What if you wanted to light several light bulbs? Could you simply add more light bulbs to the circuit you made before? Let's try and see.

Try This!

You will need: An adult's supervision, the circuit you've been working with, 2 more lights and sockets, and 2 more pieces of copper wire.

First, unhook one wire from one side of the light bulb that's already connected. Now add one more light bulb. Switch on the light. What happens? Repeat the process by adding another light bulb.

What happened when you added more light bulbs to the circuit? When you increased the load, you found that the battery didn't supply the same amount of electricity to all the light bulbs. The light bulbs were dimmer, or not as bright. Each light bulb that was added produced more resistance to the flow of electricity. Remember, each light bulb is considered a resistor because it decreases the flow of the current when the current is transformed into light energy. Three light bulbs added much more resistance than one light bulb.

Explain what you've learned so far about circuits.

Series Circuits

What you created in the last experiment was a series circuit. A **series circuit** is a circuit that has more than one resistor, and the electricity takes one path through the resistors. The current left the battery, then traveled through the wire to the first bulb. It lit the bulb, then continued to flow out of that bulb through the wire into the next bulb—and into the next. It flowed through a series of bulbs before it circled back through to the

Math It!

There's a well-known relationship between current (I), voltage (V), and resistance (R). It's called Ohm's law: $V=IR$ or $I=V/R$. The unit of resistance is named after the German physicist George Simon Ohm. The law states that when a 1-volt battery produces 1 ampere of current through a resistance, that resistance is 1 ohm.

If one of these lights burns out, the other won't work because they're in a series.

battery. With each new resistance, the current was not as strong. The higher the resistance, the smaller the current.

One major problem with the series circuit is that if one of the bulbs burns out, it opens the circuit and the flow of electricity stops. You see, the filament in the bulb is conducting electricity. It continues the flow out of the circuit. When the filament in the bulb burns out, the conducting path is no longer closed. The current stops flowing because the circuit has been opened, and the other bulbs don't get electricity. This is how most Christmas lights are made. When one bulb burns out, the entire string of lights turns off.

But there's another kind of circuit that can be used to keep the flow of electricity strong as it flows through each resistor. Let's explore parallel circuits now.

Parallel Circuits

What if I want all three light bulbs to be just as bright as when I only had one bulb? What do you think I should do? Well, you may have said, "Add more batteries." That's definitely an option but not a very economical option. Would you believe me if I told you that all you need is a little more wire? Let's see if that works.

Try This!

You will need: An adult's supervision, your circuit from the last experiment, and a few extra wires.

Set up your light bulbs according to the image shown here. Flip the switch to see what happens!

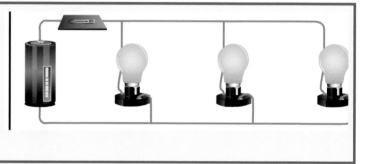

A parallel circuit is a circuit that has more than one resistor, but the electricity takes multiple paths through the resistors. You created a parallel circuit in your last experiment. Why did adding more wire work to make all the bulbs shine as brightly as when you only had one bulb? It's because as electrons flowed out of the battery and down the wire, some journeyed through the first wire to light the first bulb. Some took a different path and flowed through the second bulb, while other electrons flowed through the third bulb. When the electrons left the battery, they flowed through only one resistor (one bulb) before they returned to the battery to pick up more energy. The resistors were parallel to one another, using the same battery but getting their own flow of electricity from the battery.

The battery in a parallel circuit won't last nearly as long as the battery in a series circuit. However, if one light burns out in a parallel circuit, the electricity can still flow easily through the other lights.

Explain the difference between a series circuit and a parallel circuit.

Before we close this lesson, let's learn how electric engineers and electricians map out electrical currents on paper.

Circuit Symbols

You've learned a lot about circuits, haven't you? You now know about resistors, wires, cells, and batteries. Engineers and electricians use special symbols to represent each of the different items in a circuit. I'm going to teach you a few of these symbols so you can draw a circuit diagram. Throughout this lesson, we've represented batteries with pictures that look like batteries, lights with symbols that look like lights, and wires that look like wires. But the real way to represent a circuit is with classic symbols that are used worldwide.

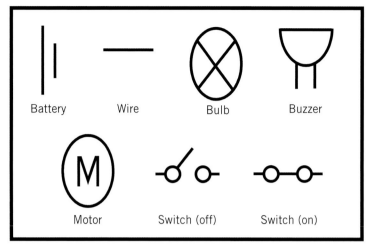

Look at the illustrations of the different symbols we've studied. Now look at the illustrations of the circuits. Do you see how the symbols represent the circuits? Can you tell me which is the series circuit and which is the parallel circuit in the images? The parallel circuit is on the left and the series is on the right.

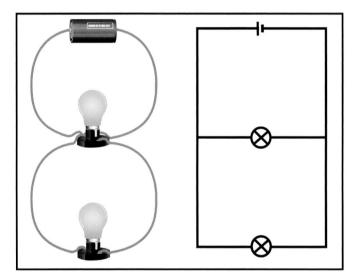 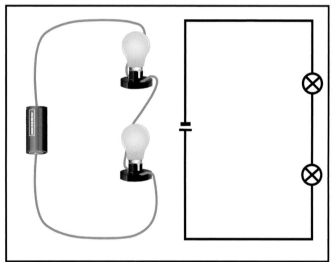

Do you notice that wires in a circuit diagram are never drawn as curves or turns? They're always drawn as straight lines even though in real life the wires tend to twist and turn. In your notebooking activity, you'll draw some circuit diagrams using these symbols.

Final Matters

You've made great headway in understanding electricity. But there's still more to learn because electricity and magnets go together. In the next lesson you'll use a lot of the same materials you used in this lesson to study electromagnetism. So keep your materials close by and your circuits set up. In the meantime, let's finish the lesson with some questions, activities, and a fun experiment!

What Do You Remember?

What is electrostatic energy sometimes called? What is the name of a gadget that stores electricity? What is an insulator? Name something that can be used as an insulator. What do we call facilities that generate electricity? What kind of current—alternating or direct—comes through your house from the power plant? What is a load? What kind of current—alternating or direct—comes from a battery? Who created the first battery? Which kind of circuit—series or parallel—would you prefer to have for your Christmas lights? Why?

Notebooking Activities

After recording the fascinating facts you discovered and the experiments you did, draw the circuit diagrams below and label each item. Above each circuit diagram, write down whether the diagram shows a series circuit or a parallel circuit. The *Chemistry and Physics Notebooking Journal* has a page with diagrams for you to use.

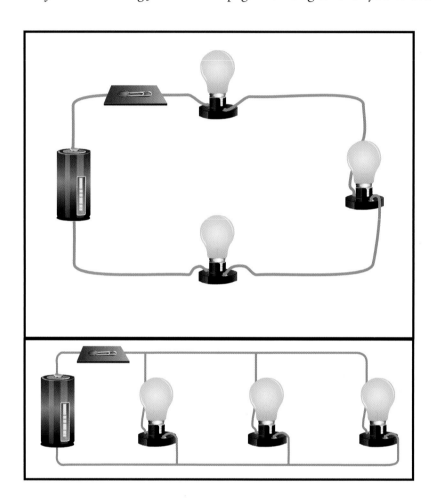

Experiment
Make a Flashlight

You will need:

- 2 D batteries
- 2 five-inch pieces of insulated copper bell wire with 1 inch of insulation stripped off the ends
- a cardboard tube cut to 4 inches in length
- a flashlight bulb
- 2 brass fasteners (brads)
- a 1-inch x 3-inch cardboard strip
- a paper clip
- electrical tape
- a bathroom-sized paper cup

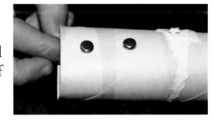

1. Push the brass fasteners through the outside of the tube near one end and attach a paper clip to the fasteners. This is your switch to turn on and off your flashlight.
2. Inside the tube, attach a wire to each fastener.
3. Tape the batteries end to end (positive to negative) and put them inside the tube.

4. Tape one end of the wire to the bottom of one battery's negative side.
5. Pass the other wire end through a hole (large enough to insert the bulb) in the center of cardboard strip. Then twist the wire around the bulb and tape it in place. Insert the bulb into the cardboard strip. This strip, when taped to the tube, will position the bulb for contact with the positive (+) terminal.

6. Use the paper cup as a reflector by inserting the bulb through a hole punched in the bottom of the cup. Secure with tape.

Mysterious Magnetism

Do you have papers and pictures hanging from your refrigerator? If so, they're probably held there by magnets. As a child, I found few things as fascinating as magnets. In this lesson we're going to explore the mysterious world of magnetism and the electrifying world of electromagnets.

This lesson comes right after the electricity lesson because electricity and magnetism are closely related. In fact, you can't have electricity without magnetism, and magnetism can become stronger with electricity! I'll explain all that in a little while. But for now, let's start at the beginning. As you've already learned, all these wonderful physics and chemistry concepts began at creation—when God made the world.

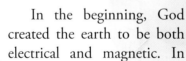

In the beginning, God created the earth to be both electrical and magnetic. In fact, the world is really one massive magnet. Before I explain that, I want you to understand how magnets work. That way, you'll better understand how the earth itself is a magnet.

Magnetic History

You may not realize this, but magnets are made out of magnetic metals and rocks. The story of how magnets were discovered goes something like this: An ancient Greek boy was walking along a path on his way somewhere. He took a path over some rocks. When he stepped on one large rock, all the nails in his shoes came out and stuck to the rock. That must have been a powerfully magnetic rock! I'm not sure if that story is true, but it's a fun story. Just imagine what the boy would have thought—a magic rock!

The ancient Greeks were responsible for giving magnetic objects the name "magnets." It may be because the first magnetic stones were found near the city of Magnesia. Or the name could have come from the story of the boy, who was called Magnes. Either way, the Greeks noticed that pieces of iron would jump onto certain black, metallic rocks. They also observed that smaller pieces of this kind of rock would jump onto larger pieces of iron. For thousands of years magnetic materials were considered a big mystery. Let's explore these magnetic materials— called magnetite.

Magnetite

Magnetite is a black rock with a shiny surface. It's made up of iron and oxygen. Most magnets we use in our homes are a mixture of powdered magnetite mixed with plastic or ceramic. Really strong magnets are sometimes made up of metal alloys like alnico or rare earth metals. You'll need a rare earth magnet later in this lesson. If you have a magnet, examine it for a bit. What are the properties you notice about this special rock?

Scientists describe a **magnet** as any object that attracts and repels certain metals. Magnets also produce a **magnetic field**. This field is like a force around the object. Just as an electrical field surrounds everything charged with electricity, so a magnetic field surrounds magnets. When magnetic objects get in that field, they're either pulled toward the magnet or are repelled and pushed away from it. This depends on which side of the magnet they're facing. We call objects that are attracted to magnets **magnetic**. The magnet itself is also considered a magnetic object.

This rock is a piece of magnetite. It's strongly magnetic and is used to make magnets.

All speakers are made with magnets, even tiny earphones.

Magnets Everywhere

You probably use magnets more than you realize. In fact, many things around your house use magnets to operate. Consider your refrigerator door. How does it close so tightly? Examine the door by opening and closing it. You probably discovered that long magnets running the length of the door keep the door tightly shut. Without these magnets, your food would spoil. Some cabinet doors use magnets. All the speakers in your house depend on magnets to produce sound. In fact, every single machine in your house most likely has magnets in it. That's because motors are made with magnets. We'll learn all about these special motor magnets at the end of this lesson.

Magnets are used in medicine as well. Magnetic resonance imaging or MRI scanners are used to see inside the body. They can detect if anything is wrong without causing the body harm.

Farmers even use magnets. Farmers make their cows swallow magnets when they're young. This is so the tiny nails or small pieces of barbed wire they might accidentally swallow won't harm them. The magnet sits in the large stomach chamber, attracting the small iron pieces. This keeps the iron from traveling farther into the cow's body.

Some of the most amazing vehicles today are those that

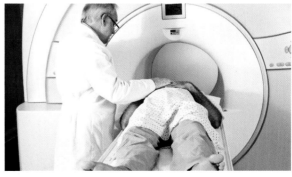

This MRI scanner will use magnets to detect if there's anything abnormal in this man's body.

rise into the air and zoom away as if they're flying. These vehicles use maglev or magnetic levitation technology. In fact, the fastest trains in the world, traveling over 300 miles per hour, run on giant magnets that levitate (or raise) the train above the track. Astrophysicists dream of building a giant space elevator that would take people from earth to space using special magnets.

This Transrapid high-speed train runs on magnetic levitation, floating on a frictionless magnetic cushion.

You've already learned that magnets have helped mankind in many ways. They are truly a magnificent creation of a majestic God! Let's take some time to learn about the characteristics of magnets.

Explain all that you've learned so far about magnets.

Magnets have a north pole and a south pole. The opposite poles are attracted to each other, and the other poles are repelled by each other.

North and South

You've learned that atoms can be positive or negative. Like atoms, magnets have opposites too. All magnets have a north pole and a south pole. Some magnets even have the letters N and S on each end, showing you which end is which. Do you remember that opposites attract? Well, it's the same with magnets. The north pole of a magnet is attracted to the south pole of other magnets. Again, just like atoms, like poles are repelled by each other. Let's explore this concept with real magnets.

Try This!

You will need: An adult's supervision and 2 magnets, with each end labeled north or south.

First, try to attach the magnets to one another at the same poles (north to north or south to south). Now try to attach them at the opposite poles (north to south). What happens?

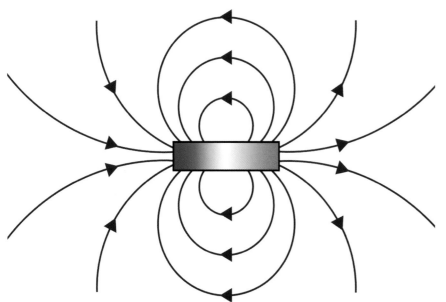

Did you notice that the magnets are attracted to one another at the opposite ends but won't stick together at the other ends? They're repelled and attracted because of their poles. Did you notice you didn't actually have to touch the magnet to the other magnet to get them together? When you got them close enough, they leaped through the air toward each other. That's because of the magnetic field I told you about earlier. It looks something like the drawing here.

A magnetic field is a region around the magnet. When magnetic materials come nearby, they experience the force of the magnet. This force causes them to move. They move either away from or toward the magnet.

The lines on the image show the shape of the magnetic field around the magnet. Look at the lines of the magnetic field. The closer together the lines, the stronger the field. When you put another magnet or any magnetic object near the magnetic field, it will be affected by the magnetic force.

You can actually see the magnetic field of a magnet by doing the following experiment.

Try This!

You will need: An adult's supervision, a bar magnet, a horseshoe magnet, a round magnet, a piece of paper, and iron shavings.

To begin, place the piece of paper on top of the bar magnet. Now drop the iron shavings on top of the paper. What happens? The iron shavings line up in the shape of the magnetic field, don't they? Try the same thing with the horseshoe and round magnets. Save your iron shavings for another experiment.

You should know this is not an exact representation of the magnetic field of the magnet. The lines you see with your iron shavings are much larger than the actual lines in a magnetic field. The shavings are attracted to the lines, but they're more like large groups of lines in the magnetic field. If you were to redo the experiment, the lines would be in different places. This reveals that the lines you see are not the *actual* lines—they only tell you about the direction of the force lines.

As you can see, when a magnetic object is placed near the magnetic field, it will experience the force of the magnetic field. It will either be pulled toward or repelled by the magnetic field it encounters. We can actually see the magnetic forces between two magnets. Let's watch!

Try This!

You will need: An adult's supervision, 2 bar magnets, a piece of paper, iron shavings, and a table.

First, place the piece of paper on the table. Now pour a pile of iron shavings on the paper. Over the paper, hold the first magnet's north pole against the second magnet's south pole. Next, slowly pull the magnets a short distance apart. Do you see the presence of the magnetic field? Now dip both magnets in the north pole shavings. Place the north pole of the first magnet against the north pole of the second magnet. What happens?

In the last experiment, you could see how the attraction between the two fields increased the strength of the magnetic field. Did you notice how the repelling magnetic forces bent the magnetic field away from the magnets? These invisible forces are always present when magnets are attracting and repelling.

My Magnetic Domain

What do you think would happen if you cut a magnet in half? Would you be able to get a south pole magnet and a north pole magnet? No matter how many times you cut the magnet in half, it still has a north pole and a south pole. If you cut your magnet in two pieces, you would not have one north pole magnet and one south pole magnet. You'd have two magnets, each with a north

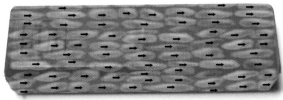

Although the domains in a magnet are much smaller, closer together, and stacked on top of each other, this image gives you a good idea of how the domains are assembled—all facing the same direction.

pole and a south pole.

Why is this? Every magnet is made up of billions of tiny magnets called **domains**. Have you ever heard the word "domain"? A domain is an area. Your bedroom is your domain. It's your area. All throughout every magnet are billions of microscopic areas. They look somewhat like the picture on this page.

Every domain is just like a miniature magnet. In a magnet, all the domains point in the same direction—with a north pole and a south pole. Because the domains are so small, it would be nearly impossible to cut the magnet small enough to break apart a domain. Even if you could, you'd probably still have a north pole and south pole in the almost invisible particle you were able to remove from the magnet.

Before we move on, explain to someone what you've learned so far about magnets.

Magnetic Materials

Iron was the first metal discovered to be attracted to magnetite. Metals that are strongly attracted to magnetite are called **ferromagnetic**, from the Latin word *ferrum*, meaning iron. So any metal that sticks to a magnet is like iron, or ferromagnetic.

Not all metals are strongly attracted to magnets. Discovering which materials are magnetic is a fun activity that may surprise you. Try the following activity to see what objects around your house are attracted to magnets.

Try This!

You will need: An adult's supervision, a magnet, and different items from around your house (keys, bottle caps, nails, paper clips, and metals from your parents' toolbox).

To begin, guess which items will be magnetic and which will not. Using your magnet, test each item to see if it's attracted to the magnet. When you're done, be sure to record whether or not your predictions were correct. There's a chart for this activity in the *Chemistry and Physics Notebooking Journal*.

Were you surprised by any of the items that were or were not magnetic? What makes certain objects magnetic? Let's find out!

Magnetic Atoms

Did you know that electricity, or anything electrical, produces a magnetic field? It's true! That means anything with electrons produces a magnetic field. Since the whole earth is filled with electrons, everything on earth is magnetic. How can that be? Didn't we just discover that some things are magnetic and others are not? Well, that's *sort* of true. Let's explore this a little more to understand it better.

Here's how it works: Whenever an electron is spinning inside an atom, it creates a tiny magnetic field around that tiny atom. Since the electrons are always spinning, magnetic fields are always being created. When these fields occur, we say the atom has a **magnetic moment**. Every atom experiences magnetic moments—becoming magnetized by spinning electrons. But an atom that experiences a magnetic moment isn't always able

These ferromagnetic nails are strongly attracted to magnets.

to attract magnetic objects. When electrons are spinning around an atom, they spin in either the same direction or in opposite directions from each other. If the electrons are spinning in opposite directions, the magnetic moments cancel each other out. As a result, the atom can't attract magnetic objects. This atom will be diamagnetic. **Diamagnetic** substances have a weak response to magnets because their electron pairs cancel each other out.

If there is an odd number of electrons, one electron will be unpaired with another electron. So the electrons can't completely cancel out the magnetism. These atoms are paramagnetic. **Paramagnetic** substances are slightly attracted by a magnetic field. It usually has an odd number of electrons, so there are no equal pairs. One lone electron is causing a slight magnetic field. Though we can't see the field with our naked eyes, scientists can detect the magnetic field with special instruments. Aluminum is paramagnetic. When you put a magnet on aluminum, you might feel a slight pull. However, it's not strong enough to hold the magnet on the aluminum. That's paramagnetism.

That's why most things are not magnetic. So each magnetic moment is cancelled out by the magnetic moments of the other electron in the pair. That makes the overall magnetic moment of the atom rather weak.

Elements with the strongest magnetism have groups of neighboring atoms with their magnetic moments in the same direction. These groups are the magnetic domains discussed earlier. As I already mentioned, we call these elements ferromagnetic.

Let's do another experiment to understand magnetism even more!

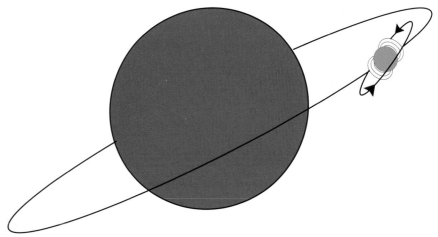

This atom has only one electron spinning in one direction. This atom has a magnetic field around it.

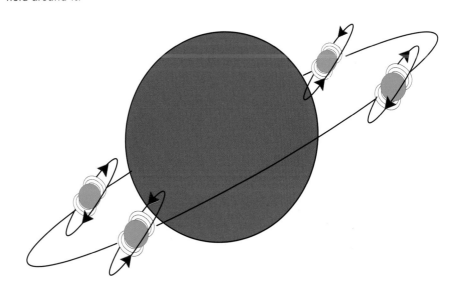

This atom has an even number of electrons spinning in different directions. Each electron cancels out the magnetic field of the others. This makes the atom diamagnetic.

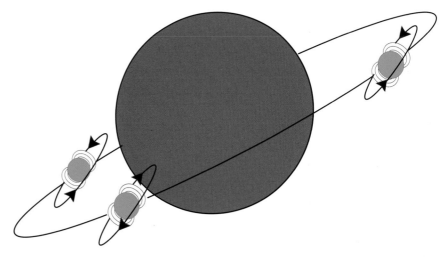

This atom has an odd number of electrons. The lone electron is producing a magnetic field around the atom. This makes this atom paramagnetic.

Try This!

You will need: An adult's supervision, a magnet, a very large steel nail, and a box of steel paper clips.

First, place your magnet in the box of steel paper clips. Now carefully lift up the magnet, taking special note of how the paper clips are sticking to the magnet. Did you notice that many of the paper clips stuck to the magnet while others stuck to other paper clips? Now place your steel nail in the box of paper clips, then lift it back out. Did anything happen? Rub your magnet in one direction on the nail several times. Put the nail in the paper clip box again and lift it out. What happened? If you rubbed the nail correctly, you should have observed the paper clips sticking to the nail. If it didn't work, try again.

When you rubbed the nail with a magnet it became magnetic, acting like a magnet! Let's find out how this happened. Since you've studied atoms so much, this won't be difficult for you to understand.

First, let's go back to domains. Throughout every single substance, there are billions of domains. Remember, domains are tiny areas. Each one of these domains has its own north pole and south pole. If the substance is ferromagnetic, almost every domain has atoms spinning in the same direction. However, every domain is doing its own thing. Look at the picture.

Do you see in the first image of the nail how each domain is going in a different direction? One domain has the north pole

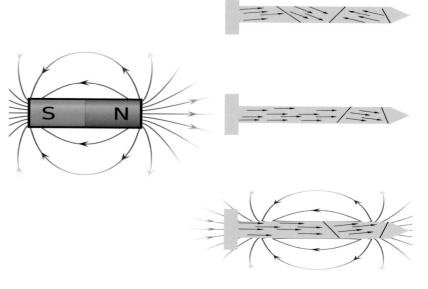

The domains on the steel nail are not naturally facing one direction. When you redirect all the domains by rubbing it with a magnet, the nail becomes magnetic.

going up, another has it going to the left, and others have it going to the right. However, most of the atoms inside each domain spin in the same direction, making each domain magnetic. Each domain has a strong magnetic moment, but not all the domains are pointed in the same direction. As you can see, you can actually change the direction that the domains point. That's what you did when you rubbed the magnet on the nail.

You made the domains line up in one direction when you rubbed the magnet on the nail in that direction. The magnetic field applied a force to the nail and repositioned the domains to face the direction of that force. If you hadn't rubbed in one direction, it wouldn't have worked. Your nail will stay magnetized until something jostles the domains out of position.

Believe it or not, there are other ways to magnetize a nail. Let's try another method now.

Try This!

You will need: An adult's supervision, a hammer, a nail, a compass, a box of paper clips, and a rock.

To begin, use the compass to find which direction is north. Now hold the nail flat against the edge of the rock with one end pointing north. Strike the nail several times with the hammer. Now carefully dip the nail in the box of paper clips. What happens?

How did pounding the nail magnetize it? The act of pounding the nail shook the atoms loose long enough for them to shift their positions. Atoms that have been shaken typically like to orient themselves toward the earth's magnetic poles. All the domains shifted to face the same direction.

Now that we're on the subject, let's talk about the earth's magnetic poles and how it was discovered that the earth is magnetic.

Before moving on to study the magnetic earth, explain to someone all that you've learned so far about spinning electrons and domains.

Compass Points

Back when ancient folks discovered magnetite, it wasn't long before they realized that a piece of magnetite in water always pointed in one direction: north. Because magnetite had this property, these pieces were renamed **lodestone**, which means leading stone.

People quickly figured out they could create devices with lodestone in them to help people find their way around. This is how compasses were invented. A **compass** is a device people use to find their way when traveling. It contains a small magnetized needle that always points north. Sailors and explorers have used compasses to navigate around the ocean and the land. Knowing which way is north helps keep them on track. Without a compass, a person could walk in circles and never realize it.

Did you know you can create your own compass? Let's do that now.

Try This!

You will need: An adult's supervision, a large needle, a pencil eraser, a flame, a plate, a bowl of water, a bottle cap, and a compass.

To begin, stick the needle into the pencil eraser. Next, with an adult's help, hold the needle in the flame until it's red hot. Put the pencil eraser with the red-hot needle on a plate, lined up north/south. Let the needle cool. Now lay the needle flat in the bottle cap and put it in the water. What does the needle do?

In the last experiment, you could have magnetized the needle with a magnet, but heating it did the same thing. Can you think of why that might be? Do you remember that pounding the nail loosened the atoms, causing them to reorient themselves toward the North Pole? Heating the needle does the same thing. Let's explore our magnetic earth a bit more.

Northward Facing

Why does the compass always point north? Early scientists thought there must be a magnetic field around the earth—and they were right! God did create a magnetic field around the earth. However, scientists discovered something very interesting when they were trying to make compasses. Let's find out what they discovered.

Making compasses became big business early in history. That's because people were always trying to get from one place to another. Typically, they used the stars to tell which way was north. But on a cloudy or stormy night, people couldn't tell which way to go because the stars were hidden. During the day, the placement of the sun in the sky helped them know which way was north. But even then, clouds and storms could hide the sun, making it difficult for people to find their way. The invention of this amazing device that always pointed north was a great help.

The earth's magnetic field makes it a giant magnet!

This compass is equipped with an inclinometer.

However, compass makers discovered several problems when creating their compasses. If you have a manufactured compass, you may have noticed these same problems. They would use a flat, arrow-shaped piece of magnetized metal attached to a tiny pivot. This way the needle could swing around in whatever direction it needed to swing in order to point north. Strangely, the needle always pointed down instead of straight ahead north. It wasn't long before scientists realized why: The needle was pointing down because it was pointing toward the earth. The earth itself was magnetic! The earth is a giant magnet, with North and South Poles.

But that's not all that was learned about the earth through the use of compasses. Compass makers learned that the needle didn't dip down at the equator. However, when someone was really close to the North or South Pole, the needle would bend all the way down, standing on its end. They realized when the lodestone is closer to the pole, the pull is stronger. When compasses are in the center of the earth at the equator, there's less pull. This is because they're so far away from the earth's poles. This discovery helped navigators develop compasses that let them know how far away they were from either pole. This special compass includes an inclinometer. The word "incline" means to lean or tilt. An **inclinometer** measures the tilts of the needle. This tells you not only which direction you're heading, but also where in the world you are!

The compass and inclinometer are great discoveries that have helped many people get from place to place. Animals, however, don't need a compass to get around. Scientists have found that many animals have built-in compasses. Animals such as sea turtles, whales, birds, dolphins, and even some bacteria seem to navigate the globe without the use of landmarks, smells, or anything else. They simply know where to go. Scientists have discovered that these animals are able to detect the earth's magnetic field to find direction. What's even more fascinating is that these animals have traces of magnetite in their brain cells. God made the earth a giant magnet for many reasons that help both man and beast.

This young green sea turtle will swim untold miles to return to the beaches where she was born to lay her eggs.

Before discovering more about our wonderful magnetic earth, explain what you've learned so far.

Shielding Magnet

Believe it or not, if earth were not a giant magnet, we wouldn't be able to live on it. That's because of the **magnetosphere**—the giant magnetic field surrounding the entire earth. God created the magnetosphere to be an enormous protective shield. It guards us from harmful particles coming from the sun. The stream of these dangerous particles is called the solar wind. The solar wind blows toward the earth every day. When these dangerous particles get close, they hit the magnetic shield and are deflected. So they travel around the earth rather than bombard it. Some particles get trapped inside the shield and end up in the very upper atmosphere of the earth. But this happens only when the solar winds are extremely rough. When this happens, these particles become electrified in our upper atmosphere. They

These are the northern lights, also called the aurora borealis. They're caused by solar winds trapped in our upper atmosphere.

beautifully light up the sky in the far northern and southern parts of the world. We call these electric lights in the sky auroras. The lights in the north are called aurora borealis, and the ones in the south are called aurora australis.

These solar winds are strong and powerful as they blow toward us. In fact, they're so strong that they affect the shape of the earth's magnetic field. Look at the image of the earth's magnetic field near the sun. Be sure to notice how tiny the earth is and how large the earth's magnetic field is. Also, look at the shape. Do you see how the magnetic field trails behind as if it's being blown by the wind? It's being blown by the solar wind!

The powerful solar winds blowing toward the earth affect the shape of the earth's magnetic field.

Upside-Down Poles

The most confusing part of the earth's magnetism is where the poles are actually located. We know that the north end of a magnet will be attracted to the south end of another magnet. So the north end of a compass needle should point toward the South Pole, not the North Pole. That means that compasses should not point north. The magnetic South Pole of the earth is located at the top of the Northern Hemisphere, while the magnetic North Pole is in Antarctica. The magnetic North Pole is near our geographical South Pole, and the magnetic South Pole is near our geographical North Pole! It's all backwards, but that's why compasses always point north. No matter where you are on earth, the point of the compass needle will always be pulled toward the north and repelled or pushed away from the south.

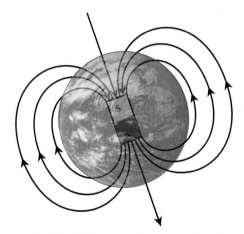

The South Pole of the magnet in our earth is located at the North Pole on our map. The magnetic North Pole is located near our map's South Pole.

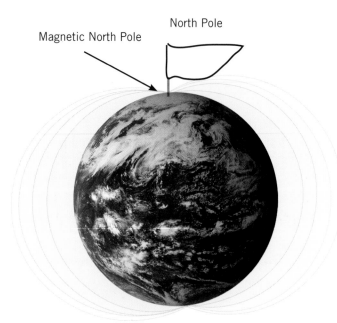

The geographic pole and the magnetic pole are not in the same place.

Off-Center Poles

Here's another small problem with our magnetic poles: The place we consider the northernmost part of the world—the top of the world—is not the farthest north for a compass. Look at the image. You can see that the geographical North Pole is not the earth's northernmost magnetic pole. Our geographic North Pole is 90°N, while our north-attracting magnetic pole is a bit off. In 2005, it was 82.7°N and 114.4°W, to the west of Ellesmere Island in Canada. When a compass is directly above a magnetic pole, the needle will point straight down.

Iron Earth

You may wonder why the earth is magnetic. Is it made of magnetite? No, it's not made of magnetite, but God did make it with a lot of iron. The inner core of the earth is full of millions of tons of liquid iron. That's why the compass is pointing downward at the poles. The most magnetic part of the earth is deep inside where the iron is. Whether solid or liquid, iron conducts electricity—which makes our earth an electromagnet.

Pole Jumping

Scientists have also discovered that earth's North and South Poles periodically shift. We know this because when molten rock comes out of a volcano, it dries with many of its domains facing toward the North Pole. Do you remember how heating the needle caused it to become magnetized? Molten rock shows some of those same properties when it's cooling after being heated. Surprisingly, scientists have found molten rocks that have domains facing the other direction. This causes scientists to believe the South Pole used to be on the other side of the world, and vice versa. Somehow, the poles switched sides. We aren't sure why or how often that happens.

The outer layer of earth is the crust. It's about 10 miles deep. The next layer is the mantle. It's made of very hot rock under intense pressure. The outer core is the next layer, made of hot molten metals and rocks. The last layer is the inner core. It's made of iron and nickel but is solid because of the enormous pressure.

Electrifying Magnet

Scientists call the earth an electromagnet because there's a huge current of electricity running through the iron core of the earth. This makes the magnetic properties of earth much stronger. You may remember that magnetism and electricity are closely related. Let's dive into that subject a little more.

Many years ago, some scientists speculated that electricity and magnetism were related somehow. Other scientists believed this was quite absurd. A Danish scientist named Hans Oersted hooked up some wires and ran a current through them. He noticed that the needle of his compass changed directions when it came near the wires. After experimenting a bit, he realized the electric current was creating a magnetic field that affected the compass needle.

Before long, scientists understood that electricity creates magnetic fields. Electricity itself is magnetic.

We call this kind of magnetism electromagnetism. Electromagnets aren't like the permanent magnets found in metals and magnetite. They're only magnetic when a current of electricity is active. An **electromagnet** is a temporary magnet where the magnetic field is generated by an electric current and disappears when the current is turned off.

Let's see if we can recreate Oersted's experiment.

Try This!

You will need: An adult's supervision, the electrical circuit you made, and a compass.

First, get the electrical circuit you made. Now hold your compass close to the wires and watch to see what happens. Switch the wires to the battery around and notice what the compass does.

You found that the compass needle, which is attracted to the magnetic North Pole, was affected by the magnetic field of the current. That's because although the electrical current's magnetism is not nearly as powerful and strong as the earth's magnetosphere, it was a lot closer to the compass. This makes the current affect the compass more than the earth's magnetosphere. The compass pointed toward the current's north pole. When you switched the battery around, the compass was still attracted to the current's north pole. Yet it went the other way as you changed the direction of the current.

Whenever an electric current passes through a wire, it produces a magnetic field around the wire. Look at the image below to see how the magnetic field looks around a wire.

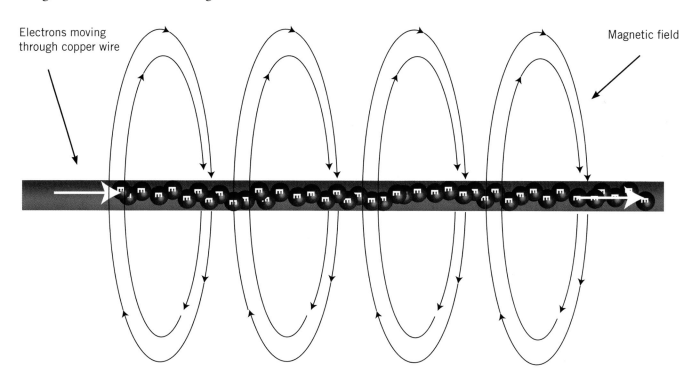

Electrons moving through copper wire

Magnetic field

Wherever electricity is running, a magnetic field surrounds the objects through which the current is running. In fact, the earth's magnetosphere is strong because of the big currents of electricity running through the earth.

The current you produced with your circuit was magnetic, but not strong enough for anything magnetic to stick to it. If the current had surrounded a piece of iron, like the iron core of our earth, it would have been much stronger.

You can create a strong electromagnet yourself. Let's do that now.

Try This!

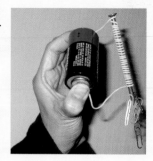

You will need: An adult's supervision; a long piece of thin, insulated copper wire; a steel nail; a size D battery; and some paper clips.

First, wrap the copper wire around the steel nail, modeling it after the image to the right. Be sure to wrap it at least 20 times. Next, attach both ends of the wire to your electric current. Now place the paper clips near the coiled wire wrapped around the nail. What happens? Turn off the current and see what happens.

You noticed that the electromagnetic field was powerful enough to pull in a paper clip. However, it wasn't a permanent magnetic field; it was only temporary. As long as the current was flowing, the nail had enough magnetism to attract the paper clips.

How would you make the electromagnetic field stronger? Which would be most effective: adding more electricity in the form of more coils, adding more voltage in the form of adding more batteries, or adding more iron in the form of adding a larger nail or several nails wrapped together?

Electromagnets are one of the most important discoveries of our modern world. Why? Because almost every machine you use—whether large or small—is made with electromagnets. Whenever you listen to music or sound coming from the speakers of your car, television, or computer, you're hearing electromagnets in action. Generators that bring electricity into our homes are made using electromagnetic force. Electromagnets are part of the reason we have such an amazing technologically advanced world. They've added a great deal of comfort, convenience, and entertainment to our lives.

Explain in your own words all that you've learned about the magnetosphere and electromagnetism.

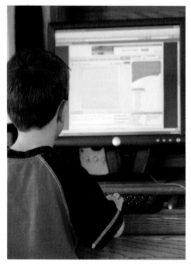

Many computer monitors wouldn't be able to give off light or create a picture without electromagnets.

Motor Moments

How are all these things made with electromagnets? What's so special about a copper wire wrapped around a piece of iron? That's a great question, and it's an important one too. Soon after scientists understood the electromagnet, they discovered something called the motor effect. The **motor effect** happens when the magnetic field of a magnet causes a wire carrying an electric current to move. Think of two magnets near one another. The north pole of one magnet is facing the south pole of the other magnet. They're not touching, but the magnets are close. There's a magnetic field between the two magnets. If you place a loop of wire between the two fields and run a current through it, you create another magnetic field. Now you have a magnetic field within a magnetic field. This will cause the wire to move toward or away from the magnets as the current flows through the wire. This causes the wire to rotate. This is the motor effect!

Toasters use electromagnets to hold the bread down until it's ready to pop up!

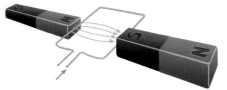

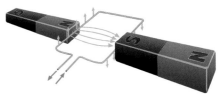

There's a magnetic field between the two magnets.

A loop of wire (the blue rectangle) is between the two currents.

When you put a current through the loop of wire, it will cause the wire to rotate.

This is difficult for many people to imagine, so, we'll do an experiment to see this in action. Let's make an extremely simple version of the motor illustrated above using a rare earth magnet. A rare earth magnet is made up of several elements that make it very strongly magnetic. These elements aren't necessarily rare. But the magnet is extremely brittle and can break apart easily. Thus, it's often coated to keep it together.

Try This!

You will need: An adult's supervision, a rare earth magnet, one AA battery, and copper wire (18- or 20-gauge).

Cut the copper wire 7 inches long. Next, put your finger in the center of the wire. Make one loop around your finger and pull the loop as tight as you can until it looks like a small circle on your copper wire. The loop should be in the center of the wire. The wire should also be in a straight line. Bend both ends of the wire downward at a 90-degree angle one inch from either side of the loop. Two inches down the wires, bend both ends inward at a 90-degree angle. Now stick the magnet to the negative end of the battery. Bend the very ends of the copper wire inward toward the battery. Stick the looped part of the wire on the positive part of the battery. Now give the wire a little push around the battery to get it spinning. Make sure the copper wire barely touches the magnet, scraping the magnet as it turns.

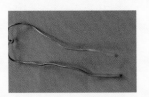

Why did the wire keep turning after you gave it a spin? The electric current was flowing through the wire and down into the magnet. The magnet sent the current back up to the battery, making a circuit. However, both the wire and magnet had electric fields surrounding them. When these two electric fields collided, they repelled each other, causing the wire to turn.

Now let's see how an electric motor fits into this picture. When turned on, an electric motor turns around and around. This makes other things turn, which then operates whatever you're trying to run. Think of a fan. It contains an electromagnetic motor. When the fan is on, the magnets make an electric wire turn because of the way the wire is shaped, which turns mechanisms that turn the blades of the fan.

Look around you. What do you see that runs with a motor? As you can see, motors have been one of the most important inventions to give us an electronic world. Try to imagine a world without motors. No cars, no boats, no electricity, no clocks. So much of what makes our modern world modern can be attributed to electromagnets!

Fans use magnets to make the blades turn.

Final Matters

Magnets and the magnetic properties of the earth are just a few of the amazing scientific phenomena created by God. In His very great wisdom, God created magnets to protect the earth, help animals migrate and locate their homes, and give travelers a compass to find their way. Because of magnets, doctors can find out if we're sick. Without this amazing creation of God, how would your life be different? The Bible tells us to be thankful for all things. Let's give thanks that God created magnets!

What Do You Remember?

What are magnetic domains? What is a magnetic field? What is a ferromagnetic substance? What is a paramagnetic substance? What is a diamagnetic substance? What is the earth's core made of? What is an electromagnet? What is the motor effect?

Notebooking Activities

Record the fascinating facts you discovered and the experiments you did in this lesson. Then do the following activity.

Create a trifold brochure describing the importance and uses of magnets in the world. Make a pocket for your notebooking journal into which you'll place your completed brochure. You can use the template provided in *The Chemistry and Physics Notebooking Journal* or a template from a word processing program. Be sure to include illustrations on your brochure and be creative!

Project
Magnetic Race Track

This is a fun activity you can do with your siblings or friends.

You will need:

- a large piece of cardboard
- markers
- strong magnets
- small toy race cars or trucks
- strong glue
- a base to elevate your race track (such as boxes)

1. Using your markers, draw a simple race track on the piece of cardboard. You can make as many lanes as you have cars, or you can make two lanes and take turns racing.
2. Place your race track on the base, making sure there's enough space around the edge for you to move your cars.
3. Glue a magnet to the center of the bottom of each car.
4. Place the cars on top of the race track.
5. Have each person racing hold a magnet underneath the cardboard directly under his car.
6. Move the magnet along the bottom of the cardboard to race the cars to the finish line. Try to race around the track as fast as you can without running off the track. If a car goes off the track, that car has to start the race over.

Simple Machines

Wow—you made it to the last lesson of your physics study! You've certainly learned a lot about the world God made. In the beginning of this book, you studied chemistry and learned all about the building blocks God used to make everything you see around you. Then you learned the physics of motion and energy, as well as the physics of electricity and magnetism. Did you know that God created the earth and everything in it for us to enjoy? God also created people in His image, which means we are creative too. With that creativity comes the ability to make things. People especially like to make machines that help us do our work. Many, many years ago people had to work very hard just to get food on their tables. They had to work hard to clean their homes. Today, machines make this work so much easier. Can you think of any machines you use in your home to help you do work? All of those machines are made up of moving parts. Those

This child is playing with a solar-powered car he created.

moving parts are really just a lot of little machines put together to make one big machine. Those little machines are what we call simple machines. In this very last lesson, we'll learn about these machines.

A machine is any gadget that allows work to be done using less force. When gardeners want to move rocks, they load them into a wheelbarrow. This helps the work of moving rocks to be done with less force. A wheelbarrow is a simple machine. When you want to pull a nail out of the wall, you use the prongs on a hammer to remove it. A hammer allows work to be done with less force. It's a simple machine. When you want to pull a heavy wagon up the steps, you may find a long board to lie over the steps and use as a ramp. The ramp allows the work of pulling a heavy wagon up the steps to be done with less force. A ramp is a simple machine.

This boy is riding on a homemade go-kart he built himself.

All these items are machines. Scientists define a **machine** as any device that changes the amount of force you have to use to get something done. Any device that helps you do work is a machine, no matter how simple.

As you know, not all machines are simple. Your washing machine is not a simple machine. It's more complex. We call it a compound machine. A **compound machine** is a combination of different simple machines working together. Long ago, people washed their clothing by hand using a bucket of water and a bar of

In many countries, electricity and washing machines are not available. Clothes are washed by old-fashioned methods. These women are washing their clothes in the river.

soap. Today, most people use a compound machine to do all that work for them.

Mankind has always used machines, both simple and compound. Today, our machines are much more complex than those used by ancient people. Most of the machines we use today are operated by motors, requiring less effort on our part.

When a machine multiplies the force exerted, we say the machine has a mechanical advantage. That just means that if a force put on the machine is increased by the machine, the machine is helping out. Let's say you try to twist a screw into a board with your hands. That would be very hard, wouldn't it? It would be easier if you used a screwdriver. A screwdriver gives you a mechanical advantage. It does the work faster and better—without much effort on your part.

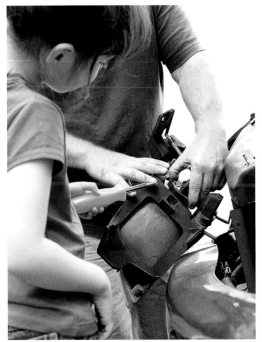

This child is helping her dad fix the car's headlight using a screwdriver.

Archimedes

It wouldn't be right for me to teach you about simple machines without first mentioning one of the most important people in history who helped us understand them. Much of what we know about them we learned from a brilliant mathematician named Archimedes. Archimedes lived off the coast of Sicily about 200 years before Christ was born. During this time, the average Greek mathematician talked a lot about math, drawing pictures and formulas. They measured things and used math to understand the world around them. But Archimedes was not average. He used his knowledge of math for practical purposes in the same way that mathematicians today use math to create great technology, like computers and rockets.

What did Archimedes do that was so amazing? He used math to build simple machines that could protect his country from the powerful Romans. The Romans were always trying to conquer the small country of Sicily and take it as their own. Rome wanted to rule the world, so they decided every country had to be conquered. There was one tiny nation on the map that was next to impossible to conquer. That's because a brilliant mathematician lived there, and the king listened to him! Archimedes created and built numerous devices that gave the soldiers a mechanical advantage in war.

Archimedes used math to build machines that would help win battles against the Romans.

Although some of the machines were not actually invented by Archimedes, he did make them bigger and better. He made them more useful for protecting his country, making life easier for the people.

The Romans were terrified of the weapons used by the little nation of Sicily. What were these weapons devised of simple machines? Just imagine being a powerful and noble Roman soldier, sailing the seas toward Sicily. You believe you'll finally and perhaps easily conquer this small country. Yet you've heard absurd stories about huge machines that could easily turn your beautiful Roman ships into rubble, sunken at the bottom of the ocean. But you don't believe those stories.

As you come near the banks of Sicily, ready to use your mighty skills and power to attack and conquer the country, you suddenly see giant boulders falling from the sky! Out of nowhere these boulders pummel your fleet, putting holes in your ships and harming your soldiers. The ships begin to sink. Those that didn't get hit draw closer to the shore. Suddenly, huge hooks on long poles fly down onto the boats and pierce the wood. The hooks, attached to giant machines called the Claws of Archimedes, move upward. They lift the ships into the air then plunge them down again. Over and over the Roman ships are smashed into the water and sunk.

Archimedes was the mastermind behind all of these devices that protected Sicily. However, Rome did win the battle with Sicily eventually. The Roman general Marcus Claudius Marcellus admired Archimedes' inventions so much that he ordered soldiers not to harm Archimedes. Unfortunately, a soldier killed Archimedes anyway.

Because Archimedes kept numerous records of his inventions and discoveries, we're able to learn all about him. He used simple machines such as pulleys, levers, and other devices for many practical purposes. We'll learn about some of Archimedes' inventions throughout this lesson.

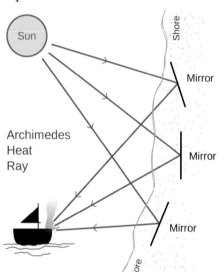

It was said that Archimedes set up huge reflective mirrors that captured the sun's rays. These mirrors supposedly reflected the rays down onto the ships until they caught fire. *Mythbusters* tried this and disproved the concept, but it's an interesting idea.

Explain what you've learned so far about machines and mechanical advantage.

Six Simple Machines

There are six simple machines we'll study in this lesson. These simple machines were identified in the Renaissance period of history over 400 years ago. The six machines are the inclined plane, the pulley, the screw, the wedge, the lever, and the wheel and axle. With these simple devices, you can create almost anything! As you learn, you'll be experimenting with all of these machines. At the end of the lesson, you'll use your knowledge to create a special compound machine using many simple machines. It's called a Rube Goldberg device. I think you're going to have fun. So let's go!

We call the object we are moving up the plane the resistance. The push up the plane is the force.

Inclined Planes

Do you know what a plane is? No, not the kind that flies in the air. I'm talking about the kind you learn about in geometry—the kind of plane that airplanes need in order to land. A **geometric plane** is a flat surface, like a table or a piece of paper. The airplane's landing pad is a plane. If you haven't heard this before, keep it in mind because you'll hear it again in geometry class.

If you take a plane—a flat surface—and put it on an angle, it becomes an inclined plane. An **inclined plane** is a flat surface whose ends are at different heights. The word "incline" means a slope or slant. An inclined plane is a ramp or a sloped surface used to raise or lower objects. It makes lifting and lowering things much easier.

Ramps have been used since the beginning of time. The ancient Egyptians used inclined planes to move huge stone blocks (weighing up to 3,000 pounds each) up to the top of a 400-foot pyramid. These ramps extended all the way up and around the pyramid.

The Egyptians also used inclined planes to travel on the Nile River. These planes were wooden slides covered with mud to reduce friction. The Egyptians used them to raise their boats out of the water and onto the bank when they encountered a waterfall. The boats could then be slid along the ground and lowered back into the water at the bottom or top of the waterfall.

The ancient Greeks also used a famous inclined plane called the diolkos. This plane moved boats over the land so they wouldn't have to sail through the dangerous Peloponnese peninsula near Corinth.

Today, buildings are created with inclined planes so people in wheelchairs can get inside. Movers also use inclined planes to get furniture off and onto a truck. If you need to place a heavy box on a shelf, you can create an inclined plane and push the box up. It would be a lot easier than lifting the box straight up.

Does pushing the box up the incline take more effort or less than lifting it up to the shelf? That's a trick question. It actually takes the same amount of effort or work, but it's spread out over a certain distance. When you spread work out over a distance, it seems easier. If you push the box up the incline, it travels a longer distance than if you lift it straight up to the shelf. But the effort is spread out. Sometimes this is the only way to get a task done. If a box is too heavy to lift, an inclined plane enables work to be done that could not be done otherwise.

Think of it this way: Imagine you're hiking up a mountain with a group

The work of moving the boxes into the truck is spread out over a distance when using the ramp.

Math It!

The mechanical advantage is the path length divided by the height. This comes from the conservation of energy: Work is the amount of energy used. In mathematical terms, this is force times distance. So if we double the distance needed, we halve the force required. This principle applies to all machines. For example, an at inclination of 30°, the length of the plane is twice the height. So the mechanical advantage is 2. Apart from friction, if you push a wheelbarrow up an incline, you'll only need half the force required to lift it yourself vertically. However, you move the wheelbarrow twice as far. So the work/effort/energy is the same in both cases.

of people. Your goal is to reach the top of the mountain. Everyone wants to reach the summit to look at the beautiful view that can be seen only from the very top. You can climb straight up the mountain and get there quickly, or you can take the trail that winds around the mountain and arrive much later. Which do you think requires more effort? They both require the same amount of energy and effort, but the trail spreads that effort out over distance and time. If you go straight up the mountain, you'll use a lot of energy all at once but will arrive much sooner. Of course, that would give you longer to rest and enjoy the view while you wait for the rest of the group. Which would you rather do? Which would your parents prefer to do? It's much easier to take the trail than it is to climb straight up because it's easier to spread the effort out over a period of time. This is how an inclined plane makes work easier.

With an inclined plane, the force needed to lift yourself or an object is lessened by increasing the distance. If a plane is really steep, it requires more force than if it's a small slope. However, an incline that isn't very steep is usually much longer, adding even more distance to your travel.

Let's test out this concept with some experiments.

Going straight up the mountain uses the same amount of energy as taking the trail around the mountain. But taking the trail spreads the energy out over a period of time.

Try This!

You will need: An adult's supervision, several large books, a rubber band cut in half, scissors, a paper clip, a ruler, duct tape, a sock filled with rocks (tied), a table, a pencil, and a board.

First, stack your books on a table. Double knot one end of the rubber band around the end of the paper clip. Hang the rubber band over the top of the ruler so the bottom of the clip reaches 4 inches down on the ruler. The other end of the rubber band should hang over the back of the ruler. Tape it to the ruler. Place the sock on the table next to the books and hook the top of the sock to the paper clip. Now hold the ruler and lift the sock straight up until the bottom of the sock is at the same level as the books. Look where the paper clip reaches on the ruler. Record that number on a piece of paper. Use the ruler to measure the distance you lifted the sock. Now place your board on the books to make an inclined plane

or ramp. Hold the ruler on the ramp and pull the sock to the top of the books. Observe where the paper clip reaches now as it pulls the sock up the ramp. Record the number and the time. Now use the ruler to measure the distance you pulled the rocks. Write this information down. What did you learn? Experiment more by changing the incline of the plane, making it more inclined and less inclined. Does this change the work or distance?

The amount the rubber band stretched shows the effort needed to lift the rocks. Did it take more effort to lift the sock straight up or to slide it up the ramp? Which required a greater distance? You used more effort to lift the rocks straight up, but it was a shorter distance. You used less effort over a longer distance to pull the rocks up the ramp.

You may not realize this, but not all inclined planes are smooth ramps. Buildings and homes often use a different kind of inclined plane to help people get up to the next level or down to the bottom of the building.

Imagine if you had to walk up a smooth inclined plane every time you wanted to get the second floor of someone's house. What do we use instead? You guessed it! A stairway is also an inclined plane. A ladder is one too. Stairs and ladders are simple machines used to get people up and down more easily. The steps make it easier to climb the plane without slipping.

Tell someone what you've learned today about inclined planes. If you're taking a break, record in your notebooking journal what you did and learned.

Twisting Planes

It's time to learn about another simple machine—the screw, which is really a twisting plane! Let's do a project to discover how this type of machine is constructed.

Try This!

You will need: An adult's supervision, a piece of paper, scissors, a ruler, a marker, and a pencil.

Start with a piece of paper shaped like an inclined plane. To do this, draw a right triangle about 5 inches high and 9 inches along the bottom. Cut out your triangle. Now with a marker, draw a line along the sloping or longest edge of the triangle. Place the 5-inch edge of the paper against the pencil. Roll the pencil slowly so that the paper wraps around it evenly. Do you see how a screw is really an inclined plane wrapped around a tubular-shaped object?

Get a screw from your parents' toolbox. Now look closely at the screw. What do you notice? Remember when we talked about the path twisting around a mountain? Does the screw remind you of that at all? A **screw** is actually an inclined plane wrapped around a cylinder or a cone. It's a lot like a trail wrapping around a mountain. As you know, an inclined plane lessens the effort needed to lift or lower something by increasing the distance over which the work is done. A screw also allows work to be done with less effort. There are many, many uses for screws—probably more than you can imagine! Screws can hold materials together, drill holes into objects, open and close faucets and jars, keep light bulbs in place, and lift materials—like a regular inclined plane.

The metal screw is used for building things or hanging pictures. The threads of the screw turn around and around as they cut into a surface. Less effort is needed to cut into the surface because of the increased distance the threads travel.

Jars also use screws. Get a jar with a lid and untwist it. Examine how the lid is created like a screw. Jars use screw systems to tighten or loosen lids. Light bulbs are screwed into sockets. A screw system is used in a car jack to raise an entire car with almost no effort at all. You turn the screw, which raises the jack, and the 2,000-pound car lifts right up!

The lid on this jar is a twisting plane that screws tightly onto the jar.

Archimedes created a special screw to help farmers lift water out of wells and up onto their crops. This screw can lift water by the act of turning. Archimedes' screws were also used to get water out of the hull or bottom of a ship. Believe it or not, Archimedes' screws are still used today to irrigate or water farms. People or animals can turn them. Let's do an experiment to see if we can create a water-lifting device similar to the screw Archimedes created.

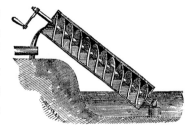

Above is an illustration of Archimedes' screw. On the right is a modern version of this device used to transport water up a slope.

Try This!

You will need: An adult's supervision, a can, a bowl of colored water, clear packing tape, and clear plastic tubing (¼ inch in diameter).

Tape the end of the clear plastic tubing to the top of the can. Now wind the tubing around the can so that it spirals like the threads of a screw. Tape the tubing into place, being sure there's a small bit coming out the bottom of the can. Now tilt the can slightly. Place the top end in the water. Turn the can until you see colored water in the tubing. Carefully lift the can so it's above the water. Keep the can tilted and continue to turn it. What happened to the water in the tube?

The water screw you made is much like Archimedes' screw. Like all screws, the water screw changes the direction of the force. When you turned the screw in a circular motion, the water moved upward in the threads.

As you can see, a screw is a simple machine that uses an inclined plane wrapped around a cylinder to reduce the effort and force people use to do work. Wider screws have a greater mechanical advantage because of the greater distance the inclined plane must move when it pushes through. When you want to hang a picture on the wall, you can either hammer a nail or use a screw. Which is easier? That brings us to the next simple machine—nails! A nail is an example of a different kind of simple machine, the wedge.

Explain what you've learned about screws.

This ax is a wedge, separating the wood into two pieces.

Wedging In

When you think of the word "wedge," what do you think of? Have you ever used the word? A **wedge** is a really simple machine used to push things apart. It's actually two inclined planes put back to back. It's wide at one end and thin at the other. The thin edge is first pushed into an object. As it moves in, the wide edge separates the materials, pushing them apart.

A wedge is like a moving inclined plane, using force to come between two things. An ax is swung into a log to split it apart. A nail is hammered into wood. A crowbar is wedged into a crack and moved up or down to split materials apart. A saw is made up of many small wedges that cut wood in half. Your teeth are a beautiful set of God-designed wedges, used to cut and chop food so you can eat it. A plow is also a wedge, cutting through the soil. Have you ever cut your food with a knife? A knife is a common wedge. A fork is too. It's a tool made of four little wedges. Razors are wedges; so are scissors. Some people use a rubber wedge to hold the door open.

The mechanical advantage of a wedge depends on how thick the wedge is. Imagine you needed to chop some wood. What type of wedge would you use? A short, thick wedge would split the wood apart faster, but you'd have to use more force. A long, thin wedge would be easier to drive into the wood, but it would take longer to split it.

Levers

Let's do an experiment to learn about our next variety of simple machines: levers.

Try This!

You will need: An adult's supervision, a kitchen table, a chair, and a broom.

First, try to lift the table using only one hand. Was it difficult? Did it take a lot of effort? Did you have to use a lot of force to lift the table? Now place the back of the chair about four inches from the edge of the table. Lay the broom over the back of the chair with the straw part facing away from the table. Place the broom handle under the table. Gently push down on the straw end. What happened?

You just made a machine called a lever! Levers are used in many, many simple and compound machines. When you use a hammer to pull out a nail, that's a lever. Have you ever opened a soda bottle with a bottle opener? Then you've used a lever. When you use a screwdriver to pry the lid off a can of paint, you're using a lever. Even a pair of scissors is a lever! Have you ever played on a seesaw? That's a classic lever. We use levers all the time.

A **lever** is simply a bar that goes up and down over a point. That point is called the **fulcrum**. The chair was the fulcrum in your experiment. The load is the thing being lifted—the table in your experiment. You probably noticed that using the broom to lift the table required a great deal less force than trying to lift the table without the lever. With the broom, you created a first-class lever, one of the most useful levers.

There are three different kinds of levers: first class, second class, and third class. Look at the three different levers pictured below. See if you can find the differences in how the load (the weight) is lifted with each lever. How does the location of the fulcrum make a difference?

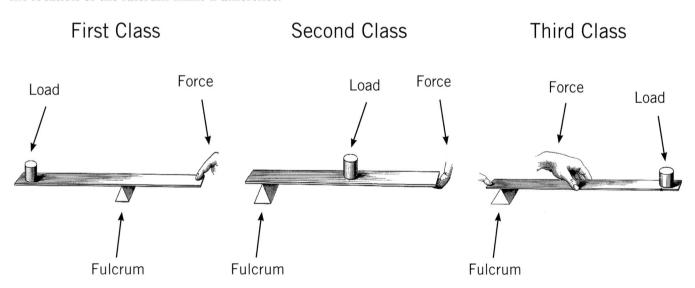

First Class   Second Class   Third Class

Let's explore the three different classes of levers.

First-Class Levers

A **first-class lever** has the fulcrum in the middle. The effort is on one side, and the object being moved is on the other. In the last experiment, your arm moving the broom down was the effort. The table was the object being moved. We call that the load. It was a heavy load, but the lever made it a lot easier to lift, didn't it?

A first-class lever changes the direction of the force you must apply to lift an object. When you lifted the table with your hand, you pushed the table up. When you lifted the table with the lever, you pushed the lever down. One end of the lever moves up when the other end is pushed down. If you've ever been on a seesaw, you've played on a lever. A seesaw is a toy that uses a first-class lever.

Pretend you're on a seesaw with a National Football League linebacker. (These guys are monstrously large!) How on earth would you lift him? Think about this for a minute. If you change your position on the seesaw, you can actually lift that linebacker. Do you think you should move closer to the load (the football player) or farther from the load? Let's experiment to see whether lengthening the lever arm makes it easier or harder to lift a load.

A seesaw is a first-class lever. The load changes from one child to the other.

Try This!

You can create a lever using a ruler and water bottle.

You will need: An adult's supervision, a stiff ruler, a can of beans, a table, tape, and a water bottle filled with water.

First, tape the water bottle onto the table so it doesn't move around. Now place the ruler midway on the water bottle. Place the can of beans on one end of the ruler. Using your hand to apply effort, lift the can of beans.

You probably noticed that when the fulcrum is farther from the effort (the effort is your arm pushing on the lever), the lever works more effectively. You're lengthening the lever arm to make the lifting easier. This allows you to lift the load with less effort. Now back to the big football player on your seesaw. If you move farther from the center, but the linebacker moves closer to the center, you can lift him up. Amazing, huh?

Here's something to test your understanding: Suppose a giant meteorite came crashing through our atmosphere and landed in your backyard. That would be really exciting, wouldn't it? But what if the meteorite landed on your garden hose? You would need to use a lever to lift the meteorite. Which of the levers pictured on the previous page would be best to use to lift the space rock off your hose?

Try This!

You will need: An adult's supervision, pennies, and the ruler and water bottle lever you made earlier.

Try balancing an equal amount of pennies on either side of your lever. Then begin moving one penny at a time over to the other side. What do you have to do to adjust the balance?

In ancient times, first-class levers were used in business. That's because they were used to make scales. Scales were a part of everyday life. When someone wanted to purchase something, the item was placed on a scale to determine how much was being bought. The merchant would put a known weight on one side of the scale, then add the amount of the purchased item needed to balance out the scale. Some dishonest merchants would alter the placement of the fulcrum, making the scale unequal. They would pretend to sell a certain amount, making it appear heavier on the scale than it really was.

God commented on this practice in the Bible. Proverbs 20:23 says, "The LORD detests differing weights, and dishonest scales do not please him."

This is a warning to always tell the truth in everything. I hope you do this already. It's important to God that you

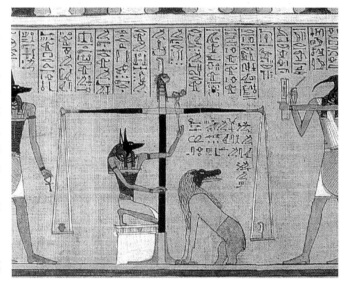

The ancient Egyptians believed a person could not get into heaven unless his heart was lighter than a special feather.

choose to be truthful even in small matters.

Archimedes discovered the value and importance of levers way back in ancient Greece. He's credited with saying, "Give me a place to stand, and I will move the earth."

Archimedes used these levers to create simple and compound machines. First-class levers were used as catapults to launch rocks onto Roman ships as they came into port. With practice, they could aim the rocks exactly where they wanted them to go. Men powered these catapults.

During the Middle Ages, the catapult design changed, and a counterweight was used to launch the rocks. This weapon is called a trebuchet. A heavy weight on the other end would cause the lever to launch the rock without much manpower.

If you'd like to build a catapult, go to www.apologia.com/bookextras. You'll find a lot of different options there.

This is a replica of an ancient catapult.

You've learned a lot about first-class levers. Be sure to tell someone all about them in your own words.

Second-Class Levers

Let's explore second-class levers by doing the following experiment!

Try This!

You will need: An adult's supervision, a yardstick or other long stick, a long string, tape, and a heavy book.

First, tie the string to the heavy book. Now lift the heavy book with the string. Did that take a lot of effort? It probably wasn't super easy. Now place the string over the stick and place one end of the stick on the table. Tape it securely to keep it in place. Next, place the string in the middle of the stick, with the table on one end and your hand on the other. Now lift the books with the stick.

You probably found it required less effort to lift the books with the stick lever than without the help of the lever. The lever you created in this activity is a **second-class lever.** These levers have the load between the fulcrum (the table) and the effort (your hand).

You'll notice that with a second-class lever, the direction of the effort doesn't change. You lifted the lever in the same direction as you lifted the books. With the first-class lever, you pushed down to make the load go up. With the second-class lever, you lifted the lever up as you lifted your arm. This kind of lever isn't as useful as a first-class lever.

Wheelbarrows are one of the best examples of second-class levers. They've been used in Europe and China for thousands of years. The fulcrum on a wheelbarrow is where the wheel attaches. The load is above or just behind the wheel. The effort is at the very end of the arms of the wheelbarrow. The effort is your hands, and the load is in the middle.

The ancient Chinese used wheelbarrow-type devices to carry officers into war and transport their arms and equipment. Today, they're still used to transport people in China, India, and Japan. These devices are called rickshaws. A rickshaw is a wheelbarrow that carries people around the city.

Do you think the handles on a wheelbarrow make a difference in how much effort you must use to lift the load? If you had to lift a pile of bricks, would you want long handles or short handles? You've probably figured out from the first-class levers that the longer the effort arm, the easier the lever is to use.

If you have a wheelbarrow, go outside and spend some time learning how it's made and how it works. Be careful carrying your brothers and sisters in the wheelbarrow, though. Make sure you don't wheel them around on a hard surface!

These young men are pulling rickshaws. They're taking these children to school in Madagascar.

Third-Class Levers

A **third-class lever** has the effort between the fulcrum and the load. That means the part doing all the work is in the middle. A great example of this is your uniquely designed arm. God created a third-class lever when He made your arm. When you lift a glass of water to your mouth, the fulcrum is your elbow. Remember, the fulcrum is the place where the bar pivots or turns. The effort is where the muscles of your forearm attach to your bones. The load is the glass of water in your hand.

Force   Load

Fulcrum

Another example of third-class levers is a fishing pole made with a string tied on a stick. When you pull the fish out of the water, the load (the fish) is at one end, while the effort (your arm) is in the middle—pulling up on the pole. Surprisingly, this kind of lever reduces the mechanical advantage. This is because it increases the force required, but reduces the distance by the same amount. It still takes a lot of work to lift heavy objects with your arms and to lift heavy fish out of the water with a pole. Tweezers are another example of a third-class lever. Can you explain why?

Explain all that you've learned about second- and third-class levers before moving on to the next section.

Math It!

There's a very easy way to work out the mechanical advantage of all levers: Distance from applied force (effort) to fulcrum divided by distance of load to fulcrum. For example, if the handle was 80 cm from the fulcrum and the load was 20 cm (either first or second class), the mechanical advantage is 80 cm / 20 cm = 4. So if the most you could lift on your own was 100 lbs., this lever would allow you to lift 400 lbs. The principle is the same for a third-class lever. However, your handle might be 6 inches away and the load 6 feet away. In this instance, the mechanical advantage is 1/12. So you need 12 times as much force, but you can move the load 12 times faster.

Pulling Pulleys

When I was a child, there was a tree house in an empty lot near our house. Attached to a tree branch next to the tree house was a special device called a pulley system. This system could bring items up into our tree house without us having to carry them. We would simply drop the loads into a bucket at the bottom and easily pull the items up using the ropes attached to the pulley. Sometimes my friend's mom would bring us lunch while we were playing in the tree house. She would come through the vacant lot and put our lunch and drinks in the bucket for us to lift up and eat. We would spend all day up there playing make-believe games or planning our futures.

What is a pulley system? A **pulley** is a simple machine that lets you pull down a rope, chain, or wire to lift something. You pull down, and it goes up! The pulley itself is a wheel with a groove. The rope fits inside the grooves of the wheel and is wrapped around a portion of the wheel. The groove keeps the rope from slipping off. The pulley wheel and rope together make a pulley system. Our tree house pulley was attached to a branch. The rope looped around the pulley. The bucket was tied to one end, and a big knot was on the other end, preventing the rope from coming out. By pulling the rope down, we could lift heavy items up into our tree house. This helped a lot! It's hard to carry things when you're climbing up boards nailed to a tree.

Years ago, when people dug wells to find water, they would use a bucket on a pulley system to retrieve the water from the well.

Single-pulley systems use only one wheel.

Our tree house had a **single-pulley system**, which has one wheel. This pulley system actually doesn't change the amount of force needed to lift a load, but it seems easier because you're pulling down instead of lifting up. When you pull down, you can use your own weight for additional force. A flagpole uses a single pulley system. Flags are not usually heavy enough to require something stronger than our own effort to raise the flag.

Would you like to make a single-pulley system? Let's try it now.

Try This!

You will need: An adult's supervision, a coat hanger, strong wire cutters, an empty spool of thread or ribbon, a small pail, and some rope.

Cut the hanger in the center of the bottom part. Now thread both ends of the hanger into the spool until both ends are sticking out the ends of the spool. Next, attach some rope to your pail. Place the rope around the pulley as shown. You just made a single pulley! Find a place to hang it up. Now gather your load and use the pulley to lift it up.

You probably noticed that the single pulley didn't change the effort required to lift the load. But you could get it up a lot faster! It probably seemed that lifting the pail was easier since you were pulling down on a string and not lifting the pail up with your hands.

It's fun to use a pulley system to raise things up. A single-pulley system is really helpful in many ways, but if you really want to make lifting things easier, you need a **double-pulley system**! A double pulley has two wheels that are connected. One wheel is attached to the load. The other is fixed to a supporting object (like the branch of our tree house). The rope passes over the top wheel, loops around

Pulleys are used for many tasks on ships and boats.

Double-pulley systems use two wheels.

the lower wheel, and goes back up through the top wheel.

Because of the way the ropes are looped through, when the rope is pulled, the load moves only half the distance compared to a single pulley rope. However, even though it's moving half the distance, you can lift twice as much weight with the same amount of force. So the overall work is the same. By increasing the number of pulleys that are connected together, more and more weight can be lifted with the same effort. The more pulleys you add, the easier the lifting becomes. With the right number of pulleys, even *you* could lift a huge ship out of the water!

Archimedes was famous for his discovery and use of pulleys. In fact, he needed to convince the king that pulleys were extremely effective and powerful. So he built a really complicated pulley system and moved an enormous ship into the sea using only his hands! Usually, it took hundreds of men to move the same ship into the sea. Archimedes also made a compound machine to lift up and smash the Roman ships when they approached the shore. You probably remember that compound machines use two or more simple machines. These particular compound machines built by Archimedes were made with levers and pulleys.

Today, pulleys are still being used to pull boats out of the water, lift sails, and many other tasks. If you would like to experiment with double pulleys and another type of pulley called a movable pulley (which is not attached to anything), visit www.apologia.com/bookextras.

A movable pulley attaches the load directly to the pulley instead of to a fixed object. The person is above the pulley, pulling up on the rope.

You've learned a lot about pulleys. Spend some time explaining to someone what you did and learned before moving on to wheels, gears, and other turning things.

Ancient Egyptians depended on the wheel and axle to pull their chariots into battle.

Wheels and Axles

Can you imagine the world without wheels? Wheels really do make life easier. Imagine pulling a wagon with no wheels. Imagine visiting Grandma without a car or bike. It would take a long time to get to her house without wheels of some sort. Think about how difficult it would be for an airplane to land without wheels. Wheels have been around a long time, and it's no wonder! They really are quite useful.

Wheels were used in the earliest history of mankind. Europeans and the ancient Chinese used wheels for carts and wheelbarrows. The ancient Egyptians used chariots that pulled soldiers into battle. Without the wheel, life would have been much more difficult. Even today, much of our world revolves around the wheel—whether it's the clock on the wall, the fan inside our air conditioner, the blade in our blender, or the bicycle we ride down the street.

When I was a child, I attempted to build a car by hammering wheels into a block of wood. My car didn't roll very well at all. That's because for wheels to be really useful, they need to be attached to an axle. The wheel and axle together are a simple machine.

An **axle** is a rigid bar that's inserted through a hole in the wheel. Cars, motorcycles, bicycles, and even skateboards must have an axle for their wheels to turn properly.

Let's experiment with wheels and axles by building a small car powered by a balloon.

This is the axle between the wheels of a bicycle.

Try This!

You will need: An adult's supervision, safety goggles, tape, 3 straws, 4 bamboo skewers, a 4x6-inch piece of cardboard, 4 bottle caps (like water bottle caps), a balloon, a hammer, and a nail.

First, have an adult help you hammer a small hole in the center of each bottle cap. These are your wheels. Set them aside. Next, tape two straws to the bottom of the cardboard to make two axle holders. Now insert the skewers inside the axle holders. Put a wheel on both sides of the axle (each end of the skewer). Put the last straw down inside the balloon with about an inch of the straw sticking out the top of the balloon. Now tape it securely so you can blow up the balloon with the straw. Tape the balloon to your car perpendicular to the wheels. Blow up the balloon, set the car down, and watch it go!

If you had tried to build the car without the axle connecting the two wheels on either side, your car would not have run properly.

Belting Belts

You already know that wheels are great for moving people and objects around. But did you know that many machines we use are made with internal wheels that are attached to a belt? A **belt** is usually a circular band made of rubber—kind of like a giant rubber band. We call this belt that turns more than one wheel a **drive belt**. Cars, sewing machines, vacuum cleaners, and bicycles are a few of the machines that use this system to rotate the wheels. Bikes can use this belt system or a chain system to turn the wheels.

Do you see how these drive belts are like giant rubber bands turning the wheels?

When we connect wheels to a drive belt, we can make wheels do a lot of work. When one wheel turns, it drags the belt around with it, carrying its turning motion to all the other parts of the machine.

A drive belt runs around the wheel somewhat like a pulley to carry the turning force from one place to another. Unlike a pulley, the belt must be tight on the wheels. There must also be friction between the wheel and the belt so the belt doesn't slip off the wheel and so the wheel can turn the belt. If the belt is too slack or loose, it won't grip the wheels. If it's too tight, it could break.

Have you ever heard of a conveyor belt? A **conveyor belt** is a machine consisting of one or more pulleys and a wide flat belt. Conveyor belts are used in many businesses to carry items from one person or station to another. You've probably seen a conveyor belt at the grocery store,

Math It!

The point of the simple machine of wheel and axle is like the others: Trade distance for force or vice versa. Without friction, the formula for mechanical advantage is again simple: The mechanical advantage is equal to the radius of the wheel divided by the radius of the axle. For example, with a screwdriver, the handle (wheel) is much wider than the shaft (axle), so you need much less force to turn it.

moving your purchases up to the cashier. Or maybe you've waited for your luggage to arrive on a conveyor belt at the airport. Have you ever jogged on a treadmill? A treadmill is a conveyor belt people run on to get exercise. These conveyor belts are large, fat drive belts with wheels on each end, turning the belt.

Let's experiment with drive belts and wheels.

Try This!

You will need: An adult's supervision, a thick rubber band, 2 spools, 2 nails (without heads and longer than the spools), a board, and a hammer.

First, hammer the nails into the board just a little farther apart than the rubber band is long. Attach the spools over the nails, then attach the rubber band to the spools. Turn one spool and watch the rubber band move the second spool.

You just created a drive belt!

Before we move on to gears, explain what you've learned so far about wheels and axles.

Gears

Do you see the gears in this pocket watch? They turn the hands on the clock in order to show the time.

A **gear** is a wheel that has teeth along its edge. When gears are put side by side, the teeth from one gear fit between the teeth of the other gear. When one gear turns, it turns the other gear. Inside a watch (the type with hands), gears of different sizes move the watch hands each minute. Gears turn either clockwise or counterclockwise. When gears fit together, they move in different directions. So, when one gear moves clockwise, the other gear moves counterclockwise. A series of intermeshing gears is called a **gear train** or **transmission**. The first wheel is called the **driver** or **input gear**. The last wheel is called the **follower** or **output gear.** If there were a third wheel, it would be called the **idler gear** and could be placed between the two other gears.

Gears are inside many machines that turn. Clocks, watches, and bicycles use gears that connect all the rotating parts. Gears transfer movement from one wheel to another. You can have as many gears as you need to get the object moving. The more complicated the machine, the more gears are needed!

Math It!

The mechanical advantage for gears is once again a simple division or gear ratio: the number of teeth on the output gear divided by the number of teeth on the input gear. The idler gears between don't change this. For example, if the input gear has 10 teeth, and the output gear has 100 teeth, the mechanical advantage is 10. So you would need 10 times less force. But the output gear would also rotate 10 times more slowly to balance out.

Try This!

You will need: An adult's supervision and a bicycle.

Take your bike outside to the driveway. Now turn your bicycle upside down. Make sure it's sturdy so it doesn't fall down on top of you. Now slowly turn the pedals to study how the gears move. What do you observe?

Did you see anything on your bicycle that might be working as a drive belt? The chain is a drive belt that moves the first gear, which turns the other gears. The gears of your bicycle are called sprockets. They're connected to one another by the chain. Different-sized sprockets move the bicycle at different speeds. Larger sprockets turn a wheel slowly, but with great force. Smaller sprockets turn a wheel quickly, but with less force. The pedal of the bike is called a crank.

Cranks are a kind of wheel too. They turn an axle around to get other parts moving.

An eggbeater is a compound machine with a crank, an axle, gears, and wheels. If you have an eggbeater, spend some time studying it to see how it all works together.

Wheels are such an important part of our lives. As you go about your life, take note of all the ways in which you use wheels.

As you can see, simple machines are important for everyday life. Not only do they make jobs easier, but they can also be combined to make the many machines we rely on every single day—from cars, dishwashers, and vacuum cleaners to airplanes, spaceships, and satellites that orbit the earth. Mankind has learned to use the laws of physics and the creativity given by God to make life easier.

This bike has many different-sized sprockets. The rider can switch to a different gear in order to ride faster using more force or slower using less force.

Final Matters

I hope you've enjoyed all that you've learned this year! I know you've gained a lot of knowledge. Perhaps you'll grow up to a be a chemist, researching to find solutions that help people and the world. Maybe you'll become a physicist, discovering important scientific phenomena that can be used for mankind. You may even become an engineer, creating products, technologies, and devices that protect people or make life better. However, even if you never become a scientist, you'll often use what you've learned in this book to help you accomplish things in your life. Remember, God has a special plan for your life. He tells us in Jeremiah 29:11, "'For I know the plans I have for you,' declares the LORD, 'plans to prosper you and not to harm you, plans to give you hope and a future.'"

God already knows your future. He'll guide you each day if you'll let Him. He'll guide you into the future He has chosen for you. "For this God is our God for ever and ever; he will be our guide even to the end" (Psalm 48:14).

Not only will God guide you, but He'll also give you all that you need and will help you become all that He desires you to be. Isaiah 58:11 says, "The LORD will guide you always; he will satisfy your needs in a sun-scorched land and will strengthen your frame. You will be like a well-watered garden, like a spring whose waters never fail."

Take time every day in prayer to talk to God. Be sure to read your Bible so He can talk to you! Stay close to Him as you grow and begin to develop interests and talents. Seek God for all you need. Even though He created atoms, molecules, and every scientific truth you've learned, He cares for you more than those things. Because God loves you so much, He sent His Son whom He loved more than anything to come and pay for your sins. He did this so you could be His child and have a relationship with Him—so that you could one day go to heaven and be with Him. The Bible says God longs to bless you. "Yet the LORD longs to be gracious to you; therefore he will rise up to show you compassion. For the LORD is a God of justice. Blessed are all who wait for him!" (Isaiah 30:18)

As you finish these final activities, remember you are a special creation loved by God!

After you finish the notebooking assignments, you'll begin designing your Rube Goldberg machine!

What Do You Remember?

How did Archimedes help his country? What is an inclined plane? What is a screw? What is Archimedes' screw? What is a wedge? What is a first-class lever? What is a second-class lever? What is a third-class lever? Does a single-pulley system or a double-pulley system make work easier? Give some examples of items that use wheels to make work easier. Be sure to include how the items make work easier.

Notebooking Activities

After recording all the fascinating facts you've learned, create a table of all the simple machines you just discovered. Write down examples from everyday life of something that uses that machine. Pages for these activities are provided in the *Chemistry and Physics Notebooking Journal*.

Experiment
Build a Rube Goldberg Device

Do you have trouble getting up in the morning? If so, you could build a Rube Goldberg device to help you get out of bed!

What's a Rube Goldberg device? Rube Goldberg was a cartoonist. He drew pictures of complicated devices using lots of different simple machines attached together to perform very simple tasks—like pouring water on a sleeping person to awaken him, or operating a napkin. In the United Kingdom, the cartoonist W. Heath Robinson drew similar devices. So the British call them Heath Robinson devices.

Rube Goldberg devices use a series of events in a chain reaction. Many movies and television shows use Rube Goldberg devices to complete simple tasks. In the movie *Back to the Future*, a long, complicated Rube Goldberg device opens dog food and pours it into a bowl to feed the dog. In the movie *Chitty Chitty Bang Bang*, a complicated device created by the dad makes breakfast for the family.

Do you have the game Mouse Trap? This game was designed using the concepts of the Rube Goldberg device.

Using the concepts of simple machines and mechanical energy, you'll design and—if you can—build a Rube Goldberg device. You'll want to design it on paper before you begin building it. Try using items you already have or take a trip to the hardware store to get items you think would help your Rube Goldberg device operate better. Your Rube Goldberg machine should complete a simple task, such as pouring water, putting toothpaste on your toothbrush, ringing a bell, turning on a light, or any other simple task.

Remember to draw your design before you begin. To get some ideas for your machine, go to www.apologia. com/bookextras. You can also look online to find ideas for building your Rube Goldberg device.

Supply List

Every student will need his own notebook (or the *Chemistry and Physics Notebooking Journal*), blank paper, lined paper, and colored pencils. An adult should supervise all projects, experiments, and "Try This!" activities. Caution: Set aside equipment to be used only in experiments, not for cooking. Never experiment and cook/eat with the same items! Thrift stores are a good source of inexpensive equipment.

Lesson 1

- water
- graduated cylinder
- small, solid object that doesn't absorb water (such as a rock)
- safety goggles
- 2 glasses
- 2 eggs
- 2 clear plastic straws
- food coloring (red, yellow, blue, and green)
- 12 plastic cups
- measuring spoons
- 1½ cups salt
- tall, thin vase or glass
- 8 ounces honey
- 8 ounces corn syrup
- 8 ounces 100% pure maple syrup
- 8 ounces whole milk
- 8 ounces dish soap
- large bottle of vegetable oil
- 8 ounces rubbing alcohol
- turkey baster
- popcorn kernel
- die from a game
- cherry tomato
- bead
- ping-pong ball or marshmallow
- bowl to hold water
- small piece of wood
- cork
- piece of ice
- coins
- small plastic toys
- 25 pennies
- large glass pan to hold water
- aluminum foil
- damp paper towel
- strong magnet
- needle
- metal tack

- metal hair clip
- 3 tall, thin plastic bottles with caps (like a soda or water bottle)
- box of Alka-Seltzer tablets
- vinegar

Lesson 2

- water
- 5 identical plastic cups
- 1¼ cup salt
- ¼ cup Epsom salt
- ¼ cup rubbing alcohol
- 1 packet Jell-O
- freezer
- clock
- 16 ounces corn starch
- glass cake pan
- measuring cup
- piece of waxed paper
- bowl
- needle
- 1 square of toilet paper
- 1 cup fruit juice
- 2 cups ice
- small zippered plastic bag
- large zippered plastic bag
- clear plastic cup
- small piece of paper
- 1 piece of gum (or peanut butter)
- uninflated balloon
- small bottle of soda
- packet of Pop Rocks candy
- 1 piece of bubble gum
- mirror or window
- large, clear plastic container or jar with a tight-fitting lid
- enough rocks to make a layer in the container
- enough sand to make a layer in the container
- enough topsoil to make a layer in the container
- plant from a plant store

- small plastic cup

Lesson 3
- gloves
- safety goggles
- small empty soda bottle
- tablespoon measuring spoon
- 1 tablespoon yeast (or potassium iodide for stronger reaction)
- very warm water
- ¼ cup dishwashing liquid
- 7 colors of food coloring
- cup
- spoon for stirring
- sink or deep-sided dish
- ½ cup hydrogen peroxide (The stronger kind from the beauty supply store makes a bigger reaction.)
- 1 large and 2 small paper plates
- marker
- glue
- 10 pieces of small candy (like Nerds)
- 10 pieces of large candy in one color and 8 pieces in another color (like peanut M&M'S or Gobstoppers)
- pile of Legos
- 2 wire coat hangers
- 12 small fruits (blueberries, grapes, cherry tomatoes, or any other small, roundish fruit)
- masking tape
- 2 pieces of copy paper
- 3 cups butter, softened
- 4 cups white sugar
- 8 eggs
- 2 teaspoons vanilla extract
- 10 cups all-purpose flour
- 4 teaspoons baking powder
- 2 teaspoons salt
- 2 cups powdered sugar
- 4 teaspoons milk
- 4 teaspoons light corn syrup
- pastry tube

Lesson 4
- magnifying glass or microscope
- ½ cup salt
- water
- pan
- stove

- notebook or notebooking journal
- pencil
- safety goggles
- ½ teaspoon borax
- 1 tablespoon cornstarch
- 1 tablespoon white glue or clear school glue
- a few drops of food coloring
- 9 small plastic cups
- spoon
- timer
- zippered plastic bag
- rubber band
- string
- balloon
- bamboo skewer
- several Styrofoam cups
- glass bowl or casserole dish
- ¼ cup pure acetone (available as nail polish remover at beauty supply store)
- saucer
- paper towel
- vinegar
- 5 copper pennies (made before 1981)
- ¼ cup milk
- ¼ cup lemon juice
- ¼ cup Milk of Magnesia
- ¼ cup baking soda
- ¼ cup ammonia-based glass cleaner
- litmus paper
- 2-liter bottle of Diet Coke
- package of mint Mentos
- hot glue gun
- 2 glass jars with lids
- 2 thermometers that will fit inside the glass jars
- 2 steel wool pads
- 2 bowls
- sink
- ½ cup potassium nitrate (stump remover)
- aluminum foil
- ⅓ cup sugar
- water
- wick
- empty toilet paper tube
- duct tape
- protective gloves
- box of alum
- large glass measuring bowl
- large drinking glass

- thread or nylon fishing line
- skewer or pencil
- magnifying glass

Lesson 5
- ½ cup flour
- ½ cup sugar
- ½ cup melted butter
- ½ cup old-fashioned oats
- ½ cup chocolate chips
- greased baking sheet
- mixing bowl
- large mixing spoon
- oven
- 8 ounces of a clear carbonated drink
- 1 glass
- 8 raisins
- ¼ cup cooking oil
- running water
- soap
- glass pie plate or similar high-lipped dish
- ½ cup milk
- 1 drop each of red, yellow, blue, and green food coloring
- cotton swab
- a few drops of dishwashing liquid
- aluminum foil
- ½ cup heavy whipping cream
- small glass jar (like a baby food jar) with lid
- powdered chocolate drink mix
- spoon
- large glass of milk
- 4 Crayola markers (original classic colors: black, brown, violet, green)
- 4 white Crayola sidewalk chalk sticks
- 4 plastic cups
- ½ gallon of swamp water or muddy lake water
- 2 two-liter soda bottles with caps
- large glass beaker or glass vase with wide mouth
- 2 teaspoons alum
- ½ cup fine white play sand or beach sand
- ½ cup coarse or industrial sand
- ½ cup small pebbles, like aquarium rocks
- coffee filter
- rubber band
- stopwatch
- scissors

Lesson 6
- 6 pennies
- 1 index card
- table
- 1 glass
- water
- tin pie pan
- raw egg
- empty toilet paper tube
- smooth, flat surface
- 13 marbles
- 1 large shooter marble
- balloon
- sidewalk chalk

Lesson 7
- bicycle with hand brakes
- small toy car
- glass or wooden table
- water
- 1 tablespoon soap or oil
- 3 pieces of copy paper
- window
- shoe box or other small box
- 20-inch string
- small rock
- tape
- 15–20 pencils
- few small toys or objects
- table
- chair
- video camera
- baseball
- tennis ball
- ledge
- penny
- balloon
- small pail with handle
- 3 pieces of heavy card stock

Lesson 8

- 2 rubber bands (1 thin)
- 2 pencils
- an object to use as a drum, such as a can with a plastic lid or a large cookie tin
- safety goggles
- wooden spool with large hole
- electrical or duct tape
- washer
- toothpick
- scissors
- tennis ball
- basketball
- zippered plastic bag
- kitchen counter near sink
- 2 straws cut at an angle to make a sharp point
- water
- 3 shoe boxes (1 that is white or light on the inside and outside)
- 2 small bottles of water
- thermometer
- black paint (enough to cover the inside and outside of a shoebox)
- 6–10 eggs
- sand (enough to fill 1 shoe box halfway)
- 1-foot sheet of aluminum foil
- bamboo skewer
- baking soda
- vinegar
- black powder paint
- small funnel
- plastic cup

Lesson 9

- large casserole dish
- water
- several pieces of Cheerios cereal
- set of dominoes
- flat surface like a table or counter
- long cardboard tube (such as a gift wrapping paper tube)
- balloon
- rubber band
- paper
- tape
- scissors
- candle
- lighter

- long garden hose
- piece of thick paper (like card stock)
- 2 metal spoons
- Sheetrock wall
- car hood
- large container filled with water (like an aquarium or plastic bucket)
- wooden table
- drinking straw
- large metal can
- small metal can
- table
- chair
- shoebox
- materials that will absorb sound (carpet, foam, cardboard, plastic, fabric, carpet padding, etc.)
- glue
- object that produces sound, like an iPod, cell phone, alarm clock, or small radio

Lesson 10

- straight-sided, thin drinking glass
- water
- 3 sheets of white paper
- duct tape
- 3 bright flashlights
- very dark bathroom
- copy paper box
- knife
- 2 prisms
- sunny day
- glass of water
- ¼ cup of milk
- white wall
- darkened room
- plastic wrap or cellophane (red, blue, and green)
- scissors
- 3 cardboard tubes
- tape
- piece of white cardboard
- sharp pencil
- 6 colors of markers, crayons, or tempera paint (purple, blue, green, yellow, orange, red)
- TV remote control
- bouncy ball
- piece of aluminum foil
- mirror, and something to prop it up with on a table

- table in a dark room
- 2 small square mirrors
- small object (such as a small plastic figure)
- long pencil
- penny
- teacup
- reusable adhesive putty
- one 18-inch length of 2-inch outer diameter PVC pipe
- two 2-inch inner diameter PVC pipe elbow joints
- 2 small, round mirrors measuring 2 inches or less in diameter

Lesson 11
- thermometer
- desk lamp that's turned on
- aquarium or other large transparent container
- room temperature water
- large bowl that will fit into aquarium (or two small bowls)
- 2 plastic film canisters with lids (or 2 four-ounce plastic GladWare containers)
- hammer
- nail
- scissors
- boiling water
- ice water
- red and blue food coloring
- balloon
- pot of boiling water
- empty glass bottle
- ¼ cup peanut butter
- metal spoon
- wooden spoon
- plastic spoon
- container of hot water
- pan
- water
- 5 empty baby food jars with lids
- masking tape
- 4 pieces of insulation material (such as fiberglass, down-filled fabric, cotton cloth, a wool sweater, or wool socks)
- a tissue
- magnifying glass
- pitcher of water
- sunny day
- paved surface outside

- jar with lid
- candle that fits inside the jar
- match
- vinegar
- baking soda
- narrow-necked glass bottle
- plastic straw
- piece of clay
- safety goggles
- 4 small paper cups
- rubbing alcohol
- nail polish remover
- oil
- freezer
- large glass of water
- thin plastic bottle with cap
- 2 cardboard boxes, one smaller than the other so it can fit inside the larger one
- aluminum foil
- glue
- pot or glass jar with lid, painted black, that will fit inside the smaller box
- newspaper
- sheet of cardboard a bit larger than the top of the larger box
- pencil
- piece of plastic wrap or clear sheet of plastic or glass about the size of the top of the larger box
- some food to cook (grilled cheese sandwich, hot dog, etc.)

Lesson 12
- balloon
- mirror
- plate
- coarsely ground black pepper
- pair of wool socks
- large carpeted area
- doorknob
- Wint O Green Life Savers
- very dark room
- 6 pennies dated after 1982
- piece of rough sandpaper
- piece of thick cardboard
- electrical tape
- small LED
- water
- scissors

- 1 teaspoon salt
- vinegar
- 6-volt lantern battery
- 8 pieces of coated copper wire
- 3 small 6-volt light bulbs and sockets
- 4 drinking glasses
- milk
- 2 paper clips
- 4 brass paper fasteners (brads)
- tape
- 2-inch piece of corrugated cardboard
- 2 D batteries
- 2 five-inch pieces of insulated copper bell wire
- 4-inch cardboard tube
- flashlight bulb
- 1-inch x 3-inch cardboard strip
- electrical tape
- bathroom-sized paper cup

Lesson 13
- 2 magnets with north and south markings
- 2 bar magnets
- horseshoe magnet
- round magnet
- 2 pieces of paper
- iron shavings
- table
- different items from around your house (such as keys, bottle caps, nails, paper clips, and metals from your parents' toolbox)
- very large steel nail
- box of steel paper clips
- hammer
- compass
- rock
- large needle
- pencil eraser
- flame
- plate
- bowl of water
- plastic bottle cap
- long piece of thin, insulated copper wire
- 1 D battery
- small rare earth magnet
- 1 AA battery
- 7-inch piece of 18- or 20-gauge copper wire
- large piece of cardboard
- markers

- several strong magnets
- several small toy cars or trucks
- strong glue for metal and magnets
- base (such as boxes)

Lesson 14
- several large books
- rubber band cut in half
- scissors
- paper clip
- ruler
- duct tape
- sock filled with rocks
- table
- pencil
- board
- piece of paper
- marker
- pencil
- can
- bowl of colored water
- clear packing tape
- clear, plastic tubing (¼ inch in diameter)
- chair
- broom
- can of beans
- full water bottle
- handful of pennies
- yardstick or other long stick
- long string
- coat hanger
- strong wire cutters
- empty spool of thread or ribbon
- small pail
- rope
- safety goggles
- 3 straws
- 4 bamboo skewers
- 4-inch x 6-inch piece of cardboard
- 4 bottle caps (like water bottle caps)
- balloon
- hammer
- nail
- thick rubber band
- 2 spools
- 2 long nails without heads (longer than the spools)
- board
- bicycle

Answer Key

This answer key includes answers for the "What Do You Remember?" section at the end of every lesson, as well as answers to other questions within the lesson text.

LESSON 1

"What Do You Remember?" page 28

Physics and chemistry are both the studies of _____ and _____. **Matter and energy.**

Matter is defined as anything that has _____ and _____. **Volume and mass.**

What is mass? **How much stuff is inside a particular material.**

Why is mass not always measured by weight? **Because objects do not have weight in space, but they have the same mass in space.**

How can we measure volume? **By immersing an object in liquid.**

Which is denser—a cube of wood or the same size cube of gold? Why? **The cube of gold is denser because the atoms in the gold are more tightly packed together, and they are more massive.**

Name as many properties of matter as you can recall. **Answers will vary; could include mass, volume, density, state of matter, viscosity, luster, color, hardness, odor, malleability, ductility, plasticity, and reactivity.**

LESSON 2

"What Do You Remember?" page 41

What are the three main states of matter? **Solid, liquid, and gas.**

What causes one state of matter to change into another state? **Heating and cooling.**

Which state of matter is composed of atoms that are frozen in place? **The solid state.**

Which state of matter is composed of atoms that are bound together but do not have a specific form? **The liquid state.**

Which state of matter is composed of atoms that are freely moving about, expanding to take up as much space as is available? **The gas state.**

What is freezing point? **The temperature at which a liquid becomes a solid.**

What temperature is the freezing point of water? **32°F or 0°C .**

What is melting point? **The temperature at which a solid becomes a liquid; the same as the freezing point.**

What is boiling point? **The temperature at which a liquid becomes a gas.**

What temperature is the boiling point of water? **212°F or 100°C.**

What is the condensation point? **The temperature at which a gas becomes a liquid; the same as the boiling point.**

LESSON 3

page 55

How many protons does it [iron] have? **26.**

How many protons does helium have? **1. (Its symbol is He.)**

How many energy levels does helium have? **1.**

Which element has 87 protons? **Francium.**

Which has 10 protons? **Neon.**

How many energy levels does that element have? **2.**

Which element has an atomic mass that's a little below 56? **Iron.**

What's the atomic mass of tin? **118.69.**

"What Do You Remember?" page 59–60

What is an atom? **The smallest particle of an element that still keeps the properties of that element.**

What is an element? **A substance that contains only one kind of atom.**

What is the charge of a proton? **Positive.**

What is the charge of a neutron? **Neutral.**

What is the charge of an electron? **Negative.**

What is the nucleus of an atom made of? **Protons and neutrons.**

What are electron shells? **The energy levels where the electrons orbit the atom.**

How many electrons can fit in the first energy level or electron shell? **Two.**

How many electrons fit in the second energy level of an atom? **Eight.**

What are valence electrons? **The electrons in the outer shell.**

When is an atom stable? **When it has all the valence electrons it needs to fill up the outer shell.**

When is an atom unstable? **When it does not have all the valence electrons it needs to fill up the outer shell.**

What is the difference between a covalent bond and an ionic bond? **Covalent bonds share electrons. Ionic bonds give and take electrons.**

What is an ion? **An atom with a charge because it has lost or gained an electron.**

What is a cation? **A positively charged ion.**

What is an anion? **A negatively charged ion.**

What do the numbers inside the box of an element on the periodic table of elements represent? **The atomic number and the atomic mass.**

LESSON 4

page 70

Paper towel: **2–4 weeks.**

Orange peel: **2–5 weeks.**

Banana peel: **2–5 weeks.**

Paper bag: **1 month.**

Newspaper: **6 weeks.**

Apple core: **2 months.**

Milk carton: **100 years.**

Wool sock: **1–5 years.**

Plastic bag: **10–20 years.**

Plastic film canister: **20–30 years.**

Nylon fabric: **30–40 years.**

Leather: **50 years.**

Tin soup or vegetable can: **50 years.**
Foamed plastic buoy: **80 years.**
Aluminum soda can: **200 years.**
Disposable diaper: **450 years.**
Plastic bottle: **450 years.**
Rubber boot sole: **50–80 years.**
Plywood: **1–3 years.**
Styrofoam container: **50 years.**
Glass bottle: **1 million years.**

"What Do You Remember?" page 79
What is a compound? **A pure chemical substance with two or more different elements combined.**
What is a crystal? **A solid with a regular, repeating arrangement of atoms.**
Name some crystals you have in your house. **Answers will vary.**
What is a polymer? **A molecule made of repeating small molecules combined.**
Name some natural polymers. **Answers will vary; could include proteins, starch, cellulose, and natural rubber.**
Name some man-made polymers. **Answers will vary; could include plastics, nylon, and synthetic rubber.**
What is a chemical reaction? **A reaction that occurs when two or more chemical substances interact with each other and change into different chemical substances.**
What is a physical reaction? **A physical change that does not change the chemical substance but only the appearance of the substance.**
What are some physical changes? **Answers will vary; could include melting, boiling, dissolving.**
What is a reactant? **The chemicals (elements/molecules) that are being mixed in a chemical reaction.**
What is the product of a chemical reaction? **The chemicals (elements/molecules) resulting from a chemical reaction.**
What is an endothermic reaction? **A chemical reaction during which heat energy is absorbed.**
What is an exothermic reaction? **A chemical reaction during which heat energy is released.**
What factors can influence the rate of reaction? **Answers will vary; could include increasing the concentration of the compounds that are being combined, heating, catalyst.**
Name some acids you know about. **Answers will vary; could include vinegar, lemon juice, stomach contents, car battery liquid.**
Name some bases in your home. **Answers will vary; could include ammonia, baking soda, caustic drain cleaner.**
What is the pH of pure water? **7 (neutral).**

LESSON 5

page 83
Milkshake: **heterogeneous.**
Sugar cubes: **compound.**
Clouds: **compound.**
Toothpaste: **homogeneous.**
Chocolate chip cookies: **heterogeneous.**
Sand: **heterogeneous.**
Dirt: **heterogeneous.**
Milk: **homogeneous.**

"What Do You Remember?" page 93
What is the difference between a mixture and a compound? **Mixtures are compounds that are not chemically combined but rather physically mixed.**
What is a heterogeneous mixture? **A mixture where the individual parts of the mixture can be easily seen.**
What is a homogeneous mixture? **A well-mixed mixture in which the individual parts cannot be seen as separate.**
What are alloys? **Mixtures of different metals.**
What is a concentrate? **A solution that has a large amount of solute in the solvent.**
What is a saturated solution? **A solution in which no more solute can be dissolved in the solvent.**
What are some ways to separate the component parts of a mixture? **Answers will vary; could include evaporation, filtration, sifting, magnetism, chromatography.**

LESSON 6

page 102
Why are you forced back against your seat when the car you're in suddenly accelerates? **Because of inertia, your body is seeking to stay in the same position it was in. Eventually the force of the car's movement will put your body in motion.**

"What Do You Remember?" page 106
The study of motion is called the study of _____. **Mechanics.**
What is Newton's first law of motion? **Something at rest stays at rest unless something forces it to move, and something in motion stays in motion in a straight line unless something forces it to stop moving.**
What is a force? **A push or pull on an object.**
If you were riding in your car with books on your lap, what would happen if your car suddenly stopped? Why? **Your books would fly forward because of inertia.**
What is Newton's second law of motion? **Force is what causes an object to change speed or direction. The change is resisted by the mass of the object.**
What is acceleration? **The change in speed or direction something is going.**
What is Newton's third law of motion? **For every action, there's an equal and opposite reaction.**
Who was Isaac Newton? **Answers will vary; could include a great creationist physicist and mathematician; discoverer of the spectrum of light and the laws of motion, gravity, and cooling; inventor of the reflecting telescope; coinventor of mathematical calculus.**

page 108
Which law do you see when the marbles are all lined up, just sitting still before the game starts? Newton's first law of motion (inertia). **Which law explains why the shooter rolls in a straight line?** Newton's first law of motion (inertia). **Why do marbles that are stationary suddenly start rolling when the shooter strikes them? Because a force is acting on them.**

LESSON 7

"What Do You Remember?" page 123
What is the force that resists movement between two objects? **Friction.**
What is a lubricant? **A substance that reduces friction.**
Name three lubricants mentioned in this lesson. **Water, soap, and oil.**
What is adhesion? **The sticking together of two different materials.**

What is the law that tells us all objects are attracted to other objects according to their mass and distance? **The universal law of gravitation.**

Which of the two objects would hit the ground first if pushed from the same height—a bowling ball or a basketball? **They would hit at the same time.**

What kind of resistant force does an object traveling through water encounter? **Water resistance or drag.**

What kind of resistant force does an object traveling through air on the earth encounter? **Air resistance or drag.**

How do people reduce air or water resistance? **Through aerodynamic design (reducing the surface area facing into the air or fluid).**

What is the speed limit of falling objects called? **Terminal velocity.**

When an object is in free fall, what two resisting forces will the object encounter? **Air resistance and gravity.**

What was the force that was in effect when David was twirling the sling? **Centripetal force.**

LESSON 8

page 128
Boy with soccer ball: **kinetic energy.**
Binder on shelf: **potential energy.**
Person riding a bike: **kinetic energy.**
Ball in the grass: **potential energy.**
Books falling: **both potential and kinetic energy.**
Bikes in the grass: **potential energy.**

"What Do You Remember?" page 144
What is energy? **The ability of someone or something to do work.**
What is kinetic energy? **Energy in motion.**
What is potential energy? **Stored energy.**
What is the law of conservation of energy? **Energy cannot be created or destroyed, only transformed.**
What are some forms of energy that come from animals and plants buried long ago? **Fossil fuels: oil, coal, natural gas.**
What kind of energy is found in the nucleus of an atom? **Nuclear energy.**
What is renewable energy? **Energy made from sources that don't run out.**
Name some forms of renewable energy and the problems associated with each. **Answers will vary; could include wind energy (can be harmful to some flying creatures) or solar energy (can be very expensive to install).**

LESSON 9

"What Do You Remember?" page 162
What is sound? **Vibrations that travel through materials from a source.**
What phase of matter does sound generally travel through best? **Solids.**
What measurement do we use to measure loudness? **Decibels.**
What is frequency? **The pitch of a sound.**
Which has more waves per second—a high-pitched sound or a low-pitched sound? **A high-pitched sound.**
What do we call a sound too high pitched for human ears to hear? **Ultrasound.**
What do we call a sound too low pitched for human ears to hear? **Infrasonic.**
Name one way we use what we know about sound to help us. **Answers will vary; could include sonar, ultrasound, and bioacoustics.**

LESSON 10

"What Do You Remember?" page 181
What are the two most common elements found on the sun? **Hydrogen and helium.**
What is nuclear fusion? **Two different nuclei of atoms fusing or joining together to become one nucleus.**
What is the order of colors in the electromagnetic spectrum? **ROY G BIV: red, orange, yellow, green, blue, indigo, violet.**
Name two kinds of invisible light. **Ultraviolet and infrared.**
What kinds of surfaces reflect light the best? **Smooth and shiny.**
What happens to light when it enters a different medium? **It refracts—speeds up/slows down and bends.**

LESSON 11

page 188
Hot air balloon: **The fire is the heat source; the balloon is the heat sink.**
Ironing a shirt: **The iron is the heat source; the shirt is the heat sink.**
Feet by the fire: **The fire is the heat source; the feet are the heat sink.**
Shish kebabs: **The coals are the heat source; the chicken is the heat sink.**
Sun and earth: **The sun is the heat source; the earth is the heat sink.**
Toaster: **The toaster is the heat source; the bread is the heat sink.**

page 199
Why do you think power lines might be droopy on hot days but straight and tight on cold days? **The power line cords expand when they're hot, causing the material to be less firm. When it's cold, the power line cords shrink and are tight and firm.**
What might happen if water is left in the pipes outside your house and the temperature outside drops below freezing? **The water pipes could burst as the metal contracts and the water expands.**
Why do you think your car's windshield washer container is made out of plastic? **The plastic container is elastic and will easily expand without cracking if the water freezes.**
Why does a car require a substance called antifreeze in its radiator? **Cars get hot when they are running, so they must be cooled. Water is a good coolant, but because it expands when it freezes, it could harm the metal parts of the car. Antifreeze has a much lower freezing point. It is mixed with water to lower the freezing point of the water so it will not harm the car when it is cooling the engine.**

When a jar won't open, why do you run hot water on the metal lid?
The hot water on the lid of the jar causes the metal to expand, enabling it to open the jar. Since metal expands more than glass, even if the glass expands, the metal lid will still be loosened.
If one glass is stuck inside another, how could you use thermal expansion to separate it? **Running hot water over the outer glass causes it to expand and loosen from the inner glass. You could also pour cold water in the inner glass to cause it to shrink.**

"What Do You Remember?" page 199
Which law tells us there is no transfer of heat between two objects in thermal equilibrium? **The zeroth law of thermodynamics.**
What is the first law of thermodynamics? **Energy and matter can never be created or destroyed. They can only change from one kind of energy or matter to another.**

What is the second law of thermodynamics? **The universe is always becoming less and less ordered or organized.**

What is the third law of thermodynamics? **The entropy (or disorder) of something approaches its minimum as it's cooled toward absolute zero.**

How is radiant heat transferred? **Through electromagnetic radiation.**

Describe how heat is transferred through convection. **Answers will vary; should include movement of warmer fluids to cooler regions.**

Describe how heat is transferred through conduction. **Answers will vary; could include atoms and molecules transferring energy by collisions.**

What are the three things a fire needs to ignite? **Oxygen, heat, and fuel.**

What is temperature? **The measurement of how active the molecules are in a substance.**

Which temperature scale has water freezing at 32 degrees? **Fahrenheit.**

Which temperature scale has water freezing at 0 degrees? **Celsius.**

Which temperature scale has water freezing at 273.15 degrees? **Kelvin.**

Explain thermal expansion. **Answers will vary.**

What substance expands when it freezes? **Water.**

LESSON 12

"What Do You Remember?" pages 217–218

What is electrostatic energy sometimes called? **Static electricity.**

What is the name of a gadget that stores electricity? **A capacitor.**

What is an insulator? **A protective shield against the flow of electrons.**

Name something that can be used as an insulator. **Answers will vary; could include rubber, plastics.**

What do we call facilities that generate electricity? **Power plants.**

What kind of current—alternating or direct—comes through your house from the power plant? **An AC or alternating current.**

What is a load? **A resistor or device that uses electrical energy.**

What kind of current—alternating or direct—comes from a battery? **A DC or direct current.**

Who created the first battery? **Volta.**

Which kind of circuit—series or parallel—would you prefer to have for your Christmas lights? Why? **Parallel. If one bulb burns out, the rest will stay lit.**

LESSON 13

"What Do You Remember?" page 234

What are magnetic domains? **Tiny areas all over a magnet that work as individual magnets.**

What is a magnetic field? **The region around the magnet that produces a magnetic force.**

What is a ferromagnetic substance? **A substance strongly attracted by magnets.**

What is a paramagnetic substance? **A substance that has a slight magnetic attraction.**

What is a diamagnetic substance? **A substance that repels a magnet because the electrons' magnetic moments cancel out each other's magnetic moments.**

What is the earth's core made of? **Liquid iron (and some nickel).**

What is an electromagnet? **Any magnet powered by an electric current where the field disappears when the current is turned off.**

What is the motor effect? **The effect that happens when a wire carrying an electric current experiences a force from the magnetic field of a magnet.**

LESSON 14

"What Do You Remember?" page 253

How did Archimedes help his country? **He built simple machines that were used to defeat the Romans (temporarily).**

What is an inclined plane? **A ramp that is used to lift or lower objects.**

What is a screw? **An inclined plane wrapped around a cone or cylinder.**

What is Archimedes' screw? **A giant screw used to lift water.**

What is a wedge? **A machine comprising a moving inclined plane used to push objects apart.**

What is a first-class lever? **A machine that has the fulcrum in the middle of the load and effort.**

What is a second-class lever? **A machine that has the fulcrum at one end, the effort at the other, and the load in the middle.**

What is a third-class lever? **A machine that has the effort between the fulcrum and load.**

Does a single-pulley system or a double-pulley system make work easier? **A double-pulley system.**

Give some examples of items that use wheels to make work easier. **Be sure to include how the items make work easier. Answers will vary.**

Photograph and Illustration Credits

Photos by Jeannie Fulbright: 19, 20 (top), 34-35 (all), 37 (both), 40 (bottom), 48 (middle), 52 (bottom), 53 (all), 55, 56 (top), 61, 63, 66 (bottom), 67-68 (all), 82-83, 94, 100, 106 (left), 109, 117, 118, 124, 132, 136, 140, 143 (both), 146-147 (all), 151 (top), 154 (top), 156 (bottom left and right), 159, 164, 165 (bottm), 180, 195, 198, 207 (right), 209

Photos by Tamara Adelberg: 202 (bottom), 212 (bottom all), 213 (bottom), 215 (all), 219 (all)

Photos by Debra Bash: 147 (top), 148 (bottom), 149 (all), 163 (all), 182 (all), 200 (all)

Photos by Rebecca Brandt: 188 (top), 189 (bottom), 190 (bottom), 191 (top and middle), 193 (top), 194 (middle and bottom), 195 (top), 197 (middle), 198 (bottom)

Photos by Lauren Carlson: 33 (top), 37, 46 (bottom), 69, 72 (top), 80, 88 (top), 91 (bottom all), 96, 108, 114 (bottom), 130 (top), 134 (bottom)

Illustration by Shiela Catanzarite: 75 (middle)

Photos by Sally Conroy: 152 (top), 158 (bottom)

Photo by Bryson Davis: 150 (middle)

Illustrations by Brenda Ehly: 53, 56 (middle)

Photos by Calvin Fulbright: 233 (middle all)

Photos and Illustrations by Jeannie Fulbright: 20 (top), 22 (all), 23, 26 (fourth bottom), 29, 36 (all bottom), 40, 42 (all), 47 (top), 48 (all), 49 (top, middle), 50 (all), 51 (top, bottom), 52 (top, all), 61 (all), 77, 81, 93 (bottom), 103 (middle), 104 (top), 145 (all), 151 (bottom, all), 155 (bottom, all), 156 (bottom, all), 169 (middle), 171 (middle), 177 (top), 202 (top), 213 (top), 220 (top), 223 (bottom), 225 (all), 229 (bottom), 230 (top), 231

Photos by Sandra Hua: 223 (top), 226 (top), 227 (bottom), 232 (top), 235 (all)

Photo by Sheila Jones: 21 (top)

Photos by Yetty Oladeji: 244 (middle), 245 (top), 246 (top), 248 (middle), 250 (top all)

Illustrations by Rebecca Purifoy: 20 (middle), 24 (third middle), 39 (bottom), 40, 58 (top), 79, 86 (middle, bottom), 117 (bottom), 118 (top), 124 (all), 125, 133(bottom), 147 (bottom), 156 (top), 160 (middle), 173 (top), 189 (top), 190 (top and middle), 192 (top), 207 (top), 211 (middle), 213 (top), 216 (bottom), 217 (all), 218 (all), 220 (bottom), 233 (top all), 238 (bottom), 239 (top), 241 (top), 244 (bottom), 248 (top right)

Photo by Jessica Rondina: 44 (bottom)

the National Archives/Charles Levy – top), 137 (kallerna – middle), 139 (courtesy of the Bureau of Reclamation – bottom), 141 (courtesy of NASA – top), 141 (courtesy of NASA – bottom), 142 (courtesy of U.S. Airforce/ Airman 1st Class Nadine Y. Barclay – top), 143 (Gretar Ívarsson – top), 143 (courtesy of NASA – bottom), 153 (mboverload – middle), 153 (courtesy of the U.S. Marine Corps/LCPL John McGarity – bottom), 160 (courtesy of the U.S. Government – top), 161 (courtesy of NASA – bottom), 165 (courtesy of NASA), 169 (courtesy of the University of Denver – top), 175 (Shark D and Jacobolus, Dacium), 176 (courtesy of the U.S. Air Force – top), 188 (courtesy of NASA – second bottom middle), 192 (Elinor – bottom), 196 (Stilfehler – bottom), 197 (terex – top), 208 (courtesy of the U.S. Nuclear Regulatory Commission), 209 (Wtshymanski – top), 210 (Tawker – top), 211 (Guiseppe Bertini/Johnnyb11 – bottom), 222 (Allatka – top), 237 (courtesy of Gemalde-galerie Alte Meister/Dominico Fetti – bottom), 241 (Reinraum – bottom right), 242 (courtesy of Chambers' Encyclopedia – top left), 242 (Carlito20 – top right), 243 (courtesy of University of South Florida/Florida Center for Instructional Technology – all), 245 (courtesy of the British Museum/National Geographic – middle), 246 (courtesy of University of South Florida/Florida Center for Instructional Technology – middle right), 247 (courtesy of University of South Florida/Florida Center for Instructional Technology – top)

Photos published under the Creative Commons Attribution-ShareAlike 3.0 Unported, 3.0 Brazil, 2.5 Generic, 2.1 Japan, 2.0 Generic, 2.0 Germany (http://creativecommons.org/licens-es/by-sa/3.0/): 21 (pcb21 – second bottom), 24 (Rob Lavinsky – first middle), 25 (Alchemist-hp – first top), 25 (imagesofelements.com – second top), 25 (Chris Reno – first middle), 25 (Aram Dulyan – second bottom), 25 (JJ Harrison – second bottom), 26 (Omegatron – middle), 32 (Darren Hester), 34 (Isaka Yoji – top), 43 (Alan Chia – top), 44 (Own Work – top), 54 (Alan Chia – bottom), 56 (Pslawinski – top, both), 59 (Dennis s.k Collection/Dnn87 – top right), 62 (JJ Harrison – top), 62 (Didier Descouens – bottom), 63 (Stannered – top right), 63 (Siim Sepp – bottom), 64 (zdjecia Stowarzyszenie Spirifer – first bottom), 64 (Mmlynczak – second bottom), 64 (StrangerThanKindness - third bottom), 65 (Mario Sarto – top), 65 (Doug Wertman – middle), 65 (Vladimir – bottom), 66 (Juergen Schoner – top), 66 (350z33 – middle), 67 (Mohd Hafiz Noor Shams – top), 67 (Bob J. Galindo – bottom), 78 (Michael Murphy – bottom), 83 (Antilived – second top), 84 (Jan Kronsell), 87 (SuperManu – left), 89 (Alchemist-hp – bottom), 114 (Ricardo Liberato – middle), 118 (Shane Torgerson – bottom), 119 (Malin Ager), 123 (courtesy of the Library of Congress and the American Colony/ Jerusalem Photo Department), 132 (David Iliff – top), 133 (Ovulator – middle), 134 (Divulgaçao Petrobra – top), 135 (Xlxgoggaxlx – middle), 137 (Zvesoulis – bottom), 138 (Bill Ebbesen), 139 (Pierre 79 – top), 140 (Leaflet – top), 140 (Hans Hillwaert – bottom), 142 (Pratheepps – bottom), 152 (Calermo – bottom), 154 (Cmglee – top), 154 (Chabacano – bottom), 155 (Jim Boudreaux Photography – top), 158 (Charles W. Hardin – top), 174 (Bb3cxv – bottom), 176 (BOY –middle), 180 (Brocken Inaglory – bottom), 195 (Gustavb – bottom), 198 (Matt H. Wade), 202 (Emmanuel Boutet – middle left), 202 (Anders L. Damgaard – middle right), 203 (Geek3 – middle), 204 (Mataresphotos – second middle), 204 (Rainer Knapper – fourth middle), 207 (Christoph Filnkobl – bottom), 208 (MBizon – top), 209 (Glogger – middle), 209 (Kristoferb – bottom), 211 (Gbleem – top), 221 (Rob Lavinsky – top), 221 (Zuzu – middle), 222 (Aney – middle), 222 (Ischa1 – bottom), 228 (Jaypee – middle), 228 (Mak Thorpe – bottom), 229 (Jerry MagnuM Porsbjer – top), 238 (Finnrind and Pbroks13 – middle), 245 (ChrisO – bottom), 246 (Bernard Gagnon – bottom), 247 (Zephyris – middle), 248 (Cesar Rincon – top left and bottom left), 248 (GK Bloemsma – bottom right), 249 (Cesar Rincon – top), 250 (Ukexpat – bottom)

Photo published under the GNU Free Documentation License Version 1.2: 157 (Muhammad Mahdi Karim – top), 241 (Jonathunder – bottom left)

Index

WHY IS APOLOGIA SCIENCE RIGHT FOR ME?

Sure, you've heard that Apologia is the homeschooler's #1 choice for elementary science curriculum, but what makes the Young Explorer Series the right choice for *your* family? Our science books are filled with hands-on activities, and they're written to the student in an engaging, conversational style that makes learning fun for the whole family.

NOTEBOOKING JOURNALS

Instead of taking tests, Young Explorer students use notebooking journals for taking notes, documenting activities and experiments, and recording their thoughts on God's marvelous creation. With lesson plans that walk your family through the entire year, materials for making mini books, and tons of additional activities, the notebooking journals are an essential part of the Young Explorer Series.

✱ Try our junior notebooking journals for beginning writers! These feature coloring pages and less writing, but include all the same hands-on activities as our regular notebooking journals. Junior notebooking journals are recommended for grades K–2nd.

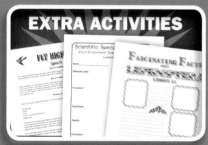

EXTRA ACTIVITIES

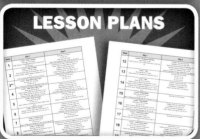

LESSON PLANS

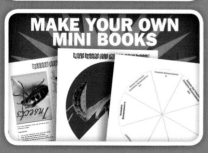

MAKE YOUR OWN MINI BOOKS

Order your family's next science course at apologia.com!

apologia

TRANSITION TO
JUNIOR HIGH
AHEAD

THE TRANSITION TO MIDDLE SCHOOL IS A HUGE STEP ON YOUR CHILD'S PATH TO LEARNING INDEPENDENCE. Apologia's junior high science curriculum paves the way to the future with an enjoyable approach to higher learning. Our textbooks are written directly to the student, so no teacher's manuals are required. And experiments use household materials, keeping your costs to a minimum. Now Apologia's junior high science features Student Notebooks to help your student bridge the transition between elementary and high school.

GENERAL SCIENCE
Recommended for
7th Grade

PHYSICAL SCIENCE
Recommended for
8th Grade

Creating a good lab notebook and learning how to study are invaluable skills required for success in high school and college science. Our Student Notebooks make it easy with step-by-step guides to every chapter.

FEATURE 1:
LAB REPORT GUIDES

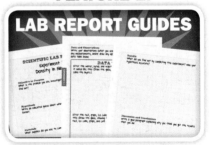

FEATURE 2:
NOTETAKING GUIDES

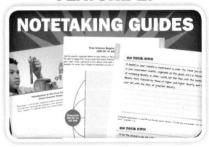

FEATURE 3:
DAILY LESSON PLANS